A Social History of the English Working Classes 1815–1945

Eric Hopkins

Lecturer in Economic and Social History
at the University of Birmingham

Hodder & Stoughton

LONDON SYDNEY AUCKLAND

Acknowledgements
The Publisher's thanks are due to J. M. Dent for permission to use John Pudney's poem 'For Johnny' from *Collected Poems* and The Owen Estate and Chatto & Windus Ltd for eight lines from Wilfred Owen's poem 'Anthem for Doomed Youth' from *The Collected Poems of Wilfred Owen*.

British Library Cataloguing in Publication Data
Hopkins, Eric
   A social history of the English Working Classes, 1815-1945
   I. Labor and laboring classes—England—History
   I. Title
   301.44'42'0942   HD8389
   ISBN 0 7131 0316 7

First published 1979
Ninth impression 1992

© 1979 Eric Hopkins

Printed in Great Britain for the educational publishing division of Hodder and Stoughton Ltd, Mill Road, Dunton Green, Sevenoaks, Kent by Athenaeum Press Ltd, Newcastle upon Tyne.

This book is respectfully dedicated to the memory of the English working classes of the nineteenth century upon whose labours was built the first industrial state in the world.

Preface

Between 1815 and 1945 an extraordinary change took place in English society. In the first half or so of this period the working classes, of whom the majority had hitherto worked in agriculture, moved into the towns, and mostly became industrial workers. The expansion of industry and of the towns was such that the government was forced to take action so as to secure minimum standards in working and living conditions, education and welfare. For their part, the working classes in their new environment struggled to protect themselves through trade unions, self-help societies, and political activity. In the second part of the period, from 1900 onwards, they had their own Labour Party, which in 1945 secured a decisive victory in the General Election at the end of World War II and formed the first majority Labour Government. Meanwhile, all working men and women had gained the vote, state education had become compulsory and free, and the standard of living and quality of life of the average worker had improved greatly. For the first time in English history, the working classes had acquired a recognition of their existence as human beings with rights, status, and dignity. This book attempts to trace the ways in which this transformation of the role of the working classes in society—it might even be called a social revolution—came about.

The book is intended primarily for 'A' Level students, there being few if any recent books available on this particular subject as opposed to the general economic and social history of the period. It concentrates exclusively on the working classes rather than society as a whole. Economic history is introduced only when necessary to make the social history intelligible, and a brief preface to each Section gives an account of the principal economic events of the period covered by the Section. How far the book is successful in achieving its aims, the reader must judge for himself. All the writer can do is hope that it will be found helpful by 'A' Level aspirants, and also of some service, perhaps, as an introductory sketch at first-year degree level.

I should like to make the customary but no less real acknowledgement of the help given me by my wife Barbara in the production of this book, not only in the chores of proof-reading, index compiling, and so on, but also in bearing philosophically my prolonged absences from the family living-room, especially during vacations, while the book was getting itself written. I sometimes think that there should be a Society for the Protection of Authors' Wives. God bless them all, and especially mine.

E.H.

Stourbridge

Contents

Public Health Reports of the 1840s – further reasons for delay in legislation – the Public Health Act, 1848 and its terms – its subsequent history – the dissolving of the Board of Health in 1858.

The nature of government social reform – arguments for individualism – later modification of these views – Benthamism and its application to public health – modern explanations of government intervention.

Schools for the working classes about 1800 – arguments against working-class education – changes in public attitudes – the Church societies – the monitorial system – the First Grant to Education, 1833 – the Committee of the Privy Council, 1839 – the setting-up of HM Inspectorate – beginning of the pupil–teacher scheme, 1846 – the status of the teacher – a summing up: the influence of the church societies, limited nature of working-class education, parental attitudes to education.

The working classes and the churches – significance of non-conformist beliefs for the working classes – the 1851 Religious Census – contemporary and modern views of working-class attendance at church and chapel – attendance outside the towns and cities – qualifications to customary views regarding the working classes and religion.

Tudor poor law legislation – the Act of Settlement, 1662 – 18th century legislation – the Speenhamland system, 1795 – other methods of helping the poor – criticisms of Speenhamland after 1815 – the Royal Commission on the Poor Law, 1832 and its Report, 1834 – modern criticisms of the Report – the Poor Law Amendment Act, 1834 – enforcement of the Act – attacks on the New Poor Law – outdoor relief allowed again – the Andover Scandal and the new Poor Law Board, 1847 – gains made by the 1834 Act and criticisms of it – poor relief outside the poor law system.

Modern controversies over the standard of living in the first half of the 19th century – the optimist/pessimist controversy and its results.

Section II: Equipoise and After 1850–1900

The course of reform in the second half of the 19th century – textile factory legislation extended to other places of work – the Workshops Act, 1867 – inspection of workshops – 'factories' redefined agricultural gangs – wages boards – sliding scales – the Alliance System – the Eight Hours Act – the Sweated Industries Act – the working week at the end of the century – the extent of regulation.

Public health reform and Dr John Simon – model dwellings – public health acts in the 1850s and 60s – the Royal Sanitary Commission, 1869 and its Report – legislation of the 1870s – deep drainage – the housing problem in London and its results – housing in 1914 – improvements in health, and in death and infant mortality rates by 1914.

Leisure activities – professional sport and mass audiences – cycling – sportsmanship – the music halls – the new popular press – home and outdoor activities.

situation of the time – school meals, medical inspection of children, and the Children's Act – Old Age Pensions – the Eight Hours Day and Minimum Wages for miners – the Trades Boards Acts – Labour Exchanges – insurance against unemployment and ill-health under the National Insurance Act – other minor reforms – the reforms assessed – the extent of collectivism and the controversy over New Liberalism – working-class attitudes to the reforms.

groups – government attempts to succour the unemployed – the Means
Test – the Unemployment Act, 1934 – the failure to cure unemployment – the Distressed Areas – life on the dole – unemployment and the
young, the old, and the housewife.
Social reform – unemployment and health insurance – housing – Old
Age Pensions – Education – Labour demand for secondary education – the Hadow Report – its implementation – the overall effect of
social reform.
The extent of poverty – Rowntree's Survey of 1936 – Boyd Orr's survey of
nutritional needs – some conclusions.
The Labour Movement – post-war troubles and the mining industry – the
failure of the Triple Alliance – the state of the unions – the first Labour
Government – the Zinoviev Letter – the General Strike – events after the
Strike – the second Labour Government – its collapse – the part played
by Ramsay MacDonald.
Leisure interests – pre-war patterns continued – new interests – the
radio, talking pictures, the motor car and the motor cycle – dirt-track
racing, hiking, and dancing – the popular press.

Military service – conscription – the theatres of war – attitudes to the
war – casualties.
The Blitz – evacuation of children – raids on London and elsewhere – the
ordeal of the urban working classes – V1s and V2s – the effects of raids on
morale.
Life at work – female labour – dilution and government control of
labour – wages and working conditions – strikes – the role of the trade
unions – Labour representation in the government.
The standard of living – improved health of the nation – rise in earnings – leisure activities – football, cricket, the radio – CEMA and cultural
activities – ENSA.
Social reform – rejection of pre-war attitudes – Priestley's *Postscripts* – proposals for reform – the Beveridge Report – the White Paper
Chase – the Education Act, 1944 – the Family Allowances Act – the end
of the war and the Labour electoral victory in 1945.

Section I
The Birth of the New Society
1815–1850

During this period both agriculture and industry suffered depression immediately following the end of the Napoleonic Wars in 1815, but industry recovered in the early 1820s, and industrial growth continued until the late 1830s. By then the most prominent industries (the staple industries) were textiles, iron, and coal, with the cotton industry in particular being the most mechanized in the world. Agriculture took longer to recover, but it, too, began to be more profitable by the 1830s, only to suffer depression again from 1836 onwards. This depression also affected industry, and proved to be the most severe of the century. The years 1839–42 were especially gloomy, and agriculture, industry, and trade were all very seriously affected. The newly developing industrial society faced a crisis, and appeared dangerously near to breakdown. However, the depression eased after 1842, and free trade policies, combined with the technological advantages of the growing railway system and of the steamship, brought a return to prosperity in the later 1840s.

Chapter I
Life at Work

Occupational Structure of Society

It is not without significance that the term 'the working classes' first came into use in the early nineteenth century. Before that time the factory system was almost unknown, and so were the great concentrations of working people in industrial towns which are so familiar today. Up to then the typical working man lived in the country, and he worked on the land, together with his wife and children. Industrial occupations existed, of course, but they accounted for only a minority of workers when compared with agriculture. All this changed dramatically in the first half of the nineteenth century, and was already changing when the 1811 census was taken. Although the attempt in this census to show the national occupational structure in terms of families was somewhat crude and unrefined, nevertheless the results of the census give an unmistakable indication of the new pattern of employment:

Occupations in Britain in 1811

	England	*Wales*	*Scotland*
Families employed chiefly in agriculture	697 353	72 846	125 799
Families employed chiefly in trade, manufacture, or handicrafts	923 588	36 044	169 417
All other families	391 450	20 866	106 852
	2 012 391	129 756	402 068

Of all the families, the majority of course were families of the working classes, who were roughly four-fifths of the entire nation. What distinguished the working classes from the other classes was that they were usually manual workers, ranging from the highly-skilled and semi-skilled to the completely unskilled labourers. It is clear from the figures that families engaged in agriculture in England were distinctly

fewer than families in trade, manufacture, and handicrafts, and constituted little more than one-third of all families. By 1851 when a much
more accurate occupational analysis becomes available, the swing to
industry is even more pronounced:

Principal Occupations in Britain in 1851

Agriculture	1 790 000	Milliners	340 000
Domestic Service	1 039 000	Wool	284 000
Cotton	527 000	Shoemakers	274 000
Building	443 000	Coal miners	219 000
Labourers	376 000	Tailors	153 000

Totals in Industry

Mechanized Industry (including mining)	1 750 000
Non-mechanized Industry	5 500 000
	7 250 000

It is true that agriculture was still the biggest single occupation in
1851 (with domestic service, surprisingly, the second largest) but the
remaining eight occupations in the list taken together outnumber
agriculture completely. Moreover, agriculture accounted for only
1·79 m out of a total population in Britain of 21 m, that is, less than one
in 10 worked in agriculture as compared with about one in three in
1811. The table of Totals in Industry allows an even more striking
comparison to be made: in 1851 there were four times as many
industrial workers (7·25 m) as there were agricultural workers
(1·79 m), and these industrial workers numbered nearly a third of the
entire population. Britain had indeed become an industrial nation, the
first of its kind in the world.

It must be emphasized, however, that this is not the same as saying
that British industry was now based on the factory system. The third
table shows that this was not so at all. Mechanized industry—that is,
industry using steam-driven machinery—employed less than a quarter
of those working in industry as a whole, even when mining is included
as a mechanized industry (in fact, steam was used only for pumping,
winding and ventilation in this industry). The remaining three-quarters
of the industrial workers were employed very largely in workshops of
the traditional kind, and not in factories. Sometimes these workshops
could be quite large with up to 100 men, but the majority were much
smaller than this.

The implications of all these figures should now be clear: they are
that during the first half of the nineteenth century an extraordinary

change occurred in the lives of large numbers of working people in this country. From being engaged in the traditional routines of life in the countryside, they found themselves living in grimy industrial towns and working in workshops, foundries, shipyards, brickworks, and the new textile factories in Lancashire and the West Riding. In fact, very important changes took place in life at work during the half-century, and it is against this background that life at work for the different categories of working people may now be examined.

Workshop Industries

The vast majority of industrial workers in 1851 were employed in workshops, and these varied greatly in size and in working conditions. The one safe generalization about all of them is that by the standards of today they were dirty, insanitary and inconvenient. The smallest were family workshops situated either in the workers' cottages or close at hand in the backyard. Nailers' workshops were typical of the latter kind, and nailshops near Wolverhampton in 1843 were described as follows:

> The best kind are little brick shops of about 15 feet long by 12 feet wide in which seven or eight individuals constantly work together, with no ventilation except the door and two slits or loopholes in the wall; but the great majority . . . are very much smaller, filthily dirty, and looking in on one of them when the fire is lighted, it presents the appearance of a dilapidated coal-hole, or little black den. . . . The effluvia of these little work-dens, from the filthiness of the ground, from the half-ragged, half-washed persons at work, and from the hot smoke, ashes, water, and clouds of dust (besides the frequent smell of tobacco) are really dreadful.

These small workshops were little different from those in which many other iron trade workers worked, such as hammer makers, file cutters, anvil and vice makers, spade makers, blacksmiths, and chain makers—all these needed a fire for heating the metal, and benches at which the metal could be cut and shaped. Other trades required merely bench space—bootmakers, glovers, skinners, seamstresses, and dressmakers. Some of these trades were carried on in non-domestic workshops or garrets away from home and under the control of a small master or employer; and this was especially so in Birmingham, where there were many workshops specializing in brass goods, guns, buttons, and jewellery and trinkets of all kinds—the famous Birmingham 'toy' trade. In London, conditions varied according to whether the workmen were properly trained and skilled, or unskilled and therefore underpaid—the so-called honourable and dishonourable branches of the trade. In 1840 Dr Southwood Smith, a well-known authority on public health, reported on the lack of ventilation in a large London tailoring shop:

> I find it stated, for example (and the description here given of one occupation, that of the journeyman tailor, is applicable to many), that in a room 16 or 18 yards long and 7 or 8 yards wide, eighty men worked together; the men were close together, nearly knee to knee. In summer time the heat of the men and the heat of the irons made the room 20 or 30 degrees higher than the heat outside; the heat then was most suffocating, especially after the candles were lighted.

Whether they were large or small, very long hours had to be worked in these workplaces. The average working day varied from place to place, but 12 hours was common at the mid-century, with an hour or an hour and a half off for meals. The one mitigating circumstance was that in the smaller workshops the working week was usually flexible, so that provided the set amount of work was done by Saturday, the worker could vary the hours he worked each day to suit himself. Thus in many family workshops, Monday would be a day of rest (nicknamed St Monday), Tuesday a fairly leisurely day, and the remainder of the week very hard work, with work maybe all night on Friday so as to finish on time on Saturday. This mode of work was characteristic of nailers, and a well-known Black Country saying is that the nailers would throw their hammers in the air on Monday morning, declaring that if they stayed up in the air they would work that day . . .

Nevertheless, the general picture presented by workshop industry is one of unremitting toil in wretched conditions, and more and more men, women and children from about the age of six or seven were employed in the workshops in the first half of the nineteenth century because the demand for many kinds of articles could still be met by simple hand production. It is very hard to say whether working conditions actually grew worse in this period. The length of the working day might seem at first sight to be a good way of judging this, but in fact it varied greatly with the amount of work on hand. In slack periods workers would be on short-time or off work completely for days or even weeks; when trade was brisk they could be working sixteen hours or more a day for what was still in many cases a bare living wage. Better-paid workers did not work noticeably shorter hours than poorly-paid workers. The one clear instance of a decline in conditions can be seen when the competition of the factory with its steam-driven machinery drove a hand-trade out of existence. The classic case is that of the hand-loom weavers who worked desperately long hours in the vain effort to compete with iron and steam. The frame-work knitters producing stockings in Nottingham and Leicester are another example. By the 1840s both trades were in severe decline, and the earlier affluence of the hand-loom weavers had been replaced by grinding

5

poverty, leaving the older weavers only the memory of their former prosperity.

Larger Work Places

An important section of the working classes found employment in establishments larger than workshops but not factories in the usual sense. Such places included ironworks, shipyards, ropewalks, pottery works, quarries, glass works and brickyards. In ironworks, the 12-hour shift was hard and exhausting, and boys were employed from the age of eight. According to a report of 1842, there was considerable danger of burns:

> Of minor accidents, burns are the most frequent. The upsetting or bursting of the bucket in which the melted metal is conveyed from the furnace to the casting place is the most common cause of these injuries, and the intense heat of the material makes it very rapidly and deeply destructive . . .

Blast furnaces were worked by teams of men who filled and tapped the furnace, while work on puddling furnaces was similarly organized on a team basis. Puddling furnaces were designed to produce wrought iron from pig, and required careful judgement of the right time to boil the molten mass, and then to withdraw it for hammering out the impurities. A puddler describes his work in 1842:

> I am seventeen. I am an assistant puddler. I come sometimes at four, sometimes at five or six, according as the other set is able to leave. . . . The iron begins to heat perhaps in 20 minutes, but it may be 40 minutes or three-quarters of an hour. I have to break it and make it soft by beating, and it becomes soft, and at last boils up like unto a pot. It will keep boiling ten minutes or a quarter of an hour. My master takes the work in hand when it boils. I relieve him a short while at this work. After it has stopped boiling, he divides the iron into six balls, and rolls them about and draws them out one by one and lays them on the forge hammer.

In the glass industry, table-ware was made by men working in 'chairs' or teams of four, the head of the team being known as the gaffer or workman, the youngest being a boy aged 10 or so, called the 'taker-in'. Chairs worked shifts of six hours on, six hours off, usually from Tuesday morning to Friday midday. Six hours was considered the maximum period possible on such delicate production, though the actual working conditions were always warm and dry, and better than in many jobs. In making crown glass for windows, however, a different routine was followed in which the unit of work was the *journey*, this being the using-up of the contents of one furnace of molten glass. There were usually three journeys in a week, each lasting from 10 to 16 hours or more.

In brickyards, much of the work of making the bricks (as opposed to firing them) was performed by women and girls. The women made the bricks on their moulding tables, while the girl assistants, or 'pages', brought them the clay and carried off the finished bricks for firing. The women commonly worked to a stint of so many hundred bricks a day. It was hard work, especially for the girls, who began work at the age of six or seven. They carried heavy loads of six or more bricks at a time, while the wet clay left their clothes saturated by the end of the day. Wet clay made working conditions bad in the potteries, too. A Chesterfield doctor who had attended both those working in the pits and in the pottery works thought that

> the latter are more subject to rheumatism; this he considers owing to their working so much in the wet. He also considers the kiln boys injure their general health, partly by loss of sleep and resting in the confined air between the kilns.

In these larger workplaces the nature of the manufacture would determine whether the work was by day or by shift. Where furnaces were in use, shift work was customary, otherwise working was by the day; though sometimes (as in the case of brickmaking) the length of the day depended on the time taken to complete the stint. Once again, the working day was often about 12 hours, though longer hours were not at all uncommon in other jobs. For example, a boy of 13 working in a West Midlands skinworks told a Commission of Enquiry in 1862 that his hours were usually from 6 am to 7 pm, but that week he happened to be working from 5 am to 8 pm, going home for meals. Many children younger than this were at work, of course, there being no restrictions at all before 1850 on the age of children employed except in the mines and the textile factories.

Mines and Textile Factories

These workplaces were in a class by themselves. The most dangerous work of all was probably that of the miner; he had to face explosions, flooding, and roof falls as part of the ordinary hazards of the working day. Roof falls were especially likely when pillar and stall methods were used. This method is described in a report of 1842:

The chief miners, the undergoers, were lying on their sides, and with their picks were clearing away the coal to a height of a little more than two feet. Boys were employed in clearing out what the men had disengaged. Portions (of coal) are left to support the great mass until an opening is made on each side of the mass, and also part is taken away from the back. This undergoing is a dangerous part of the work, as notwithstanding all that experience and judgement can do, occasionally too much is taken away, and a mass of coals will suddenly fall and crush the men and boys engaged. Fortunate are they if they escape with their lives, but broken bones they cannot fail to have to endure.

It is no wonder that although miners in this particular coalfield were said to have 'fine muscular development', they also suffered from 'a proportionate diminution of stature and a crippled gait'. They were also prone to lung diseases and ruptures, and many were unable to go on with the work after the age of 40. Accidents were an everyday occurrence: miners fell down shafts, were struck by falling coal or timber at the pit bottom, fell from the rope or skip when going up or down the shaft (cages were not used till later), or were crushed against walls by passing trucks of coal.

One of the most objectionable aspects of the mining industry was the employment of women and children in some of the pits (though not in all). Women were used to carry coal in baskets or to drag trucks full of coal. The baskets might hold up to three hundredweight, and this load had sometimes to be carried up several ladders. In 1842 it was calculated that one girl of 12 carrying coal in this way had to travel up four ladders and along passageways a total distance which exceeded the height of St Paul's Cathedral. As for drawing trucks of coal, a woman of 37 described her work as follows:

> I have a belt round my waist, and a chain passing between my legs, and I go on my hands and feet. The road is very steep and we have to hold by a rope, and when there is no rope, by anything we can catch hold of. . . . The pit is very wet where I work, and the water comes over our clog tops always, and I have seen it up to my thighs; it rains in at the roof terribly; my clothes are wet through almost all day long. . . . I have drawn till I have the skin off me; the belt and chain is worse when we are in the family way. My feller (husband) has beat me many a time for not being ready.

Older children might also be used for this work, and the description of these children given in the First Report of the Children's Employment Commission (1842) is well-known:

> Chained, belted, harnessed like dogs in a go-cart, black, saturated

with wet, and more than half-naked—crawling upon their hands and feet, and dragging their heavy loads behind them—they present an appearance indescribably disgusting and unnatural.

Younger children from the age of eight or nine were used as trappers—that is, opening and shutting the trap doors which controlled the circulation of air in the mines. They also filled the trucks. The children were often beaten as they were in other industries, but in the pits a good deal of cruelty might take place in secret. As one observer put it:

> The colliers are uneducated people, and are vicious in temper . . . what passes underground in the dark tunnels in which the people work is not known even to the underground over-looker . . .

It was also alleged that immorality was rife in some pits. Men sometimes worked quite naked alongside women who were commonly naked from the waist up, so that (it was said) the women became debased and degraded. However, the numbers of women below ground were not large—only 2340 in all in 1841.

The employment of children was also very common in the new textile factories. Some contemporaries found nothing to object to in this. Dr Andrew Ure, who claimed to have visited many factories over a period of several months, stated in 1835 that he had never seen a child subjected to corporal punishment, nor had he ever seen children in an ill-humour.

> They seem to be always cheerful and alert, taking pleasure in the light play of their muscles—enjoying the mobility natural to their age. The scene of industry, so far from exciting sad emotions in my mind, was always exhilarating. . . . The work of these lively elves seemed to resemble a sport, in which habit gave them a pleasing dexterity. Conscious of their skill, they were delighted to show it off to any stranger.

Other observers disagreed strongly with this rosy picture of life for the children, and thought that the so-called apprentices, in particular, were very ill-used. The factory reformer, John Fielden, who had himself worked as a child in his father's mill, explained how the apprentices were recruited and set to work:

> The small and nimble fingers of little children being by far the most in request, the custom instantly sprang up of procuring *apprentices* from the different parish workhouses of London, Birmingham, and elsewhere . . . being from the age of seven to the age of thirteen or fourteen years old.

9

The custom was for the master to clothe his apprentices, and to feed and lodge them in an apprentice house near the factory. Overseers were appointed to see to the works, whose interests it was to work the children to the utmost, because their pay was in proportion to the quantity of work they could exact.

Mr John Moss, who had been in charge of apprentices at Backbarrow in Lancashire in 1814–15, described their life for the benefit of a Select Committee of the House of Commons in 1816:

What were the hours of work?—From 5 o'clock in the morning till 8 at night all the year through.
What time was allowed for meals?—Half an hour for breakfast, and half an hour for dinner.
Had they any refreshment in the afternoon?—Yes, they had their drinking taken to the mill, their 'bagging' they called it.
You mean luncheon?—Yes.
Did they work while they ate their afternoon refreshment?—Yes.
They had no cessation after dinner till 8 o'clock at night?—No.
Did they, beyond working those 15 hours, make up for any loss of time?—Yes, always. They continued working till 9 o'clock, sometimes later.
Did the children actually work 14 hours in the day?—Yes.
And one hour was allowed for the two meals, making 15 hours in the whole?—Yes.

Mr Moss went on to say that the apprentice house was about a hundred yards from the mill, and that he got them up, winter and summer, at half-past four every morning so that they would be at the mill at five o'clock.

Since these children had no fathers or mothers to look after them, they were often treated brutally by the overseers. In the more humane mills they might be prodded with a stick to keep them awake, or encouraged to sing hymns. Since it was calculated that in some mills they walked 20 miles during their day's work, it is not surprising that they became very tired. In the more ruthless establishments they would be cuffed on the head, or beaten with the iron rod known as the billy-roller; or they might suffer even worse treatment as did Robert Blencoe:

What are the forms of cruelty which you spoke of just now as being practised upon children in factories?
I have seen the time when two hand-vices of a pound weight each, more or less, have been screwed to my ears at Lytton Mill, in Derbyshire. There are the scars remaining behind my ears. Then three or four of us at

once have been hung on a cross beam above the machinery, hanging by our hands, without shirts or stockings. Mind, we were apprentices, without father or mother to take care of us; I don't say that they often do that now. Then we used to stand up in a skip, without our shirts, and be beat with straps or sticks; the skip was to prevent us from running away from the straps. . . .

It would be wrong to think that this treatment was typical of all mills. Indeed, there were witnesses other than Dr Ure who testified that the children in some mills were really well looked after. The children in Mr Moss's mill at Backbarrow, for instance, were not harshly treated, that is, if we are to believe the following certificate from a visiting doctor:

I do hereby certify that I have attended the apprentice house of Ainsworth Catterall & Co of Backbarrow upwards of six years, and during that time the children have been particularly healthy, and the number of deaths very few. I consider the treatment of the children very good in all respects. John Redhead, surgeon. Cartmel, May 25, 1816.

The local minister also certified that the children attended church regularly, were well-behaved, and appeared neat and clean. If this gentleman and the doctor are to be believed, it appears that the children were not treated too badly, though the hours were still very long.

Free children were those who were not apprenticed, but were often taken to the factory by their parents, and were able to earn a small wage. Their treatment, in fact, does not seem very different from that accorded the apprentices. A girl of 17 who had begun work in a Manchester mill at the age of eight afterwards described her experiences:

Were you ever late of a morning at M'Connells?—Yes, sir.
Did they scold you?—The spinners always licked me; they always lick the piecers when they are too late of a morning. Generally with a strap—either a strap or a rope, very seldom with the hand.
How many blows did they give you when they licked you?—Well, sir, I never took particular notice. I have been licked for five minutes together as hard as he could lick me. . . .
Did all the masters lick you?—I never worked with a master yet but what he licked me when I was late in the morning. One master used to lick me of all colours if I was two minutes late. I've gone off from home half-dressed he used to be so very savage. Mother has held me to put on my clothes, but I would be off first.

It has been alleged by some modern writers that the stories of cruelty to children in the early factories have been much exaggerated, and it is true that the reformers were anxious to bring the worse cases of ill-treatment before the public, understandably paying far less attention to cases of considerate and humane treatment. Nevertheless, there seems little doubt that children were indeed overworked and treated brutally in many factories, even judging by the harsh standards of the day. Of course, the hours of adults were equally long, and young and old alike were subjected to a discipline quite foreign to those accustomed to the more easy-going life of the small workshop. There was nothing new in itself in a lengthy working day, or in foul conditions, or in the employment of children; what was new was the unrelenting pressure of work throughout a 15- or 16-hour day, and the discipline imposed by overseer, factory bell and whistle. Steam was expensive, so was gas. Hence, while the machinery was running, full use had to be made of it. As a writer on the factory system said in 1832, 'Whilst the engine runs, the people must work—men, women and children are yoked together with iron and steam.' It was common enough for fines to be exacted for breach of factory rules. These examples are for a spinning mill near Manchester in 1823—

	s.	d.
Any spinner found with his window open	1	0
Any spinner found dirty at his work	1	0
Any spinner found washing himself	1	0
Any spinner putting his gas out too soon	1	0
Any spinner spinning with gaslight too long in the morning	2	0
Any spinner heard whistling	1	0
Any spinner being five minutes late after last bell rings	1	0
Any spinner found in another's wheel gate	1	0
Any spinner being sick and cannot find another spinner to give satisfaction	6	0

This kind of work-discipline was entirely new, of course, to the workers subjected to it. The discipline of the workshop system was basically task-orientated; as we have seen, the worker had to perform certain tasks by a given time, and how many hours he worked at a stretch was his own affair. Under the factory system, however, workers had to adjust themselves to a new concept of time, for what was important was not so much the completion of certain pieces of work by a given date, but intensive labour within set hours. Now that precise time-keeping had become necessary the knocker-up made his appearance in the Lancashire mill towns, and the sale of cheap watches and clocks boomed. Thus, the new work-discipline was much more time-orientated than before. A further change is that previously the worker had some personal contact with his employer, who usually supplied the raw material, and in most cases the worker also owned his tools. But under the factory system he might know no one save the overseer who was in authority above him, and he certainly owned no part of the machines he tended. He was now merely a small cog in a large organization, and his relationship with the factory owner was reduced to the simple sale of his labour for cash—the classic cash nexus of industrial capitalism.

The Agricultural Labourer

At this point we turn from industry to agriculture. The farm labourer's routine of work had remained largely unaltered through the centuries. Although free from the concentrated toil of life in the factories, his work entailed much hard labour and often very long hours. In the 1850s he still had to start work very early:

> The ordinary adult farm labourer commonly rises at from four to five o'clock; if he is a milker, and has to walk some little distance to his work, as early as half-past three. Four was the general rule but of late years the hour has grown later. He milks till five or half-past, carries the yokes to the dairy, and draws water for the dairymaid, or perhaps chops up some wood for her fire to scald the milk. At six he goes to breakfast. . . . If a milker and a very early riser, he is not usually put on the very heavy jobs, but allowances are made for the work he has already done. The other men on the farm arrive at six.

The milker might then work in the fields till milking time came round again at about three o'clock. At last the day's work would come to an end at between half-past five and half-past six. The other men would leave at six as a rule, but in haymaking or harvest time they would be expected to stay until the job in hand was finished, often till eight or half-past.

Unlike many other workers, the farm labourer spent much of his time working in the open air. This could be agreeable enough in summer, but it was very different in winter:

> To put on coarse nailed boots weighing fully seven pounds, gaiters up above the knee, a short greatcoat of some heavy material, and to step out into the driving rain and trudge wearily over field after field of wet grass, with the furrows full of water; then to sit on a three-legged stool with mud and manure half-way up to the ankles and milk cows with one's head leaning against their damp, smoking hides for two hours, with the rain coming steadily drip, drip, drip—this is a very different affair.

In contrasting the work of the agricultural labourer with that of the factory worker, it is easy to over-emphasize the relative freedom of the countryman. This freedom was largely illusory. If he was not the slave of a machine, his physical labour was often as hard and his hours as long.

Some Conclusions

This survey of the main categories of employment in the first half of the nineteenth century goes some way to confirm the view that there was no such thing at this time as *the* working class—that is, one body of workers all exhibiting the same characteristics. This is not to deny that society was changing rapidly as the entrepreneurial class grew in size and wealth, and the working classes gradually acquired a sense of their own separate identity as a class—that is to say, they became more and more class-conscious. It has already been noted that those who worked in factories commonly had little or no contact with the factory owners, so that for these workers, at least, the old personal relationship had gone. It may be that this made factory workers increasingly aware that they constituted a separate class. Nevertheless, there were more than three times the number of workers outside the factories in 1851 than there were inside them, and conditions were very varied in both domestic workshops and in the larger workplaces. Relations between employer and workman also varied from trade to trade—they were traditionally good in the small metal workshops of the Birmingham area, but less good in the coal mines of South Staffordshire. Many skilled trades had their own internal hierarchies, the skilled worker being considered socially superior to his under-hand or assistant, while all highly-skilled craftsmen would hold themselves superior to common labourers. In view of this almost bewildering variety of different facets of life at work, any broad generalizations must be undertaken only with the greatest caution.

It is safe to say, however, that much of industry in the mid-nineteenth century was still organized on traditional patterns, and in particular on the basis of the small team. This was obviously true of domestic workshops where father, mother and children all worked together, but it is also true of blast furnace workers, puddlers, glassmakers, brickmakers, and others. Miners worked in small groups, often father with son. The leader of the team drew wages for the group as a whole. Only in the cotton factories was work by the small team noticeably absent. Families did work together in the early cotton mills, but as the spinning mule was improved upon, the number of children required to help with each machine was larger than could be provided by the average family, with the result that the family was split up.

Another outstanding characteristic of industry at the mid-century was the widespread employment of young children. This seems shocking to us at the present day, but was not so at the time, for child labour was in no way new in the nineteenth century. It was certainly not the invention of Victorian employers eager for profits and anxious to tap a new source of labour. In agriculture it had always been customary for children to work as soon as they could be entrusted with some simple task, for example, opening and closing a gate, scaring birds, helping to glean or pick up potatoes. In domestic industry the practice of employing children was also very widespread. Long before the textile industry was transformed by the factory system, Defoe described work in the home in the West Riding early in the eighteenth century:

> Though we met few fellows without doors, yet within we saw the houses full of lusty fellows, some at the dye-vat, some at the loom, others dressing the cloths; the women and children carding and spinning; all employed from the youngest to the oldest; scarce anything above four years old but its hands were sufficient for its own support.

Child employment was generally accepted at the beginning of the nineteenth century, and it was only in the cotton factory (and later in the mines) that the intensity of children's labour began to arouse disquiet, as we shall see in Chapter IV. Since working by children was taken so much for granted, the struggle for the regulation of their labour in factories proved to be long and bitter.

Closely associated as a subject with the employment of children is the length of the working day. It scarcely needs repeating that working hours were very long in factory, workshop or elsewhere. To the modern observer who is used to working hours being under legislative control, or subject to trade union agreement, the length of the early Victorian working day is deplorable; and he is often quick to ascribe it to the ruthlessness of hard-faced employers who were prepared in the words of one factory reformer 'to exact more labour from their hands than they were fitted by nature to perform'. In fact, whatever the exactions of individual factory owners, working hours had always been long, both in agriculture and in industry. This was thought normal and inevitable—it was part of the natural condition of mankind that work should be the price of human survival. Man had to work to remain alive, and hard toil was unavoidable for those born into the humbler stations of life. It is difficult to tell, of course, what the unskilled labourer thought about his conditions of work, but one may guess that he probably accepted them as part of the natural order of things. His grievances were more likely to be over the insecure and ill-paid nature of his employment than about the number of hours he had to work.

The fact remains that what was new about working conditions in the first half of the nineteenth century was not the length of the working day but the peculiar nature of work in the factory. Admittedly this affected only a minority of industrial workers, but for them work brought additional tension and fatigue and, it could be, an increasing alienation from their masters. Life in the factory with its tireless and demanding machinery was very different from life in the small workshop where the worker could knock off work when he wanted to smoke his pipe or feed his pigeons. It may well be argued that it was in the factory and in the squalid living conditions of the factory towns that the seeds of class consciousness are to be found. Yet from suffering and hardship, good may come forth in the end. The excesses of the factory system led ultimately to a mass of legislation covering not only factories but virtually all places of work, so that the child factory workers did not suffer in vain.

Chapter II
Life at Home

Population and Housing

For many working men and women in the first half of the nineteenth century, life at home was life in an urban environment. For the first time in the history of the nation, the average working man was becoming a townsman, and the Victorian town or city was in itself a new creation, a unique product of industrialization. It was not merely that the population doubled in this period, rising from 10·5 m in 1801 to 21·0 m in 1851, so that the existing towns increased proportionately as a result; to this natural growth there was added a flood of newcomers from the surrounding countryside. Older historians used to speak of a mass migration from the agricultural South to the industrial North during the Industrial Revolution. We now know that this did not occur, and it was much more a matter of short-distance migration from nearby country districts to town industry. The older authorities were at least right in suggesting that the cause of this movement was basically the attraction of industrial jobs, though again the temptation to move to the nearby town would be stronger at some times than at others, depending on whether local agriculture was in a state of prosperity or depression, and whether industry was booming or slack. Formerly it was believed that enclosure drove many smallholders off the land and into the towns in search of work, but today it is known that the number of dispossessed agricultural labourers has been exaggerated, and that the deeper cause of migration was the growth of a rural surplus population, so that there were too few jobs for the increasing numbers of labourers. Of course, some went into the towns not so much because of the chances of a better job, but simply because the town promised a different way of life—a wider choice of employment, new friends, more varied entertainment, as life away from the enquiring eye of squire or parson. For many different reasons, therefore, men, women and children left the countryside for the town, and this in spite of anything they might have heard about life in the factory or in the new industrial housing.

The consequences for town growth were enormous. The figures given below show that Bradford actually increased by eight times in 50 years, and that another four towns were more than quadrupled in size:

Population in Thousands

	1801	1811	1821	1831	1841	1851
Birmingham	71	83	102	144	183	233
Bradford	13	16	26	44	67	104
Glasgow	77	101	147	202	275	345
Leeds	53	63	84	123	152	172
Liverpool	82	104	138	202	286	376
Manchester	75	89	126	182	235	303
Preston	12	17	25	34	51	70
Sheffield	46	53	65	92	111	135
Wolverhampton	13	15	18	25	36	50

These figures show that in this period an extraordinary episode in English urban history took place which is still largely unchronicled in its detail. It is probably true to say that the average Englishman is more familiar with the creation of new clapboard towns in the American Wild West than with the expansion of towns in his own country in the same century. In came the immigrants in an unceasing tide, sometimes singly, sometimes in whole families, the majority on foot, but some by cart or waggon. The question was of course, where could they be housed?

Broadly speaking, there were three possibilities. The first is that the newcomers could go into lodgings or share existing accommodation in some way. This often meant gross overcrowding, and the Reports of the time are full of accounts of this. A typical case of 1842 is that of a father, mother and 12 children in the Black Country sleeping in a room 12 feet square with one small window seldom opened, and the roof so low that a man could stand up only in the middle. It was stated in Preston in 1842:

> The streets, courts and yards examined contain about 422 dwellings, inhabited at the time of the enquiry by 2400 persons sleeping in 852 beds, i.e. an average of 5·68 inhabitants to each house, and 2·8 persons to each bed.

> In 84 cases, 4 persons slept in the same bed.
> 28 cases, 5 persons slept in the same bed.
> 13 cases, 6 persons slept in the same bed.
> 3 cases, 7 persons slept in the same bed.
> 1 case, 8 persons slept in the same bed.

Another possibility was that of opening up parts of a house normally used for storage such as attics or cellars and turning them into living accommodation. Cellars were frequently used for this purpose in

Glasgow and Liverpool. In the latter city it proved one way of housing the large influx of Irish workers who were used to very cramped living quarters. Cellar accommodation was usually grossly unsatisfactory, not merely because of overcrowding, but also because of the prevailing damp, lack of light, and seepage from nearby drains.

The third possibility was to find somewhere to live in the new working-class housing put up by speculative builders. Much of it was thrown up speedily to satisfy immediate needs, and it was often of indifferent quality with poorly seasoned timber and cheap bricks. This criticism applies particularly to housing erected during the French Wars at the beginning of the century, when building materials had become relatively scarce and had risen in price. In Manchester it was said that:

> New cottages are erected with a rapidity which astonishes persons who are unacquainted with their flimsy structure. They have certainly avoided the objectionable mode of forming underground dwellings, but have run into the opposite extreme, having neither cellar or foundation. The walls are only half a brick thick . . .

Builders frequently used as cheap materials as possible so as to make the maximum profit from rents which had to be low if tenants were to be found at all. It should be said, however, that the landlord charging the rent was not necessarily the builder, but might be anyone with a little capital to invest in land and property, even at times a working man who had saved from his wages. In some areas such as Birmingham a group of houses might be erected by a small building society formed for that purpose by a number of skilled workers. Another and much more common way of building economically was to cram as many houses as possible on the land available—hence the long lines of terraced houses in narrow streets still standing in some Lancashire mill towns today; and sometimes 'in-filling' took place—that is, a row of houses would be squeezed in across the back gardens of existing houses. One notorious kind of house was the back-to-back, a house with only one room up and one room down, built back to back with another, usually in terraces. Leeds in particular had thousands of these houses, but they were common elsewhere as well. Houses often faced each other across narrow spaces called courts, while there were numerous passage-ways or alleys between blocks of houses, and these were sometimes built over at first floor level so as to form tunnels. These covered alleys might be the only way into an otherwise completely closed court.

Early nineteenth-century housing for the working classes was not in itself very different from eighteenth-century building in the number and size of rooms, or in its lack of amenities such as tapped water and water closets. What was different was the sheer scale of the building operations and the cramming together of very large numbers of houses—and as a consequence, sanitary conditions of a truly appalling kind.

Sanitary Conditions

To understand why conditions were so bad in the new towns, it must be remembered that sanitary arrangements in the eighteenth-century village or small town had always been simple and crude, but they could be tolerated and not thought unsatisfactory so long as the number of inhabitants remained small. It was otherwise when these arrangements were adapted for use in a very large and heavily congested town area. The results with respect to drainage, scavenging, the supply of water, and the provision of privies, were calamitous. One of the best summaries of the resulting conditions is to be found in the First Report of the Health of Towns Commission, 1844. To start with drainage: the wording of the questions asked by the Commissioners in itself gives a good indication of the conditions already known to exist. It should be noted that the word 'sewer' in this extract means an open channel, and not a closed drain.

	Question 6 What are the regulations for draining the town or district? Are the streets, courts, and alleys laid out with proper inclinations for the discharge of surface water, or are they uneven and unpaved and favourable to the retention of stagnant moisture and accumulations of refuse thrown from the houses? Are there any stagnant pools or open ditches contiguous to the dwellings, or in the vicinity?	*Question 7* Are there any arrangements for under-drainage, and are they efficient or defective? Are there any sewers or branch drains in the streets?
BRADFORD	No regulations, accumulations of refuse thrown from the houses.	No arrangements for under-drainage.
BURY	No regulations; good sewers in some streets; stagnant open ditches in many places.	No arrangements for under-drainage.
LIVERPOOL	Drainage defective, particularly in the north end of town; full of pits of stagnant water.	Sewers in the main streets, courts and alleys neglected; refuse rots on the surface; the liquid matter is absorbed and finds its way into the cellar.

MANCHESTER	No special regulations, except for private sewers.	Main streets have sewers, out districts imperfect; many streets have no sewers.
PRESTON	No regulations. Drainage very insufficient.	There are sewers in some streets.
SHEFFIELD	No regulations.	No arrangements provided in the act of parliament.
WOLVERHAMPTON	No adequate regulations.	None in the new streets of small houses.

Questions on scavenging in all these towns produced very similar answers. Whether there was a cleansing service or not, the courts and alleys where the poorer classes lived were all described as neglected and insufficiently cleaned. Bury was said to have no regular scavengers; the streets were in a filthy state with the channels choked up. Refuse was wheeled from the courts and alleys into the streets, this being described in the answer to the question as 'a sad nuisance'.

The questions and answers on the supply of water were as follows:

	Question 26 From what source is the town supplied with water?	*Question 32* Are the poorer classes supplied with stand pipes placed at particular stations, from pumps, or draw wells; or are they in the habit of begging water from tradespeople with whom they deal; or how otherwise do they obtain it?
BRADFORD	Inadequate supply; works in progress.	From carts, 3 gals for 1d.
BURY	Private pumps and Joint Stock Company.	From pumps and springs; in some instances, landlords pay for supply.
LIVERPOOL	Two public companies; water extremely pure.	No public pumps or fountains. May of the poor beg or steal it.
MANCHESTER	Supplied by water companies.	The poor very badly supplied.
PRESTON	Water company.	No reply.
SHEFFIELD	Water works; joint stock coy.	By Branch Pipe.
WOLVERHAMPTON	Private supply very deficient.	From pumps.

The picture of town life presented in the Report is thus one of drains being few and inadequate, with open ditches and stagnant pools abounding, refuse left to rot in the streets, and water available to the poorer classes to only a limited extent. It is no wonder that in these circumstances many working men and women were habitually dirty. The lack of water must also have been heartbreaking for the conscientious housewife who had her floors sullied by filth brought in on boots from the street, and her clean washing spoilt by smuts from local chimneys. But there was a worse horror as yet unmentioned—the nauseating state of the privies. These were the earth closets set up in the courts and shared by all the houses nearby. In theory, these were emptied regularly by night soil men who sold the contents to farmers to use as fertilizer. In practice, the privies were often neglected and overflowed into the courts, and in summer the smells and flies could turn the strongest stomach. The same could be said of the numerous middens or dung heaps, and of the cesspools of liquid filth. The fact was often commented on that immigrants from the countryside soon lost the colour from their cheeks, and became pale and wan in this atmosphere. Presumably the only creatures who could remain indifferent to these conditions were the pigs which were kept in the sties near at hand or were left free to roam about. A newspaper reporter, describing typical scenes in a Midlands town in the middle of the century, mentioned several pigsties in a filthy court with pig wash in open barrels, an open cesspool attached to a privy, three further privies, dirty and leaky and used by a score of families, all close to a bakehouse in which a batch of bread was observed. In another part of the same court were three tons of night soil and ashes on which barefooted children were playing, while in a corner there was a horse in an improvised stable and a heap of moist manure, immediately over which were two broken windows of sleeping apartments. The most notorious conditions of all, perhaps, were described by Engels, visiting the worst parts of Manchester in 1844:

A hoard of ragged women and children swarm about, as filthy as the swine that thrive upon the garbage heaps and in the puddles. . . . The race that lives in these ruinous cottages behind broken windows mended with oilskin, sprung doors and rotten door-posts, or in dark wet cellars in measureless filth and stench . . . must really have reached the lowest stage of humanity. . . . In each of these pens, containing at most two rooms, a garret and perhaps a cellar, on the average, twenty human beings live. . . . For each 120 persons, one usually inaccessible privy is provided . . .

These sickening conditions became widely known through a series of Reports on the state of towns in the early 1840s. However, not all towns were as bad as this. Sometimes a public-spirited town corporation would have a private act of parliament passed appointing Improvement Commissioners with powers to pave, clean, and light the streets, so that at least the main thoroughfares were kept decent. In other places a strong-minded landlord might exert a beneficial influence. In a passage rarely quoted, Engels himself described Ashton under Lyne, where the Earl of Stamford exercised a firm control over all new housing, as having a much more agreeable appearance than most other manufacturing towns:

> The streets are broader and clearer, while the new, bright-red cottages give every appearance of comfort.

Again, even in a town where the poorest lived in the foulest of slums, the skilled workman might live in much better housing with perhaps a cellar, two living rooms, two bedrooms, and a small garden. Such houses were comparatively well-built, and some are in good structural repair today. In Nottingham, for example, lacemakers lived in better houses than the impoverished framework knitters, while in London the amount of living room increased roughly in step with money wages and the security of employment of the occupants. So much attention has been paid to the worst kind of housing that the investigation of better quality working-class housing has been somewhat neglected. Another point which is worth making is that it was not always industrialization which must be blamed for bringing foul living conditions. Some market towns were equally insanitary. Shrewsbury, for example, was subjected to a public health enquiry in 1854 because death rates were so high. Lastly, although there was much less congestion in the agricultural village, living conditions were by no means ideal, as the average labourer's cottage suffered from rising damp, vermin-infested wattle and daub walls, and a leaky thatched roof.

Mortality Rates

The urban conditions described so far inevitably affected the general health of town dwellers. Food was quickly tainted in such unhealthy surroundings, and the smoky atmosphere led to chest complaints. There were no municipal baths or wash-houses before Liverpool pioneered them in 1842, and the new towns had no public parks and few open spaces for recreation. Much more serious than this, however, was the disease spread by overflowing privies and the pollution of water supplies from the same source. It was this which produced the killer disease of cholera which swept through the country in 1830, 1848, and 1866, being noticeably more virulent in the overcrowded urban centres. A further contributory factor was the great public nuisance of overcrowded burial grounds in which bodies were crammed on top of one another in shallow graves with bones often showing above the surface. Add to this the streams and rivers polluted by industrial effluent and human excrement—in a famous passage describing the river Irk in Manchester, Engels referred to

> a long string of the most disgusting, blackish green, slime pools . . . from

the depths of which bubbles of miasmatic gas constantly rise and give forth a stench unendurable even on the bridge forty or fifty feet above . . .

—and there is little wonder that death at an early age was common in the industrial towns, especially among the working classes. The contrast between Kendal, Bath and the textile towns is very marked in the following figures for 1842:

Average age at death

Towns	Gentry and professional persons	Tradesmen	Labourers etc.	General average
Kendal	45	39	34	36
Bath	55	37	25	31
London (4 poor law unions)	44	28	22	25
Leeds	44	27	19	21
Bolton	34	23	18	19
Manchester	38	20	17	18
Liverpool	35	22	15	17

Recent writers have commented on the Victorian attitude to death and the liking among even the poorest families for showy and expensive funerals—the Victorian celebration of death—but this is not altogether surprising, given the high mortality rates in towns, especially among the children who often died before they were one-year old. There is thus a somewhat macabre contrast to be made between the ever-increasing numbers of children characteristic of a rising population and the numbers struck down before they were many months old by a combination of disease and malnutrition.

Diet and Recreation

Given the wretched housing conditions of many of the working classes at this time, life at home was necessarily lived at a low level of existence—'a low and grovelling mode of living', according to one contemporary observer. Of course, it would vary very much with the wages of the head of the family (the skilled worker had a much better standard of living than the labourer), and with the number of children, whether they were earning or not, and with the state of trade and employment. Generally speaking, the poorest classes lived on bread, potatoes and weak tea, and this was so whether they lived in countryside or town. It is wrong to assume that the village labourer always ate better than his town counterpart. Although he might be able to grow his own vegetables, fresh meat came his way only rarely, unless he was prepared to run the risk of being caught poaching which was very severely punished. The weekly budget of a careful agricultural family in Lavenham, Suffolk, in 1843 (a hard year) shows how careful a family had to be if it was to keep out of debt:

Name	Age	Earnings		Expenditure		
		s.	d.		s.	d.
Robert Crick	42	9	0	Bread	9	0
Wife	40		9	Potatoes	1	0
Boy	12	2	0	Rent	1	2
Boy	11	1	0	Tea		2
Boy	8	1	0	Sugar		3½
Girl	6			Soap		3
Boy	4	———		Blue		½
		13	9	Thread, etc.		2
				Candles		3
				Salt		½
				Coal & wood		9
				Butter		4½
				Cheese		3
					13	9

An interesting contrast is provided by the weekly spending in 1842 of a West Midland nailer who wrote to his local paper to protest at the low level of his wages. He had a wife and five children, four of these working, and as a family they earned an average of £1 0s. 6d. a week. (*See table overleaf, p. 26.*)

(*See table overleaf, p. 26.*)

The writer explained that these expenses were 'exclusive of utensils for use in the house, clothing and other materials that are necessary. They do not include meat, or medical expenses, or carriage to and from the warehouse—4d per cwt. If family have any butcher's meat, it must be taken from the estimate'. When trade was moderate or slack, life was something of a struggle to make both ends meet. In times of real depression, and 1842 was an exceptionally bad year for trade in the Midlands, then the worker and his family came near to starvation.

In times of prosperity, more could be spent on food, and this was done quite freely, sometimes drawing shocked comments from middle-class observers. Miners in particular liked to spend lavishly when they had the money, and the Mines Inspector, Mr Tremenheere, referred to the 'sensuality and extravagence' of South Staffordshire

	s.	d.
Coal	4	0
Rent	2	0
Tools	1	0
Waste of iron		9
Expenses for domestic use		
Soap for washing and cleaning		6
Candles		3¼
Starch, blue, cotton, soda, thread, pins, needles, tape, etc		2¼
3 pecks of wheat flour	7	6
Vegetables	1	6
Butter	1	6
Sugar & tea	1	0
Cheese		7
Oatmeal 3*d*, milk 3*d*		6
Shoes	1	0
To nurse one child	1	6
	£1 3	9½
Average weekly income	1 0	6
Expenses over receipts	3	3½

miners when trade was good. He went on to describe what he considered to be their reckless spending:

> Poultry, especially geese and ducks; the earliest and choicest vegetables (e.g. asparagus, green peas, and new potatoes when they first appear on the market); occasionally even port wine, drunk out of tumblers and basins; beer and spirits in great quantities; meat in abundance, extravagently cooked; excursions in carts and cars, are the well-known objects on which their money is squandered.

The modern reader is perhaps less inclined to criticize their self-indulgence, given the nature and perils of their work.

Of course, leisure hours were few when compared with the present day, and the ways in which they were spent would depend upon the family income, and whether the family lived in the town or countryside. If the latter, then leisure occupations in the first half of the nineteenth century would still be traditional in nature. The village inn was the centre of what limited social activity existed, while the chapel (and to a lesser degree before the mid-century, the church) would provide an alternative place for sober recreation during the week with its choir practices, visiting speakers, tea parties, and so on. Otherwise there were the annual feasts such as harvest homes, and shearing suppers, with markets and fairs to bring a little colour and excitement. In some parts annual hiring fairs were common at which farm labourers would be hired for the ensuing year. The traditional sports of the countryside were those of hunting, shooting, and fishing, but these were for the gentry rather than the farm labourer. He might follow the hunt on foot, but his freedom to fish was limited, and as already noted, poaching was severely punished.

In the towns, leisure activities expanded and diversified as urban populations grew, and they were a necessary counterpart to the strains of industrial life. Most of these activities took place away from home rather than in the home where they were confined to reading (where literacy permitted it), cards, or drinking. Outside the home a wider variety of entertainment was available. A good deal of it was educational or 'improving' in nature—'rational recreation' was a favourite phrase of the time. This is not surprising in view of the earnestness of the age. Public lectures and meetings were common, often aided by the magic lantern. These were often free, though sometimes a modest fee would be charged as in 'penny readings'. Public libraries were very rare, but circulating libraries might be available for the better-off artisan, and employers occasionally provided a small library and newspapers in a reading room in their works. Mechanics' and workmen's institutes customarily had their own libraries, too. In the 1840s there seems to have been a boom in brass bands, a popular form of working-class music-making, while the great choral societies in the provincial cities no doubt had some members drawn from the skilled working classes.

Not all entertainment was of a cultural nature, of course, and there was plenty of what might be called light entertainment ranging from 'penny gaffs' (short theatrical shows) and street performances of musicians and tumblers to more extended theatre programmes which might include as many as three or four short plays in the one bill. Entrance to the gallery of small provincial theatres would be only 6d, the pit costing 1/-. Travelling circuses were also popular, and usually cheaper than the theatre, the lowest price seats costing only 3d.

Perhaps the principal place of recreation and relaxation for the urban masses was the public house. There the working man could find companionship, warmth, light and comfort. The Victorian public house became the working man's club, its only rival as a social centre being the nonconformist chapel. It was the pub where working-class 'sick and draw' clubs and Christmas clubs were organized, and where trade grievances could be aired and action decided upon. It was here that great quantities of beer were consumed, often adulterated with a variety of substances to give it an artificial strength and taste, not excluding sulphuric acid to give it 'bite'.

Excessive drinking was indeed a serious social problem, but it must be remembered that beer was a drink of great antiquity, and some form of drink was essential in trades requiring heavy physical labour, often at or near furnaces or steam engines; so that men drank freely at work as well as at the public house or at home. Employers recognized this, but sought to limit it where they could. Large iron works often had their own printed lists of rules for workmen, and it is common enough to find rules limiting the amount of ale which might be brought to work, and specifying the fine for breach of the rule. A typical example reads:

> Any person bringing in more than one quart of ale at any one time, or any spirituous liquor into the works (except leave is given) shall forfeit 5/-

Beer was easily obtainable not only in the public houses which were open all day, but also in the very numerous beer shops. There was increasing middle-class concern at the extent of drinking among the working classes, and a powerful temperance movement developed in the middle years of the century which had considerable influence on the Liberal Party, and even opened up a new and respectable career to the working man as a full-time, paid temperance worker. Nevertheless, if drink became a social problem among working-class men and women, it was not because of any special self-indulgence characteristic of the first half of the nineteenth century. Rather it was because drinking was a traditional form of relaxation which took on a new and alarming dimension with the dramatic expansion of the urban communities.

A more occasional form of leisure activity took the form of outings or, as Tremenheere put it, excursions. These would be to local beauty spots or places of interest, and were often organized by employers for their workmen. The coming of the railways in the 1830s and 40s gave an enormous boost to outings of this kind, the cheap-day excursions providing a new kind of holiday for the day, often to the seaside; hence the development later in the century of resorts such as Blackpool, Scarborough and Margate. The most famous place to visit in 1851, however, was the Great Exhibition held in the Crystal Palace in Hyde Park. Many thousands of working people went by train from all parts of the country to visit the Exhibition (the total attendance was over six million), all very well-behaved, and with no disorder—contrary to the expectations of the more nervous among the middle classes. Henry Mayhew described the behaviour of some of the 'shilling folk'—that is, visitors on one of the cheap days:

> Here you see a railway guard, with the silver letters on his collar, and his japan pouch by his side, hurrying with his family towards the locomotive department. Next you come to a carpenter in his yellow fluffy flannel jacket, descanting on the beauties of a hugh top, formed of one section of a mahogoney tree. . . . Peeping into the model of the Italian Opera are several short-red-bodied and long-black-legged Life Guardsmen; whilst among the agricultural implements, saunter clusters of countrymen in smock frocks.

For many working people a visit to the Great Exhibition would have been an exceptional treat, and the most memorable event of the year. Holidays of more than a day's duration for the working man or woman were most unusual, and a week's holiday with pay unknown till the end of the century, and then only for skilled, well-paid workers. However, some urban workers managed a kind of paid working holiday by helping each year with the harvest. Miners, for instance, would go into the fields in August when the demand for coal was at its slackest. Black Country nailers would leave their nail shops and go hopping, or help with the fruit harvest. They would return in procession, singing hymns and 'other more questionable songs' (as one observer put it):

> Anon, the work being completed, and an almost incalculable quantity of cider consumed, and after sleeping almost promiscuously together in barns and such-like places, they return pretty much as they went, but with the addition (among others) of bags of apples, carried on almost every head, and with long strings of the same fruit arranged around the necks of the females, like monster coral necklaces.

It might be expected that some time would be given where possible to sport, but it was not really until the 1850s and 1860s that cricket and football began to assume their modern forms of organization, though of course village cricket did exist, and so did various forms of football. Certain older forms of sport of a crude and violent nature lingered on in the first half of the century. Bull-baiting continued into the 1830s, while cockfighting, ratcatching, and matches between fighting dogs went on a good deal longer. They all provided occasions for betting, and this also applied to the popular sport of pigeon-flying in the Black Country. Of this last sport, the *Edinburgh Review* observed that:

> Sometimes the bet turns on which of a rival pair of 'tumblers' makes the greatest number of summersets in the air; sometimes it is a race between two pigeons, turned out to fly to their usual feeding place; or several are let loose at once, and the owner of the bird which arrives at a designated spot pockets the stakes.

Town Life in Perspective

To the modern reader, the early Victorian town may well appear as a nightmareish creation, a horrendous mixture of noise, dirt, and smells in which even the main streets were befouled with horse manure, thus necessitating the services of a crossings sweeper if one was to cross the road with clean boots. From this point of view, life at home must have been of a very poor standard, lived in wretchedly unhygienic surroundings. That there is a strong element of truth in this cannot be denied, but it is essential to see the facts in perspective. In the first place, although no one denies that conditions could be very bad, it is wrong to suppose that noisome slums did not exist in London and other cities in the previous century—they certainly did, but in the nineteenth century the difference is that the pressure of numbers made the scale of the problem far greater than ever before, and indeed made it quite intolerable. The result was the movement for public health reform to be discussed in Chapter IV. It would be equally wrong (as we have seen) to imagine that all the working classes lived in filth and disorder—this is not true of the better-paid, skilled workman whose wife took pride in her house and its furnishing, and in the cleanliness of her children. Admittedly, such households often had to put up with unpleasant odours from earth privies and middens, but so did many middle-class families who also lacked water closets, and in the smaller industrial towns frequently lived as near the works as their work people. Middle-class houses sometimes had cesspits in their own cellars into which chamber pots were emptied, and the resulting stench was accepted cheerfully enough. Victorians of all classes were surprisingly robust in their attitude to the excretory processes. Perhaps this helps to explain why it was that in spite of all the insanitary horrors, the new towns still attracted immigrants in such large numbers, for many must have considered life in them with all the drawbacks still preferable to life in the countryside.

There is another point to consider: it has often been alleged by liberal historians that the bad state of the towns was due to the greed of landlords and builders who exploited the working-class demand for housing. As one historian put it: 'the avarice of the jerry-builder catering for the avarice of the capitalist.' In fact, houses were not everywhere noticeably worse in quality than they had been before, though in the big towns they certainly were more congested. One comes back again to the basic causes of discomfort and disease—the lack of deep drainage, the absence of a piped water supply, and the failure to provide scavenging, all characteristic of town life in the previous century, and not especially the responsibility of the individual landlord in the early nineteenth century. The greed of landlords cannot be made to bear the blame for all this, unless indeed landlords are deemed always to be exploiters by the very fact that they are capitalist owners of property.

Lastly, it is worth reiterating that life at home for the working classes in this period was not uniform in nature or quality. The major determining factor was always the trade of the worker, for the skilled worker, the aristocrat of labour, enjoyed a higher and steadier income and could live in a better home than the unskilled labourer. Life at home was also influenced by the trade cycle, for in times of prosperity even the labourer would find it easier to keep his job and could eat a little better; whereas in times of depression he might be near starving and faced with the workhouse. Yet whether skilled or unskilled, the background to life in the town for the industrial worker was one of noise, dirt and inconvenience unthinkable at the present day. In the countryside the environment was admittedly better, but housing was still very bad. Work took up so much time in the lives of both industrial and agricultural workers that there was not a great deal of time left for leisure and recreation. Nevertheless, being human and adaptable, they used their leisure time as best they could, and life had its moments of enjoyment even in the grim surroundings of the towns.

Chapter III
Working-Class Protest and Self-Help

Working-Class Protest

During the long wars against the French, agriculture had been very prosperous, though the agricultural labourer had no share in the profits. Indeed, his position had worsened, partly because prices had doubled and wages had failed to keep pace, and partly because the growth of population made labour supplies in the countryside very plentiful. However, some industrial workers were better off, depending on the nature of their work. Iron workers clearly benefited from the war because of the demand for munitions, while weavers profited from the greatly increased supplies of yarn resulting from the mechanization of spinning. Yet even these more prosperous workers had to face the rise in prices, and the end of the war in 1815 brought hardship to all the working classes.

This was because the boom in agriculture was soon over, and farmers were faced with the threat of competition from imported corn. By the Corn Law of 1815 the government attempted to protect the home price of corn by forbidding foreign imports until the home price had reached 80/- a quarter. This led to accusations that the price of bread was being kept artificially high in order to protect landowners' profits; though the subsequent fluctuations in the price of corn seem to have been due partly to the working of the Corn Law and partly to other factors such as bad harvests. Meanwhile the re-opening of trade routes to Europe led to a period of readjustment in foreign trade. Industries which had flourished because of the war now had to find new customers. Competition for jobs intensified as the armies were disbanded and more than a third of a million men came into the labour market. Depression spread in both agriculture and industry, and unemployment increased. In these circumstances working-class protest grew, commonly taking the form of a demand for political reform which, it was hoped, would lead to better conditions for the working classes.

At first it may seem strange that social distress should lead to campaigns for the reform of the electoral system, but it must be remembered that the old unreformed system with its rotten boroughs, restricted franchise, and open voting confined political power to the property owners—that is, the middle and particularly the upper classes.

Only a handful of working men had the vote, mostly in the boroughs, and no women at all. Yet the ideals of the French Revolution—liberty, equality, and fraternity—had made a deep impression in this country, so that in addition to the middle-class radicals who wanted an extension of the franchise, there were many thoughtful working men who believed it to be unjust that they should not have a vote. It seemed obvious to them that they should be given a greater say in government, not only as a simple matter of political justice but also so that they could draw attention to their economic grievances. It hardly needs to be said that these views were regarded with great suspicion by the vast majority of the middle and upper classes who feared that they might lead to revolution and the overturning of the Constitution.

Certainly the government in the post-war period was very hostile to demands for political reform. Some attempts to improve the electoral system had been made in the 1780s, but were abandoned when war broke out. The government's fear of revolutionary ideas during the war was so strong that reform societies were banned, radical leaders were put on trial for treason, Habeas Corpus suspended, and large public meetings forbidden; anyone who denounced the British Constitution could be transported for seven years. In 1793 Lord Braxfield, having given his view that 'the landed interest alone has a right to be represented', went on to assert that:

> Two things must be attended to which require no proof. First, that the British Constitution is the best that ever was since the creation of the world; and, it is not possible to make it better.

When one bears in mind this background, and remembers that the war against France and French political notions had lasted some 22 years, it is not surprising that after 1815 the government was highly sensitive to working-class protest.

The Prime Minister of the Tory government of these years was Lord Liverpool, with Lord Sidmouth as Home Secretary, and Lord Castlereagh as Foreign Secretary. An older generation of historians have always regarded this ministry as peculiarly reactionary in nature. Liverpool had seen the fall of the Bastille, and this is said to have strengthened his intensely conservative views; one French observer said of Liverpool that had he been present at the creation of the World, he would have begged God to conserve Chaos. . . . Another jest was that the secret of Liverpool's policy was that he had none. Sidmouth was similarly thought to lack any constructive policy, being content to leave matters to the working of Divine Providence. Castlereagh at the Foreign Office had little to do with home affairs, but as leader of the House he had to defend government policy, and was closely associated with it. Shelley, attacking this government in his bitter *Masque of Anarchy*, described Castlereagh as follows:

I met murder on the way—
He had a mask like Castlereagh—
Very smooth he looked, yet grim;
Seven blood hounds followed him . . .
He tossed them human hearts to chew
Which from his wide cloak he drew.

Yet in fact Liverpool's government was not as repressive as these views seem to show. Liverpool was neither cruel nor insensitive by nature, and was certainly no reactionary tyrant. When faced with political disorder, his policy took the traditional form of restoring order and waiting for things to return to normal. The modern historian of the period 1815–22 takes it for granted that much of the political agitation of the time was due to the sufferings of the working classes resulting from economic depression. Liverpool, however, did not think there was any necessary connection between social distress and political disturbances. He considered that the government could do little or nothing about the former; most miseries of mankind were beyond the reach of legislation, and government intervention into economic matters nearly always did more harm than good. As for the latter, he thought political agitation merely the work of a discontented minority which would die down, given time to do so.

There still seems no doubt today that the large numbers attending political meetings of the time included many hungry and unemployed workers, and the Spa Fields meetings in London towards the end of 1816 were no exception. In November the famous radical MP for Preston, Henry Hunt addressed a large crowd in Spa Fields on the need for political reform. Hunt's ability to rouse a crowd was well-known. According to a contemporary report, he said that he was opposed to the use of force save as a last resort, but went on:

Those who resisted the just demands of the people were the real friends of confusion and bloodshed . . . but if the fatal day should be destined to arrive, he assured them that if he knew anything of himself, he would not be found concealed beneath a counter, or sheltering himself in the rear.

The meeting was adjourned till 16 December when 'Orator' Hunt was again to speak. But before Hunt arrived at the December meeting, other reformers put in an appearance, notably Dr James Watson and his son. They were members of the small Society of Spencean Philanthropists, which advocated the public ownership of land. Both had been drinking before the meeting, young Watson especially so. He immediately made a speech to the crowd and led off a party towards the Tower of London. Gunsmiths' shops were broken into, and rioting broke out and continued for some hours in the Minories, not far from the Tower. Hunt arrived later and addressed the crowd who had remained, who later broke up peacefully. The rioting seems to have been the result of young Watson's drunken tirades, and some of the crowd were drunk, too, but no doubt many of the participants were protesting members of London's unemployed.

The Cabinet was certainly alarmed by the rioting, especially as at the end of the year parties of unemployed textile workers from Lancashire began to organize themselves to march on London and present petitions to the government. Since they each carried a blanket, they were soon nicknamed the Blanketeers. They did not get farther than Stockport and Macclesfield, where the march was broken up and the leaders imprisoned (March, 1817). Meanwhile, Sidmouth took precautions against further outbreaks. Habeas Corpus was suspended and a number of acts passed (the 'Gagging Acts') to prohibit seditious meetings, attempting to weaken the loyalty of troops, and so on. Dr Watson and some of his fellow reformers were put on trial for treason (the younger Watson had fled to America) but were all discharged when the chief witness for the prosecution was discredited as a person of notoriously bad character. The case against them therefore collapsed.

In the same week as this trial (June, 1817) another alarming outbreak occurred—the Pentrich Rebellion in Derbyshire. The origins and true nature of this rising by between 200 and 300 villagers, many of them unemployed stockingers, and led by one Jeremiah Brandreth, are still obscure. Their intentions seem to have been to march on Nottingham, 14 miles away, and later on London where they would 'wipe off the National Debt'. Brandreth, the 'Nottingham Captain', seems to have believed that Nottingham would rise in their support, and waverers among his supporters were encouraged by promises of roast beef and ale, pleasure trips on the Trent, and the setting up of a provisional government (understood by some to mean a government which would provide provisions). Little is known of Brandreth's background, save that he himself was a stocking maker, but he was a powerful leader and a stern disciplinarian, constantly reminding his followers that:

> Every man his skill must try,
> He must turn out and not deny;
> No bloody soldier must he dread,
> He must turn out and fight for bread.
> The time is come you plainly see
> The government opposed must be . . .

They marched through a rainy night to Nottingham, calling on farms on the way, Brandreth shooting through the window of one farm house and killing a farm servant when he was denied entry. On the morrow it was clear that Nottingham had not risen in support, and Brandreth's supporters began to melt away, in spite of his threat that he would shoot deserters. The game was up when some Hussars appeared on the scene, and the leaders were arrested, put on trial in Derby, and either executed or transported. Sympathy was aroused for Brandeth and the others when it was revealed in the *Leeds Mercury* that the notorious spy Oliver had been involved in the events leading up to the rebellion. Some historians consider that he had acted not merely as an informer (and in the absence of an organized police force the government relied heavily on informers, who sometimes manufactured information), but also as an *agent-provocateur*. Whatever his role, it seems that a rebellion would have taken place in any case, and the historian E. P. Thompson considers that it was one of the first attempts in history to mount a wholly proletarian insurrection without any middle-class support. He also thinks that the rebellion was not an isolated incident, but rather a part of a nation-wide revolutionary conspiracy. If this is so, then the government were to some extent justified in their harsh punishment of the ringleaders, though the older view is that the government purposely exaggerated the threat to the established order so that severe sentences could be passed as a deterrent and warning to others.

The good harvest of 1817 helped to prevent further disturbances, and 1818 passed without serious incident. In 1819 agitation increased again, and a massive meeting was arranged for 16 August at St Peter's Fields, Manchester. Between 50 000 and 60 000 men, women and children attended this famous meeting, marching into position with military precision, but unarmed except for their banners bearing such slogans as LIBERTY AND FRATERNITY, PARLIAMENTS ANNUAL, SUFFRAGE UNIVERSAL. Although the vast crowd was cheerful and orderly, its size and organization greatly alarmed the watching magistrates. They ordered in the mounted Manchester Yeomanry to arrest the speaker, Henry Hunt, on a charge of endangering the public peace. This was done without much difficulty, Hunt being passed along a line of special constables to the house containing the magistrates. But this left many of the yeomanry on their horses in the depth of the crowd, unable to move one way or the other. A contingent of cavalry, the 15th Hussars who had fought at Waterloo, were waiting in a side street, and they were hurriedly summoned to extricate the yeomanry. The chairman of the magistrates called down from his window to the colonel in charge—

Good God, sir! Do you not see how they are attacking the yeomanry? Disperse the crowd!

The result was Peterloo. The Hussars cleared the field within a matter of minutes. They had orders to use only the flat of their swords but inevitably the edge was used, while the freed yeomanry used their swords, too. They were only amateur cavalry, consisting of local manufacturers, ironmongers, publicans, and shopkeepers—'the stupid boobies of yeoman cavalry', the *Manchester Observer* called them—but not too stupid to pay off old scores if they had the chance. The people were at first too densely packed together to avoid the horses and the swinging sabres, but finally scrambled away along the surrounding streets. Eleven were killed and 400 wounded. The working-class radical Samuel Bamford, writing in 1839, described the scene in a memorable passage:

> In ten minutes . . . the field was an open and almost deserted space. . . . The hustings remained, with a few broken and hewed flag-staves erect, and a torn and gashed banner or two drooping; whilst over the whole field were strewed caps, bonnets, shawls, and shoes, and other parts of male and female dress, trampled, torn, and bloody. The yeomanry had dismounted—some were easing their horses' girths, others adjusting their accountrements, and some were wiping their sabres . . .

The disaster caused enormous indignation and was soon nicknamed 'Peterloo' in derision, because the Hussars had fought at Waterloo. A famous cartoon by Cruickshank entitled 'Massacre at St Peter's or Britons strike home' shows the Hussars hacking away at men, women and children with dripping battle-axes, while they are ordered by an officer to

> Chop them down, my brave boys . . . and remember the more you kill the less poor rates you'll have to pay . . .

The government made matters worse by supporting the actions of the magistrates, and then passing the Six Acts. Of these, the first three were of a kind to be expected, dealing with procedure for bringing cases to trial, the forbidding of military exercises, and the issue of warrants for searches for arms. The last three were more far-reaching in extending the stamp duty to more papers and periodicals, giving magistrates power to seize blasphemous and seditious literature, and restricting meetings to present petitions to the inhabitants of the parish in which the meeting was held.

Peterloo remains to this day the most notorious example in British domestic history of the forcible dispersal of a large crowd with heavy casualties, 11 of them fatal. E. P. Thompson has argued that there is no other term for the attack on the people but class war, and that the government in effect 'willed' Peterloo because they knew in advance that the Manchester magistrates were prepared to use force, and they welcomed the chance of a confrontation. He also thinks that revolution was very close in 1819. It is true that Peterloo was followed by the arrest of a number of radical leaders in addition to Hunt, but Thompson's assertions are really unprovable given the present state of the documentary evidence; and he himself admits that Sidmouth wrote to the magistrates 12 days before the meeting advising them not to disperse the crowd (though Thompson thinks this instruction might have been secretly withdrawn). The wider issues raised by Peterloo remain open, but working-class memories of it were bitter and long-lasting.

From the 1820s onwards the severe post-war depression began to lift, though in 1820 there occurred the last and in some ways the most baffling political event of the period—the Cato Street Conspiracy. Arthur Thistlewood, a failed gentleman-farmer, and an ex-militia officer, was one of those accused of treason along with Dr Watson after the Spa Fields riots. Having been found not guilty, he subsequently went to prison for 12 months for challenging Lord Sidmouth to a duel. He came out of prison determined to take revenge for Peterloo, and hatched a plot whereby the Cabinet would be assassinated. As he put it himself:

> High Treason was committed against the People at Manchester. I resolved that the lives of the instigators of massacre should atone for the souls of murdered innocents.

Little is known of Thistlewood personally or of his fellow-conspirators, save that they all seem to have been very poor, one of them literally starving at the time of the plot. Their political views are equally obscure, though Thistlewood was a Spencean and they all apparently believed in universal male suffrage. What political action was supposed to follow the assassination never seems to have been thought out, and one historian has recently referred to 'the desperate, pathetic, and totally shambolic fantasy-world of the Cato St Plot.' The conspiracy was penetrated by a government spy named Edwards, and the conspirators were spurred into action by a specially inserted notice in a newspaper to the effect that members of the Cabinet would be attending a dinner party on a certain date. They were all arrested in a house in Cato Street (off the Edgware Road), one of them running through a Bow Street runner in the process. Thistlewood and four others were condemned to death, and another five transported for life. Thistlewood died bravely and impressively on the scaffold, quietening one of the plotters who insisted on singing 'Liberty or Death', and declaring that he knew he was leaving Albion in chains, but that: 'I desire all here to remember, that I die in the cause of liberty . . .'. The Cato Street Conspiracy was the last political disturbance of any note in the troubled post-war period. Trade improved after 1820, and working-class distress was diminished. In 1822 Liverpool reconstructed his government, and Sidmouth was replaced by the more liberal Peel, and Castlereagh by Canning, another liberal Tory. There were no further attacks on the Tower, no more rural rebellions, no repetitions of Peterloo; nor were there any more repressive acts like the Six Acts. Working-class protest took other, more peaceful forms. In particular, the trade union movement began to advance in the 1820s.

Trade Unionism

Trade unions were by no means the creation of the nineteenth century. Their origins go back to the eighteenth century, and even earlier, for although they are to be distinguished from the old craft gilds, which were associations of both masters and men, they do bear some resemblance to journeymen gilds. Certainly it was in the eighteenth century that journeymen (employees working by the day, or *journée*) began to combine together for protection against their employers. Such combinations were viewed with suspicion by the employers who had them banned by act of parliament in a number of trades such as those of hatters, paper makers, and shoemakers. Indeed, in an age of increasing industrialization and of growing *laissez-faire* beliefs, combinations were thought to be basically wrong; and in trades not covered by act of parliament, employers might bring actions against them under the law of conspiracy, as they were in restraint of trade. They could also have them prosecuted under the Statute of Artificers, 1563, for leaving work unfinished, or even proceed against them for breach of contract. Combinations therefore led a somewhat precarious existence in the eighteenth century.

Nevertheless, they existed in considerable numbers, and were very difficult to suppress. In part this was because they were to be found only among skilled workers who had served their apprenticeships, and were not easily replaced. An employer would need to think twice before antagonizing workers of this kind, and it might serve his purpose better to enter into friendly relations with them. There is the further point that combinations or trade societies (an alternative name) often existed in the form of friendly societies, that is, societies providing insurance against illness, unemployment, or death. Such societies were given legal recognition by the Friendly Societies Act, 1793. Members' subscriptions might therefore be used not only for the perfectly legal purpose of helping their members in times of adversity, but also (with rather doubtful legality) for strike pay.

This then was the situation on the outbreak of war against France in 1793. It was not long before the government became concerned at the possible spreading of revolutionary ideas, and the war began to go badly, with mutinies in the Navy at the Nore and at Spithead in 1797, and a landing of French troops in Ireland in 1798. It was thought that trade societies could easily become revolutionary conspiracies, and in 1799 the Combination Act was passed:

All contracts, covenants and agreements whatsoever . . . made or entered into by any journeymen manufacturers . . . for obtaining an advance in wages . . . or for lessening or altering their or any of their usual hours or time of working or for decreasing the quality of work, or for preventing or hindering any person or persons from employing whomsoever he, she, or they shall think proper to employ . . . shall be and the same are hereby declared to be illegal, null and void.

This Act therefore made illegal all combinations in all trades, and it also provided for conviction by only one magistrate. An amending Act was passed in 1800 increasing the number of magistrates to two, and permitting a maximum of three months imprisonment, appeal to Quarter Sessions, and arbitration in industrial disputes. The Act also applied to combinations of employers as well as workmen.

The Combination Acts, 1799 and 1800, have long been regarded as a milestone in the history of trade unions—the Webbs called them 'a new and momentous departure'. Unfortunately, the Webbs, who published their great *History of Trade Unionism* in 1894, were wrong, probably because they did not take sufficiently into account the previously vulnerable position of the unions. The Acts added little to the existing laws, and the penalties imposed were very light. In any case, convictions might be quashed on appeal to Quarter Sessions, so that comparatively few prosecutions were ever brought under the Acts, which simply provided an additional deterrent to combination, but nothing more.

Combinations therefore continued after 1800. Sometimes they were prosecuted, as in 1810 when printers of *The Times* received up to two years imprisonment apiece for conspiracy ('A most wicked conspiracy to injure . . . those very employers who gave you bread', according to the judge). In other cases the employers were quite prepared to negotiate peacefully with their workers, or they might even be intimidated into doing so. There were the practical difficulties, too, of finding evidence for a prosecution. When Sidmouth was asked in 1816 to strengthen the laws still further against combinations, he found himself unable to do so, and referred to

the great practical inconvenience which is felt arises from the difficulty of proving the necessary facts to convict offenders.

There was always the danger, of course, that workmen might bring counter-charges of conspiracy against the masters, though in the event this rarely, if ever, happened.

When economic conditions improved in the early 1820s, the situation seemed favourable for a review of the law. The lead was taken by Francis Place, a radical London master tailor, whose ally, Joseph Hume, MP, persuaded the House of Commons to appoint a Select Committee on Industry, including the review of the working of the

Combination Acts. Place took good care to present witnesses before the Committee who argued in support of repeal. The Committee's report was critical of the Acts which they thought

> had a tendency to produce mutual irritation and distrust, and to give a violent character to the Combinations.

They therefore recommended complete repeal, subject to safeguards against threats or intimidation.

This was effected by the Combination Act, 1824, which repealed all the Combination Acts (not merely those of 1799 and 1800) and even protected combinations against the law of conspiracy. A notable victory had been gained, but it was also a somewhat strange achievement in view of the fact that Place actually thought combinations could do little to affect the level of wages, which must depend on supply and demand. His opposition to the Acts was an opposition in principle to statutory restrictions on bargaining, which he thought should be left to operate freely; but he himself was no great friend of combinations, and he thought strikes unnecessary. In fact, the 1824 Act led to repeated strikes, and a good deal of violence and intimidation, in spite of clauses in the Act forbidding this. It happened that repeal coincided with an up-turn in trade and a rise in prices, so that striking for better pay occurred on all sides. Another Select Committee was appointed, and the evidence given before it revealed some of the seamy side of the unionism of the time, ranging from restriction of output to sending non-union men to Coventry, or physical attacks on them, sometimes with vitriol. Another Act was passed in 1825, limiting the gains of the 1824 Act, confining the purposes of combination to bargaining over hours and wages, forbidding picketing and intimidation, and restoring the common law liability to charges of conspiracy. Nevertheless, all combinations henceforth were indisputably legal, and so in this way the repeal of the Combination Acts in 1824 and 1825 certainly constitutes a great landmark in the history of unionism.

After 1825 trade societies grew in numbers, though still confined to the skilled workers who were only a small proportion of the working classes as a whole. By now there were unionists who could see the advantages of district or even national unions, and some attempts were made in this direction. As early as 1818 the Lancashire spinners formed a 'Philanthropic Society' to bring in all workers in the Lancashire textile industry, and they were copied by London unionists who set up a similar group of societies called the 'Philanthropic Hercules'. Both bodies soon faded out, but John Doherty, an Irish cotton spinner in the Manchester area, tried again in 1829 by forming the Grand General Union of Operative Spinners of Great Britain and Ireland. In the next year he set up a general union of trades called the National Association for the Protection of Labour (NAPL). This consisted of local unions affiliated to a central Council in Manchester, contributions to a central fund being made so as to supply strike pay when wage cuts had been made.

By 1832 the Grand General Union had broken up, and the NAPL had also disintegrated. However, Doherty had set a precedent by his attempts at large-scale organization, and it is significant that he was a strong believer in political reform, so that the new move to nation-wide organization now had political overtones. When the builders formed their own national organization in 1832—the Operative Builders Union—they also set up as a governing body a Grand Lodge, or Builders' Parliament which in 1833 discussed the idea of co-operative production as an alternative to capitalist production. This was, of course, at a time when great national debates were ranging over political reform leading ultimately to the Reform Act, 1832. Thus the leadership of the trade union movement was becoming politically minded, though it is impossible to say how far this was true of the rank and file.

The most famous effort in the 1830s at a national organization of trade unions with ultimately political objectives was the Grand National Consolidated Trades Union, formed in London in 1834. It was designed to cover as many trades as possible, including women's trades such as bonnet-making (one lodge was entitled the Lodge of Ancient Virgins), and its major aim was to organize strike relief, though it was also prepared to consider the 'grand national holiday', or general strike, if necessary. The name of Robert Owen, the famous socialist factory owner, is associated with the GNCTU, but he did not become a member until it was in rapid decline, and in any case was not really interested in trade unions except as a means of propagating his ideas of socialist cooperation. The importance of the GNCTU was somewhat exaggerated by the Webbs, who claimed that its membership reached half a million, though more recent research has shown that the paid-up membership was only about 16 000, based largely on London tailors, shoemakers, and silk weavers.

Indeed, the GNCTU had an even briefer life than that of the NAPL. Its organization was poor, constituent unions would go on strike and expect financial help from Headquarters, and the final collapse came at the end of 1834 when the Treasurer ran away with what was left of the funds. Nevertheless, by this time the GNCTU had become famous because of the trial of the Tolpuddle Martyrs which had taken place in March earlier in the same year.

This case was the result of a group of agricultural labourers in the village of Tolpuddle, near Dorchester, deciding to form a branch of the GNCTU. Their leaders were the brothers James and George Lovelace. When recruiting members, a solemn initiation ceremony was used of a kind common enough at the time. The purpose was to impress the new recruits with the seriousness of the occasion, whether they understood what was happening or not. *The Times* reported one witness as saying:

Someone then read a paper, but I don't know what the meaning of it was. After that we were asked to kneel down, which we did. Then there was some more reading; I don't know what it was about. It seemed to be out of some part of the Bible. Then we got up and took off the bandages from our eyes. . . . Some one read again, but I don't know what it was, and then we were told to kiss the book, which looked like a little Bible . . .

The proceedings were innocent enough, and the rules of the society made it quite clear that the society was non-violent in aim. Thus, Rule 23 stated:

That the objects of this society can never be promoted by any act or acts of violence, but on the contrary, all such proceedings must tend to injure the cause and destroy the society itself. This order therefore will not counternance any violation of the laws.

Nevertheless, the Home Secretary, Lord Melbourne, chose to make an example of these innocent men, presumably because he feared some kind of reoccurrence of the agricultural riots (the Captain Swing riots) which had taken place in Kent in 1830, and which he had suppressed very harshly. The men could not be prosecuted for forming a union—this was quite legal—but initiation ceremonies and the swearing of fraternal oaths were always feared by the government as smacking of revolutionary conspiracy. So they were accused under an Act of 1797 of administering unlawful oaths, and six labourers were sentenced at Dorchester to the maximum sentence of seven years' transportation. There was an enormous outcry at the injustice of this, and by 1836 they were all brought back from Australia. But the cause of trade unionism had suffered a severe blow, and the hostility of the government was only too evident. Although the case of the Tolpuddle Martyrs did not destroy the GNCTU, it contributed to its rapid decline later in the year. Recruitment to other unions was also affected, and some employers took the offensive and presented their workmen with the 'document'—a promise not to join a union, made as a condition of employment.

However, the effect of the Tolpuddle case must not be exaggerated. The union movement was by no means completely destroyed—far from it. It is true that there were no more attempts for many years at grand national unions for all trades, but it is also clear that the attempts made up to this time to form such unions were premature. Sectionalism was still strong, and the forces against reorganization on the national scale were still very powerful. Instead, while Chartism held the centre of the stage in the late 30s and during the 1840s, trade unionism continued to make progress, especially after 1842. The movement was still very small, of course, and was still confined for the most part to the literate, skilled working man—the 'aristocracy of labour'. In most cases trade unionists concentrated on the day-to-day business of negotiating the best wage deals they could get from the employers, without reference to the wider issues on the rights of labour or the political future of the working classes. How far, if at all, trade unions were attracted into the political world of Chartism will be discussed in the next section.

Chartism

Chartism is the name given to the most striking and widespread working-class movement for political reform of the nineteenth century. The origins of this movement lie in the setting up of the London Working Men's Association in 1836 by a group of London radicals of whom William Lovett, a cabinet maker, was the most prominent. In 1837 Lovett drafted the famous charter which summed up the major demands of the Association. These demands were widely publicized in popular pamphlets, one of which was in the form of a dialogue between Mr Doubtful and a Radical. Mr Doubtful asks the meaning of 'Chartist':

> Radical: It is one who is an advocate for the People's Charter.
> Mr Doubtful: The People's Charter, pray what is that?
> Radical: It is an outline of an Act of Parliament, drawn up by a committee of the London Working Men's Association, and six members of parliament; and embraces the six cardinal points of radical Reform.
> Mr Doubtful: What are these points?
> Radical: They are as follows: 1. Universal suffrage 2. Annual parliaments 3. Vote by Ballot 4. Equal Representation 5. Payment of members 6. No property qualification.

By 'universal suffrage' was meant votes for all men, equal representation meant equal electoral districts, and no property qualification meant no property qualifications for being elected to parliament. None of these points was new; at least five of them figure in a radical statement of 1780. But it is not surprising that they should form the basis of new radical demands in the period of bitterness and disillusionment following the passing of the 1832 Reform Act. Although working-class political organizations had given strong support to the Whig government in passing the act, the working classes had gained little from it. It was the middle classes who were given the vote in the borough constituencies, very few working men benefiting at all. Understandably enough, disappointment over the Reform Act was a major cause of Chartism.

Chartism started on a small scale in London, but it soon grew into a massive national movement as it gained support from other reformers. They included opponents of the new Poor Law such as Richard Oastler, already famous in the Factory Reform Movement, J. R. Stephens, a Methodist minister, and John Fielden, the manufacturer; currency reformers such as the Birmingham banker, Thomas Attwood, with his Birmingham Political Union which had actively supported the Reform bills of the 1830s; and brilliant individual reformers such as Feargus O'Connor with his influential newspaper, *The Northern Star*, founded in 1837. In addition to disappointment over the Reform Act and opposition to the New Poor Law, other causes for the initial take-off of Chartism must include the hostility aroused by the case of the Tolpuddle Martyrs, the dislike of the new rural police established in 1839, and a vague but pervasive fear of the strengthening of central control resulting from the Whig reforms of the 1830s.

It was Attwood who first proposed that a petition for the enactment of the six points of the Charter should be presented to Parliament by a specially summoned Convention of Chartists. If Parliament refused to accept the petition, then a general strike should be organized to last a month (the 'sacred month'). In February, 1839 a Convention of 54 Chartists duly assembled in London, the petition having meanwhile attracted 1 280 000 signatures. Heated arguments took place over what should be done if the petition were rejected. It was proposed that all Chartist meetings should be asked certain questions—whether they would carry out the 'sacred month', start a run on the banks, boycott hostile shopkeepers; and most ominous of all, they were to be asked whether

> . . . according to their old constitutional right—a right which modern legislators would fain annihilate—they have prepared themselves with the arms of freemen to defend the laws and constitutional privileges their ancestors bequeathed them? In short, whether they had armed themselves.

The Convention moved to Birmingham where rioting broke out on 4 July, and Lovett and others were arrested. On 12 July, the Commons rejected the petition. The 'sacred month' was then decided on, but as support was not encouraging, it was never carried out. In November 1839, a Chartist rising took place at Newport in South Wales. The precise aims of this rising are still obscure, but it seems that it was intended to seize power locally and to release a well-known Chartist, Henry Vincent, from Monmouth gaol. O'Connor appears to have tried to stop the outbreak, but it was betrayed to the authorities, so that when the Chartists entered the town the soldiers were waiting for them. Fourteen Chartists were killed, and the leaders, including John Frost, a respected local draper, ex-mayor and ex-magistrate, were sentenced to death. So ended the first phase of Chartism.

The second phase began in 1840 with the setting up of a new organization, the National Charter Association by O'Connor, and it is fair to say that from now on Chartism was increasingly dominated by Feargus O'Connor. Nevertheless, he had first to contend with a rival movement in the form of the 'New Move'. This was an attempt by Joseph Sturge and other members of the Anti-Corn Law League to combine the aims of the League with a strictly peaceful agitation for the extension of the suffrage. This proved popular with a number of Chartists who disliked the militancy of O'Connor and his supporters. Complete Suffrage Associations were established, together with the Birmingham Complete Suffrage Union. At first, O'Connor denounced the whole business, calling it 'complete humbug':

> Complete suffrage would merely tantalize you with the possession of a thing you could not use. . . . Repeal of the Corn Laws without the Charter would make one great hell of England . . .

Meanwhile, another national Convention had been meeting, and a second petition was presented to the House of Commons in May, 1842, this time claiming to have 3 317 752 signatures, but it was again rejected. The problem arose once more of what to do next, particularly in view of the divided nature of the movement, Lovett and others now being attracted to the New Move. By July O'Connor himself had changed his mind, and was speaking in favour of Sturges, but what might have been a hopeful move towards reconciliation was lost in the wave of strikes which began in the Midlands and the North, these strikes being known collectively as the Plug Plot.

The year 1842 was a year of extreme depression in trade—one of the worst of the century—and unemployment and wage cuts were widespread. Driven desperate by their plight, men went from works to works in Lancashire, Yorkshire and the West Midlands, knocking out boiler plugs in order to enforce a kind of general strike. The Chartists certainly did not start the strikes, though they approved of them; for example, a Chartist conference in Manchester declared that they

> strongly approved of the extension and continuance of the present struggle until the PEOPLE'S CHARTER became a legislative enactment!

The inevitable result was that when the strikes were suppressed—one estimate is of 1 500 arrested, and 79 transported—the Chartists were blamed for them, and held responsible for the rioting and violence which had occurred. Many Chartists in turn blamed the Anti-Corn Law League for encouraging the strikes so as to discredit Chartism. In these circumstances O'Connor returned to his earlier hostility to the League, and by December the alliance between the Complete Suffrage Union and the National Charter Association was at an end. Subsequently the CSU itself faded away, leaving O'Connor in charge of what was left of Chartism. Thus ended the second phase of the Chartist movement.

It is noticeable that both the first and the second phase of Chartism ended in violence, even though the Chartists cannot be held responsible for starting the Plug Plot. Inevitably the question arises of how far Chartism was in itself a violent movement. It is true that Chartists often used menacing language. O'Connor declared that he was for peace,

> but if peace giveth not law, I am for war to the knife.

Another leading Chartist, Peter Bussey, said that

> he recommended that every man before him should be in possession of a musket, which was a necessary article that ought to provide part of the furniture of every man's house. And every man ought to know well the use of it . . .

A Manchester poster declared:

> Now or never is your time; be sure you do not neglect your arms, and when you do strike do not let it be with sticks or stones, but LET THE BLOOD OF ALL YOU SUSPECT moisten the soil of your native land.

On the other hand, the well-known slogan of the Chartists was 'Peacefully if we may, forcibly if we must', and this is perhaps a better indication of the outlook of the majority of Chartists, who did not welcome violence. It has been suggested that much of the threatening language was deliberately intended to intimidate—a rhetoric of violence—and the authorities were well aware of this. Even Lovett, always thought of as essentially a man of peace, seconded a Convention resolution in 1839 advising the people to arm. Considering the many thousands of Chartists who attended meetings over a period of 10 years or so, the amount of public violence was remarkably small. Most of the vast meetings held by torchlight outside the industrial towns were extraordinarily peaceful. The occasions when Chartists deliberately used force in an attempt to gain their ends are limited principally to the Newport rising and to smaller isolated incidents thereafter. This is not to say, of course, that bitter fighting with the police did not take place at times, and one can understand the feelings of the desperate, half-starved Chartist who declared in 1842:

> Better die by the sword than die of hunger . . . and if we are to be
> butchered, why not commence the bloody work at once?

The third and last phase of Chartism begins at the end of 1842, with
O'Connor now the monarch of a declining kingdom, as a recent
historian has put it. During the course of the next year 1843 he began to
work upon a favourite scheme for settling Chartists on the land. At first
there was a good deal of opposition among Chartists to his plans, partly
on the grounds of practicability, and partly because it was thought it
might distract attention from the Charter. However, by 1845 the
National Co-operative Land Company was in being, and branches were
established all over the country, but especially in Lancashire and in
London. In the end, there were 70 000 subscribers, and about 250
people were settled on five sites.

During these years of the mid-1840s Chartism as a political force
made little progress. Most historians explain this by the fact that the
economy was recovering from the depths of depression at the beginning
of the decade, and many have commented on the fact that the fortunes
of Chartism seemed closely linked to the state of the economy. One
distinguished historian, Elie Halévy, for this reason called Chartism
'the blind revolt of hunger'. Even at the time observers could see that
some Chartist support resulted from the sufferings of starving men and
women. J. R. Stephens said in a famous speech:

> The question of universal suffrage is a knife and fork question . . . a
> bread and cheese question . . . and if any man asks me what I mean by
> universal suffrage, I would answer: that every working man in the land
> has a right to have a good coat to his back, a comfortable abode in which
> to shelter himself and his family, a good dinner upon his table, and no
> more work than is necessary for keeping him in good health and as much
> wages for that work as would keep him in plenty . . .

Was then Chartism simply a knife and fork question? In one way it
was, because it is clear that mass support came in times of the worst
depression—in 1839, 1842, and as we shall see very shortly, in
1848—and many Chartists undoubtedly believed that political reform
was bound in the end to bring social reform. On the other hand, it is
equally clear that many of the leaders were not starving at all, and were
strong believers in the political rights of the workers; for Chartists like
Ernest Jones and Julian Harney the vote was an inalienable right, part
of an Englishman's birthright which had somehow been filched from
him. Obviously there were middle-class Chartists who had some
sympathy with this point of view. Then again, there were Chartists who
became interested in particular issues, such as educational reform
(Lovett was among these), or teetotalism, or the Christian religion.

For these Chartists, the movement was not merely a bread and cheese question. Hence Chartism was more than the blind revolt of hunger, but empty stomachs certainly provided mass support in the key years of depression.

Closely associated with the idea that Chartism was based on hunger is the idea that it was a revolt against industrialization. This introduces the interesting problem of which sectors of the working classes were the strongest Chartists. It is true that Chartism was weak in agricultural villages and market towns, but it is not true that the bulk of Chartists were factory workers rebelling against their working conditions. As we already know, factory workers were only a small proportion of the national workforce at the mid-century, and in any case, Chartism was not confined to textile factory areas like industrial Lancashire or the West Riding. All the same, the movement was strong in Lancashire, some factory workers were certainly Chartists, and no doubt their numbers increased in the worst years of depression. But the leading categories of Chartists seemed to have been depressed workers in domestic industry (handloom weavers, nailers, stockingers) and skilled workers such as carpenters, shoemakers and tailors. The first group might be held to be the victims of the Industrial Revolution, but the second group were hardly touched by technological change as yet, and were well-paid and articulate. If one remembers the middle-class supporters who included schoolmasters and doctors, it can hardly be argued that Chartism as a whole was a revolt against the Industrial Revolution. It is significant, too, that the trade unions held aloof from Chartism (though individual trade unionists were Chartists, of course). In London only the unions of weaker crafts consisting of less skilled artisans provided any support for Chartism, although the Chartists did try to enrol men in the same trade into branches of the National Charter Association.

In 1847 prospects improved for Chartism as trade began to decline, the land company recruited more and more members, and O'Connor was elected MP for Nottingham. By 1848 trade had still not recovered, and interest in political reform increased with the news of the February Revolution in France. A new Convention was summoned, and a third petition was prepared. A nation-wide campaign aroused great enthusiasm, and once more the possibility of real violence loomed up. Many Chartist speakers referred to the need for physical force, such as Ernest Jones:

> I believe that we stand upon the threshold of our rights. One step, were it even with an iron heel, and they are ours. I conscientiously believe the people are prepared to claim the Charter. Then I say, take it, and God defend the right!

Arrangements were made for a great rally on Kennington Common on

10 April followed by a march with the petition to the House of Commons. The government took the threat to public order very seriously: over 150 000 special constables were enrolled, while there were thousands of regular police, 8000 soldiers, 1500 Chelsea Pensioners, and 12 cannon, together with forces of marines and sailors. Arms were also distributed to civil servants.

When the great day dawned, a large crowd assembled peacefully on the Common, the numbers present being estimated by O'Connor as between 400 000 and 500 000, by *The Times* as about 20 000, and by the Prime Minister, Lord Russell, as 12 000 to 15 000. O'Connor addressed them in his usual manner, but prevailed upon them to accept the government's warning that it was illegal under a statute of the reign of Charles II for a large crowd to present a petition to the House of Commons. About two o'clock the crowd broke up. It was now raining heavily. The petition with its nearly 6 m signatures was loaded into three cabs and taken to the Commons. Within a few days it was announced that the petition numbered only 1 975 496 signatures, including those of 'Victoria Rex', Wellington, Peel, and would-be humorous signatures like those of Mr Punch, No Cheese, and others. The petition was rejected, and the ridicule which resulted from the forged signatures did great damage to Chartism.

Although it is often thought that Chartism as a movement came to an end in 1848 with the failure of the third petition, this is by no means true, though after 1848 it was undoubtedly in rapid decline. The Land Company got into difficulties during the year and its affairs were investigated by a Select Committee of the House of Commons. They found that the company was nearly bankrupt, and was very badly run, but it was made clear that O'Connor had acted honestly throughout; in fact, the company owed him money. By 1851 the company was wound up. By this time O'Connor, always erratic and unpredictable, was acting strangely and becoming more and more unbalanced. In 1852 he was confined in an asylum in Chiswick, and he never recovered his senses. He died in 1855. Meanwhile the Chartist movement fell increasingly under the domination of socialists such as Julian Harney and Ernest Jones. By 1860 the National Charter Association collapsed, and this at last brought the story of Chartism to a close.

Why did Chartism fail? Presumably it must be accounted a failure, because, although five of the six points of the Charter are now law, this was scarcely the direct result of the work of the Chartists. The most obvious reason for failure is that the Chartist demands were too radical for a parliament representing the middle and upper classes to accept, particularly as they were seeking not one but six separate reforms in all (the middle-class Anti-Corn Law League, on the other hand, had only one single objective, the repeal of the Corn Laws). Moreover, the Chartists lacked agreement on how they might bring pressure on the government if their petitions were not accepted. The 'Sacred Month' was never implemented, and they were divided over the use of force.

Even if they had been united on this issue, the government had the army, the police, and middle- and upper-class opinion overwhelmingly on their side. In fact, it was fortunate for the Chartists that the army in the North was commanded by Sir Charles Napier, well-known for his radical views, and actually sympathetic to the Chartist cause. He went out of his way to explain to Chartist leaders what they would be up against if it ever came to civil war, even giving them a gunnery display in Manchester, and telling them that:

> I would never allow them to charge me with their pikes, or even march ten miles, without mauling them with cannon and musketry and charging them with cavalry, when they dispersed to seek food; finally that the country would rise on them and they would be destroyed in three days.

These were the realities of the situation as Napier saw them, and the Chartists never found an answer to this. Moreover, Napier was very careful to avoid provocative action by the army, and to avoid any repetition of Peterloo. On one occasion he warned the Manchester magistrates that if they used force, they must bear the consequences, for

> not a soldier should quit the barracks till both the constables' and magistrates' heads were broken . . .

Thus the Chartists were never provoked to violence or counter-violence on a scale sufficient to make a real revolution possible. At no time was London or any provincial city really in danger.

It must be remembered, too, that Chartism lacked united leadership, as well as an agreed policy for achieving the Charter. For a time, the New Move produced two rival Chartist movements, and even after 1842 when O'Connor dominated the movement, there was still the division between believers in moral force and believers in physical force. The different varieties of Chartism—Knowledge Chartism (as O'Connor contemptuously called it), Teetotalism Chartism, and so on—all had a divisive effect, as did those Chartists who saw Chartism as a means of introducing socialism. Neither Lovett nor O'Connor was a socialist, of course, the latter being on the contrary a strong believer in individualism and capitalism. He said of his land scheme, for instance:

> My plan has no more to do with socialism than it has with the comet.

There were also variations of Chartism from region to region—areas with a good level of employment usually supporting moral force, as in

Scotland, areas suffering unemployment and distress being in favour of physical force, as in the West Riding. In Leeds the Chartists concentrated on becoming powerful in local government, and competing for seats on the Corporation. In Wales there were strong links with the Nonconformist chapels. Given all this diversity it is not surprising that with the coming of the prosperity of the 1850s the mass membership fell away, and the movement steadily declined.

Nevertheless, Chartism was a tremendous experience for the working classes, reaching into many different aspects of their lives. For years afterwards Chartists would speak with pride of the movement, and of their own part in it. Chartism gave the working classes valuable experience in leadership and in the self-discipline necessary, for example, for the organization and orderly conduct of the mass meetings characteristic of Chartism. It certainly increased class consciousness and class loyalty. It can be seen to be the natural link between working-class support for the 1832 Reform Act and popular pressure for the extension of the franchise in the 1850s and 1860s, so that it kept alive and nourished the demand for political reform throughout the period between the 1832 and 1867 Reform Acts. It also stimulated the demand for social reform, especially in the fields of public health, education, and working conditions in the factories. Thus, even if Parliament refused to accept the Six Points of the Charter, Chartism was not without its positive achievements for the working classes.

Cooperative Societies

In addition to the trade union movement and Chartism, some attempts were made by the working classes to help themselves by the establishment of cooperative societies. However, these societies were usually idealistic in nature, aiming to set up socialist communities as an alternative to capitalist society, so that the retailing of goods was only one aspect of their activities. Thus they were very different from the modern cooperative movement. Robert Owen is the best-known advocate of socialist cooperation with his ideas of planned cooperative villages (Owen's 'parallelograms') and his cooperative communities in America (1824–7) and at Queenwood in Hampshire. Owen was far more interested in cooperative production than in mere retailing, hence the setting up of his Labour Bazaar in the Gray's Inn Road in London in 1832. The idea here was for the members to make their own goods which were then valued on the basis of the cost of raw material and the labour expended on them; the final value was then divided by the current average cost of labour per hour, the resulting figure being the cost expressed in labour hours. Labour notes for certain numbers of labour hours were printed, and were intended to replace conventional money within the bazaar. The scheme proved impracticable, principally because of the difficulties of pricing goods, and the bazaar was forced to close down.

Other enterprises on a more modest scale and with more limited aims proved rather more successful, especially if they concentrated on retailing. A national congress of cooperative societies was held in 1831. By 1832 there were nearly 500 of these societies, most of them aiming eventually to establish communities on the land financed out of their profits. Many of them became associated with the GNCTU, and when it collapsed, they closed down, too. The final attempt by Owen to set up a community on the land was the Queenwood venture whereby 500 acres were purchased and £37 000 was spent, but it too had foundered by 1845.

The cooperative movement in the first half of the nineteenth century therefore achieved very little. Certainly many schemes were too ambitious, particularly those which attempted to produce their own goods. Lack of capital was often a problem, and there was a good deal of hostility among other traders, not only to the societies as competitors in trade, but also to their political beliefs. The societies themselves lacked legal status, and their members were also hampered by their inexperience in making and selling goods. It was not until the founding of the Rochdale Equitable Pioneers Society in 1844 that the modern cooperative movement really begins. Certainly the failure of the Queenwood community in 1845 seemed to spell the doom of the earlier idealist attempts at cooperation. As the standard history of the movement puts it:

> Cooperation, after 30 years of valorous vicissitude, died, or seemed to die, in 1844–5.

In fact, cooperation was far from dead, as will be seen in Chapter X.

Chapter IV
Government Intervention: Factory, Mine and Town

Early Factory Legislation

In spite of the working conditions of factory children which were described in Chapter II, factory reform in the early nineteenth century proved to be a long-drawn-out affair, and government intervention was slow, hesitant, and at first largely ineffective. This is not because governments of the time were particularly lazy or callous in attitude. As we have seen, it was taken for granted that children should work from an early age, and the fact that most of the early mills were water-powered and tucked away in the countryside prevented conditions from being widely known. Again, the new factories were often associated with the workhouses or prisons—they frequently employed pauper apprentices, of course—and this seemed to place them in a category apart from normal workplaces. Further, as will be seen shortly, there was a considerable and sustained public opposition to factory reform, not all of it from factory owners. Perhaps the most important reasons for the indifference of governments were that there was no historical precedent for parliamentary protection of workers against their employers, while at the same time *laissez faire* ideas were becoming increasingly popular at the beginning of the century. When working hours had been regulated in Tudor times, it was in order to fix minimum rather than maximum hours so as to ensure that a good day's work was done. Hence the very idea of limiting hours was a novelty, and the *laissez faire* belief in letting a man work as long or as short a day as he wished acted powerfully at first against government intervention.

The first signs of uneasiness about conditions in the new factories are to be found in the 1780s. In 1784 a group of Manchester doctors commented on

> the injury done to young persons through confinement and too long continued labour

and went on to recommend that in cotton mills there should be a long recess from labour at noon, and a more early dismission from it in the evening.

As a result the local magistrates resolved that they would not permit any children to be apprenticed in any factories where children were worked for more than 10 hours a day, or worked at night. Other magistrates followed their example, but it was not until 1802 that Robert Peel, Senior, himself a Bury factory owner, introduced the first factory Act, the Health and Morals of Apprentices Act. The most important clause in this Act provided that:

> No apprentice shall be employed or compelled to work more than twelve hours in any one day (reckoning from six in the morning to nine at night) exclusive of the time they might be occupied in eating the necessary meals.

The Act also forbade night work for apprentices, and provided regulations for separate dormitories, and also for religious instruction. There was to be inspection by locally appointed officials, and this proved to be the weakest part of the Act. Richard Arkwright's son said in 1816

> The Act has not been followed up . . . for these thirteen years, I think they visited my mill at Cromford twice.

A further weakness was that it applied to apprentices only, and not to the so-called free children.

In 1816 another Bill was introduced by Sir Robert Peel, drafted this time by Robert Owen, who was himself the owner of model mills at New Lanark, near Glasgow. The measure was delayed in the Lords, finally becoming law in 1819 after an enquiry by their Lordships into the conditions of the factory children. It declared that no child under nine should work in a cotton mill, and that children between the ages of nine and 16, both apprenticed and free, should not work longer than 12 hours between 5 am and 9 pm. This Act too was poorly enforced, and subsequent Acts in 1825, 1830, and 1831 merely altered the law in detail but without introducing adequate safeguards against overworking the children.

Why had so little progress been made by 1831? It might be thought that in spite of the government's reluctance to interfere, public protests at the cruelty inflicted on children would have forced the government to take strong action by this time. As Richard Oastler said in 1833:

> Any old washerwoman could tell you that ten hours a day is too long for any child to labour.

Yet this simple appeal to humanitarian instincts was rejected by opponents of factory legislation as being 'the erroneous dictates of the humanity mongers'. They saw that once children's hours were regulated, the hours of adults would also be affected. On principle they thought that this was wrong. Even such a person as Francis Place, known for his sympathies towards the working classes, thought that:

> All legislative interference must be pernicious. Men must be left to make their own bargains.

Later, when the Ten Hours Movement began, Brougham argued that:

> Every man has a Ten Hours Bill already. No man need work longer than he pleases.

The belief that it was wrong to interfere with the individual's right to work for as many or as few hours as he pleases was supported by most of the political economists of the day. Further, the Rev. Thomas Malthus argued in his *Essay on Population* (1798) that poverty was natural, and that every attempt to make life easier for the poorer classes must fail, since it would only result in their having larger families. This would in turn increase the competition for jobs, while the increased demand for food would put up its price. So the working classes would be as badly off as before. Population and food supply stood in a fixed relation:

> The power of population is infinitely greater than the power of the earth to produce subsistence for man. Population, when unchecked, increases in a geometrical ratio. Subsistence only in an arithmetical ratio . . . by that law of our nature which makes food necessary for the life of man, the effects of these two unequal powers must be kept equal.

In fact, Malthus argued that the only influences which kept population from constantly outstripping food supply were wars and famines, together with moral self-restraint in procreation. If the arguments were true, it was clearly a waste of time to make life easier for the working classes.

The opponents of factory legislation had other arguments of a practical nature to buttress their case. Shorter hours would bring reduced wages and increased hardship. The sensible employer would never knowingly over-work his workmen because their work would then deteriorate in quality. Since profits were made in the last half-hour, a reduction of hours would be fatal for all concerned. It would also mean a loss of trade to foreign competitors. Cobbett attacked this last suggestion with the famous remark that:

> A most surprising discovery has been made, namely, that all our
> greatness and prosperity, that our superiority over other nations, is
> owing to 30 000 little girls in Lancashire. . . . If these little girls work
> two hours less in a day than they do now, it would occasion the ruin of
> the country.

Faced with these counter-arguments, the reformers began to draw
comparisons with the conditions of slaves in the West Indies. In the
year 1830, when the anti-slavery movement was gaining more and more
support, Oastler wrote his impassioned letter on 'Yorkshire Slavery' to
a leading Northern newspaper, the *Leeds Mercury*:

> Thousands of our fellow creatures . . . are at this very moment existing
> in a state of slavery *more horrid* than are the victims of that hellish system,
> *colonial slavery*. . . . The very streets which receive the droppings of an
> Anti-Slavery Society are every morning wet by the tears of innocent
> victims at the accursed shrine of avarice, who are compelled, not by the
> cart whip of the negro slave driver, but by the equally appalling thong or
> strap of the overlooker, to hasten, half-dressed, *but not half-fed*, to those
> magazines of British infantile slavery—the worsted mills in the town and
> neighbourhood of Bradford!

Henceforth Oastler, a Tory land agent of estates near Huddersfield
and Leeds, was to become the outstanding leader of the Ten Hours
Movement which aimed to reduce the working day of factory children
to 10 hours. His interest in the state of the factory children had been
aroused by John Wood of Bradford, himself an enlightened mill owner
who gave £40 000 to the cause of factory reform. Other prominent
reformers at this time were Michael Sadler, Tory MP for Leeds, and
John Fielden, a radical mill owner in Todmorden in Lancashire. They
were joined subsequently by Anthony Ashley (the Earl of Shaftesbury
from 1851), and by John Raynor Stephens, a Tory ex-Methodist
minister. The heart of the factory reform movement was undoubtedly
in the West Riding, where Short Time Committees were set up. But not
all supporters of reform came from this area, and indeed the reformers
were of very mixed origins. Most (but not all) were Tories, some were
humane factory owners, others were landowners, while evangelical
Anglicanism was very strong among leaders such as Wood, Sadler, and
Ashley. Factory reform was never a party matter, though admittedly
Oastler and Sadler were bitterly opposed to the Whigs—Oastler
claimed to 'hate Whig politics with a most perfect hatred'—and factory
reform was sometimes a convenient stick for the Tories with which they
could belabour the Whig Governments of the 1830s.

In 1831 Sadler introduced a Ten Hours Bill into the Commons who referred the bill to a Parliamentary Committee of Enquiry, much to the disgust of the reformers who strongly suspected that their opponents would somehow stifle or distort the evidence brought before it. In fact, the Report of the Committee (known as Sadler's Committee) contained a strong indictment of factory conditions. However, Sadler failed to gain a seat in the first elections held after the Reform Act, 1832, so that it was left to Ashley to take Sadler's place and to introduce the Ten Hours Bill again in March 1833. Even then, the bill was made the subject of a Royal Commission on the grounds that the employers had not been allowed to make fair representations to Sadler's Committee. A further investigation took place, though the Commissioners met great hostility wherever they went because it was suspected that they were on the side of the factory owners. They were frequently greeted by factory children singing Condy's *Song of the Factory Children*:

> We will have the Ten Hours Bill
> That we will, that we will;
> Or the land shall ne'er be still,
> Ne'er be still, ne'er be still;
> Parliament say what they will
> WE WILL HAVE THE TEN HOURS BILL!

In spite of the refusal of the reformers to cooperate in the Enquiry, the Huddersfield Short Time Committee even going so far as to burn the Commissioners in effigy, the Report of the Commissioners was surprisingly favourable to reform. It argued that a case did in fact exist for the control of the hours of factory children, since they worked the same hours as adults, with the results that in many cases the effects of such labour were:

> permanent deterioration of the physical condition; the production of diseases often wholly irremediable; and the partial or entire exclusion (by reason of excessive fatigue) from the means of obtaining adequate education and acquiring useful habits . . .

Yet even then, Ashley's Bill was not accepted by the Commissioners since they considered that it failed to provide adequate protection or education for the children. Moreover, it was likely to result in a reduction of adult working hours. The old ideas concerning individual liberty in this connection were still held very strongly. In Macaulay's words:

> The freeman cannot be forced to the ruin of his health. If he works over

hours, it is because it is his own choice to do so. The law should not protect him, for he can protect himself.

The protests of the reformers at the commissioners' recommendations were unavailing. Ashley was forced to withdraw the bill, and it was replaced by a government Bill introduced by Lord Althorp which eventually became the Factory Act, 1833. This applied to all textile factories except silk mills, and limited hours to eight between the ages of nine and 12, and to 12 hours between 13 and 18. There was to be no night work under the age of 18, children were to receive two hours education daily, and—a very important provision which distinguishes this Act from all its predecessors—four government inspectors were to be appointed.

Curiously enough, although this Act is generally regarded as the first effective factory Act, it was bitterly opposed by the reformers. The radical paper *True Sun* called it 'the infamous White Slavery bill', and said the Whigs had refused to give the Ten Hours Bill and had passed 'a Twelve Hours Humbug'. Not only did reformers understandably object to a clause allowing two sets of children to be employed for eight hours each, one after the other, so that the adult working day might still stretch to 16 hours, but they also suspected that the inspectors would either be completely useless or the willing tools of the employers. In practice, the reformers were wrong in their suspicions, and the inspectors eventually proved effective enough, though it took some time before there were enough of them to implement the Act fully. Certainly many employers disliked the new law. Dr. Ure painted a dismal picture of the damage done by the restriction placed on hours for the nine to 12-year olds. He thought this clause would:

aggravate still more the hardships of the poor and strongly embarrass, if not entirely stop, the conscientious master in his useful toil.

As a result of this, the younger children would be dismissed from their employment and, as he put it:

thrown out of the warm spinning room upon the cold world, to exist by beggary or plunder in idleness . . .

Needless to say, there is little or no evidence to show that this ever happened.

The Gaining of the Ten Hours Bill

Throughout the remaining years of the 1830s the struggle to obtain the

Ten Hours Bill continued. Ashley led the movement in parliament, while outside parliament Oastler was still very active and increasingly violent in his language. In an attack on employers in 1836 he said:

> I never see one of these pious, canting, murdering, 'liberal', 'respectable' saints, riding in his carriage, but I remember that the vehicle is built of infants' bones; that it is lined with their skins; that the tassels are made of their hair; the traces and harness of their sinews; and that the very oil, with which the wheels are greased, is made of Infants' Blood!

However, he had now passed the peak of his reforming career, and in 1840 he was imprisoned for debt in the Fleet Prison and not released until 1844. Meanwhile, unsuccessful attempts were made to pass further factory Bills in 1838, 1839 and 1841. After the General Election of 1841 had brought the Tories to power, the reformers hoped the new government would itself introduce a factory Bill, but nothing was done, and indeed Sir Robert Peel, the new Prime Minister, made it clear to Ashley that the government was opposed to a Ten Hours Bill.

In 1842 the subject of the employment of young children came before the public again with the report of a Royal Commission on children at work, including mines. Ashley had done much to secure the appointment of the Commission, and the Report with its striking illustrations of women and children at work in the pits profundly shocked public opinion, and led at once to the passing of the Mines Act 1842. By this act the employment of women below ground was entirely forbidden, and no boy might be employed under the age of 10. Yet even here the Bill originally set the age limit for boys at 13, but the House of Lords reduced the age to 10, and it was not until 1872 that the age was raised to 12 underground, and eventually to 13 in 1903. However, government inspectors were appointed under the Act, and inspection became increasingly effective from the 1850s onwards.

In 1843 the Home Secretary, Sir James Graham, at last introduced a factory Bill to limit the hours of children to six and a half between the ages of eight and 13, together with three hours education daily. The educational provisions led to such protests from the nonconformists, who suspected that the Church of England would gain an unfair advantage in providing elementary education, that the bill had to be dropped. In the following year Graham brought in another Bill, this time without educational clauses, but again limiting the hours of eight to 13-year-olds to six and a half, and fixing a maximum of 12 hours for women as well as young people. Dangerous machinery was also to be fenced. Efforts by Ashley to amend the bill so as to limit the working day to 10 rather than 12 hours proved unsuccessful in spite of the publicity campaigns still being waged by the Short Time Committees. For example, Keighley Short Time Committee notified all members of Parliament in March 1844 that they had passed the following resolution:

That this meeting is deeply convinced that the just claims of the Factory Population require that the Hours of Labour for all Young Persons under 21 years of age, employed in Factories, should be limited to *Ten* per day, for Five Days of the Week, and EIGHT on Saturday.

Graham's bill became the Factory Act 1844. It was not the Ten Hours Bill that the reformers wanted, but all the same the clauses relating to women's hours and the fencing of machinery were an important advance.

In 1846 Peel's party was split over the repeal of the Corn Laws, and Ashley who had again introduced a Ten Hours Bill, thereupon resigned his seat as a gesture in support of Peel. Leadership of the reform movement in the Commons now passed to Fielden, who persevered with Ashley's Bill. It was narrowly defeated in May by 203 votes to 193. This gave great encouragement to the reformers; as Ashley said, although it was not a victory, 'it was the next thing to one', and in 1847 the Bill was introduced yet again. Because of the slackness of trade at the time, many factories were working only 10 hours a day, and this increased the Bill's chance of success. When it was passed later in the same year, the Ten Hours Movement was at last triumphant, 16 years after it had first begun.

Unfortunately, even then it was not a complete victory, for it was still possible to work children in relays so that the working day could be lengthened beyond the 10 hours for women and young persons fixed by the Act. A test case in 1850 confirmed that relays were still legal, and so a further bill was brought in (Grey's Factory Act, 1850) by which the normal working day was to be from 6 am to 6 pm in return for a slight lengthening of the hours of protected workers from 10 to $10\frac{1}{2}$. Ashley was heavily criticized for agreeing to the extra half-hour, though he though it a reasonable compromise in order to get the bill through; but the bill was so hastily drafted that it was not made clear that children's hours had to be included in the normal working day. It was not until the 1853 Act, which was prepared by the leading factory inspector, Leonard Horner, and introduced into the House by Palmerston, that the matter was put right. Working hours for all factory workers were normally restricted to the period 6 am to 6 pm and because young people and women had already been limited to $10\frac{1}{2}$ hours, adult men's hours were in practice the same. In this somewhat tortuous way the campaign to protect the factory children had at last brought a shorter working day for all classes of workers in the factories.

All the same, it must be remembered that this had been achieved only after a prolonged struggle and much devoted work by supporters of the reform movement. In the nature of things it is impossible, of course, to say how long reform would have taken had it been left entirely to the governments of the 1830s and 40s to take the initiative. It was pressure from without, the vigorous advocacy of Oastler and the

Short Time Committees, combined with the work of Sadler, Ashley and Fielden within Parliament which brought reform. Their achievement was unique and it set important precedents for future social reform, for never before had a government been obliged to intervene so decisively between employer and employee. Thus the factory reform movement not only provided a new pattern for agitation based on both middle-class and working-class support, but it also breached the commonly accepted rule of the time that the government should refrain from interfering into conditions of employment. This meant that the theory of *laissez faire* was being rejected in practice in this direction, at least. As yet, the regulation of working hours was confined to the factories, which employed only a minority of workers at the mid-century. In Chapter VII we shall see how regulation was extended in the course of time to many other classes of workers.

The Government and Public Health

The story of government intervention into conditions in the new towns is somewhat different from that of the coming of factory legislation. Public concern at the high death rates in the towns did not assume any importance until the 1840s, and only one public health Act had been passed by 1850, and that was largely permissive. This may seem remarkable in view of the state of the towns in the early decades of the century, but it must be remembered that in the 1820s there was a widespread and traditional acceptance of dirt and smells, and the connection between insanitary conditions and sickness and disease had yet to be hammered home. People grumbled at the filth of the towns but they put up with it. It was certainly easier in the 1820s to arouse indignation at the cruel treatment of the factory children than to stir up feeling over the evils of leaky privies and the lack of drains. Not until the 1830s did anything like a public health movement get under way.

In 1831 a major attack of cholera so alarmed the government that a Central Board of Health was set up to combat the disease, and some 1200 local boards were established by Orders in Council. These measures were only of a temporary nature, and public confidence was restored as the epidemic died down towards the end of 1832, so that no further action on a national scale was thought necessary. Nevertheless, the link between dirt and disease was stressed in a number of surveys published by doctors in Leeds, Glasgow and Manchester, and a turning point was reached in 1838 when the Poor Law Commission in London ordered a survey of some of the worst parts of London which was carried out by three doctors, James Kay (already the author of the Manchester survey in 1832), James Arnott, and Southwood Smith. Their reports (the Fever Reports) appeared as appendices to the Poor Law Commission's Annual Report in 1838, at a time when the unpopular but zealous secretary to the Commissioners, Edwin Chadwick, was already reaching the conclusion that the disease in the towns was costing the poor law authorities more and more, either in the medical care of the sick and destitute, or in the care of widows and orphans. In fact, he was beginning to argue that it would be cheaper in the long run to improve living conditions than to pay out increasing sums in relief of this kind. As he put it, somewhat laboriously:

> The amount of burdens [on the Poor Law] thus produced is frequently so great as to render it good economy on the part of the administrators of the Poor Laws to incur the charges for preventing the evils where they are ascribable to physical causes . . .

When in the next year the House of Lords ordered an enquiry into the sanitary conditions of the working classes, the Commissioners were glad to direct Chadwick's energies away from themselves and the Poor Law and into organizing the enquiry. From then on the public health movement had acquired a leader. Chadwick was unpopular because he was difficult to work with, being touchy and opinionated, but there is no doubt that he was the embodiment of the 'sanitary idea' and the most determined and influential advocate of reform. Under his forceful guidance, a wide survey of sanitary conditions was undertaken by Poor Law officials up and down the country, including the newly appointed workhouse Medical Officers, together with a host of other witnesses including employers, local doctors, and Chadwick himself. Meanwhile a Health of Towns Select Committee had been appointed in 1840, but bills based on its Report were abandoned. In 1842 Chadwick at last produced his own *Report on the Sanitary Condition of the Labouring Population of Great Britain*.

The mass of evidence in this Report made it impossible to deny that the spread of disease among the working classes was largely caused by the filth in which many of them were compelled to live; and in Chadwick's words:

> where those circumstances are removed by drainage, proper cleansing, better ventilation, and other means of diminishing atmospheric impurity, the frequency and intensity of such disease is abated . . .

Moreover, Chadwick emphasized that it was the squalor in which the poor lived which led inevitably to low moral standards, and not the other way round. Indeed, bad environmental conditions inflicted serious losses annually on the community:

> The annual loss of life from filth and bad ventilation are greater than the loss from death or wounds in any wars in which the country has been engaged in modern times.

The remedy for this state of affairs was clear:

> drainage, the removal of all refuse of habitations, streets and roads, and the improvement of the supplies of water.

In particular, the expense of removing decomposing refuse could be cut by one-twentieth or one-thirtieth by:

> the use of water and self-acting means of removal by improved and cheaper sewers and drains.

By this Chadwick meant the use of drains in which sewage could be flushed away by water.

All that Chadwick had to say in his conclusions was confirmed by the Health of Towns Commission appointed by Peel in 1843, which reported in 1844 and again in 1845. In the course of his evidence, Southwood Smith stressed yet again the dehumanizing effect of a poor environment:

> In the filthy and crowded streets of our large towns and cities you see human faces retrograding, sinking down to the level of brute tribes, and you find manners appropriate to the degradation. Can anyone wonder that there is among these classes of the people so little intelligence, so slight an approach to humanity, so total an absence of domestic affection, and of moral and religious feeling? . . . if from early infancy, you allow human beings to live like brutes, you can degrade them down to their level.

Where the two Reports of this Commission went beyond Chadwick's recommendations was that much more specific suggestions were made as to the type of regulation required. Meanwhile the reform movement was strengthened by the setting up of the Health of Towns Association in 1844, with Southwood Smith as its leader, aiming to campaign for reform through local branches throughout the country. It now seemed that legislation could not be long delayed on the basis of the recommendations made by Chadwick and the Reports of 1844 and 1845.

Yet in spite of the urgent and well-established need for action, it was a further three years before a public health Act was passed. The fact was that the forces against public health reform were still very strong. A major cause of opposition was undoubtedly the enormous cost of any substantial reform. Deep drainage (as opposed to surface channels) was bound to be very expensive, and so was the provision of more water supplies. Who was to pay for all this? Ratepayers were indignant at the thought of an increase in their rates, especially when many of them lived in relatively healthy surroundings and paid for their own tapped water supplies. Why should they have to meet the cost of new sanitary schemes? Since the government was reluctant to grant loans, it appeared that the money would have to come from the ratepayers. It was also disturbing to many of the middle classes in a commercially-minded age that this expenditure could show no tangible profit, for obviously no immediate return could be expected from investing in drainage; though Chadwick and other reformers did try to show that some money could still be made from the sale of sewage to farmers.

Sheer cost in itself was thus a formidable barrier to reform, but the lack of local authorities to enforce regulations was another obstacle. Some new towns had no corporations at all since they had grown from villages into large industrial communities. Other towns had corporations which had been reformed since the Municipal Corporation Act 1835, but political rivalries between the parties represented on the corporation made agreement over reform difficult. Rivalries between older local authorities of this kind and newer, specially-created bodies such as Burial Boards and Highway Boards raised the question of who should have overall responsibility for reform.

There was also the delicate matter of how far the central government should go in telling local governing bodies how to run their affairs. Dictation from London was much disliked in an age when local communities had few links with central government, and most government for the majority of people took the form of local government. Some of the more enterprising towns such as Leeds and Manchester went ahead with their own Improvement Acts in the early 1840s, and such towns certainly thought themselves perfectly competent to manage their own affairs as they had always done in the past. Even locally-devised building regulations were likely to be resented by property owners and builders as an interference with the rights of the individual. Again, there was the problem of the extensive engineering works which Chadwick's plans would require. Few had sufficient knowledge to judge their feasibility, or to know whether Chadwick was right in his ceaseless advocacy of the small, egg-shaped glazed earthenware pipe as the best method of drainage. Lastly, the theoretical nature of some of the reformers' arguments did not convince everyone. Disease was still thought to be spread by smells or miasmas—according to Chadwick, 'all smell is, if it be intense, immediate acute disease'—yet many considered that too much fuss had been made of smells which were often only natural and must be tolerated.

For all these reasons it is not really surprising that legislation took time, and Bills introduced in 1845 and 1846 were both speedily dropped. Another Bill introduced by Lord Morpeth in 1847 produced so much opposition that it, too, had to be abandoned. During the debates on the Bill, the principle of central control was heavily attacked. One member claimed that

> . . . a new authority was proposed to be introduced totally foreign to
> every principle of the English Constitution . . . he regarded it as a
> departure from the free principles of the British Constitution, and a
> gradual usurpation, behind the backs of the people, of the power which
> ought to belong to the representatives of the people, and one step more
> towards the adoption of the continental system of centralization . . .

When the Bill was re-introduced in 1848, again by Lord Morpeth, it
was once more strongly opposed. The *Leeds Mercury*, for example, said
that though all towns should have good sewerage and pure water

> we could not consent to purchase these blessings by a permanent
> infringement of the rights of municipal bodies, and through them of the
> people at large.

Some opponents even attacked the principle of social reform in itself as
being misplaced and misconceived. *The Economist* thought reform
might do more harm than good:

> Suffering and evil are nature's admonitions; they cannot be got rid of;
> and the impatient attempts of benevolence to banish them from the world
> by legislation, before benevolence has learned their object and their end,
> have always been productive of more evil than good.

However, the threat of another outbreak of cholera helped the bill
through, and it eventually became law at the cost of its being largely
permissive in nature. Its operation was limited to five years, and
London was excluded from its provisions as a special case requiring
separate legislation. A Central Board of Health was to be set up with
power to supervise the work of local boards, but these were to be
established only where town councils wished to adopt the Act, or where
one-tenth of the ratepayers of a particular town or parish applied for the
Act to operate. Only in a small minority of cases, where the death rate
was more than 23 per 1000, was the setting up of a local board
compulsory. The Central Board was similar to the Poor Law Board,
although there was no member of the government required to serve on
it, and Edwin Chadwick became one of the three Public Health
Commissioners. As the functions of the Central Board were largely
supervisory, its powers were really very limited, and in addition it had
little or no money to spend.

In this way the first attempt to provide a national public health
organization came into being, but for all the reasons mentioned above,
it had a very cool reception. *The Times*, usually a friend to reform at this
time, criticized the Act strongly, saying in a memorable passage that it

would rather take its chance of cholera and the rest than be forced into good health by the new Public Health Board. It portrayed Britain as suffering a 'perpetual bath night', with Master John Bull being 'scrubbed, and rubbed, and small-toothcombed until the tears came to his eyes.' In 1853 the Board's life was prolonged beyond its original term till 1854, by which time only 182 local boards had been set up, and only 13 of these had done anything about waterworks or deep drainage schemes. At this point Chadwick paid the penalty for his obstinacy and abrasiveness and he was dismissed. The Board continued till 1858 when it was dissolved, its functions being divided between the Home Office and the Privy Council. It was not until the third quarter of the century that the reforms envisaged by Chadwick were undertaken on a truly national scale; he lived to see them, but played no part in their implementation. Pensioned off in 1853 at the early age of 53, he never again held high office.

The Nature of Government Intervention

At this point we may return to consider at a deeper level the nature of government intervention into social problems in the first half of the nineteenth century. Formerly it was held that *laissez faire* reigned supreme in this period, not being replaced as a principle of government policy by increasing state intervention until the 1860s. It is quite clear that in the bald form just stated, this belief simply cannot be true, for both factory and public health legislation was enacted before the 1860s. Nowadays it is more commonly argued that the older theory might have some truth in *economic* matters—witness, for example, the repeal of the Corn Laws in 1846—but has much less truth for social policy. Nevertheless, it is still difficult to assess how far belief in *laissez faire* and individualism actually restricted government social reform before the middle of the century.

There is no doubt, of course, that belief in individualism was strong in this period. Its most popular exposition is to be found in Samuel Smiles' book *Self Help* (1859), and much earlier than this the classical economists such as Nassau Senior, James Mill, and David Ricardo, all followers of the utilitarian philosopher, Jeremy Bentham, were all strongly in favour of individualism in economic affairs. It was because of the strength of the views of both the intellectuals and the middle-class business men and factory owners that the factory reformers were careful to campaign for the restriction of the working hours of children rather than of adults. Again, Chadwick emphasized not the moral duty of the state to intervene so as to reform public health, but the economic cost of allowing squalid conditions to continue unchecked—'all smelly, decomposing matter may be said to indicate loss of money.' It seems reasonable to assume, therefore, that belief in *laissez faire* principles acted as a considerable brake on government legislation before the

1860s, and this is evident enough in the history of factory and public health legislation traced so far.

However, what permitted even strong believers in individualism to qualify their support for it seems to have been an increasing knowledge of the baleful results of unfettered individualism. This can be seen in the way in which Macaulay modified his earlier views on factory legislation. In the debates of Fielden's Bill in 1846 he reaffirmed his belief in free trade, but on the subject of hours worked and the results for the health of the worker, he went on to say:

> I hold that where public health is concerned, and where public morality is concerned, the state may be justified in regulating even the contracts of adults.

Nassau Senior similarly was prepared to admit exceptions to the rule of *laissez faire*. Commenting on the Fever Reports of 1838, he suggested that it was only to be expected that completely unregulated urban expansion would bring its insanitary horrors:

> With all our reverence for the principle of non-interference we cannot doubt that in this matter it has been pushed too far.

Above all others, Chadwick was distinguished by combining belief in individualism with belief in the need for state action as a means for the individual to practise self-help to the full. He too was a disciple of Bentham, and had been his secretary. Bentham's teachings certainly laid emphasis on the need for the state to refrain from intervention in certain areas. His general rule was that in economic matters the government should hold aloof:

> *Be Quiet* ought on those occasions to be the motto or watchword of government.

But at the same time he constantly questioned the utility or usefulness of out-of-date institutions, an approach which pre-supposes that some organs of government, at least, may have a useful role to perform, and he actually proposed the appointment of a Health Minister to be charged with 'the preservation of the national health'. Though there is controversy over this mixture of *laissez faire* and interventionist views in Bentham's teachings, there is no doubt that Chadwick managed to combine both elements in his thinking, even though the two ideas may appear contradictory. Thus in his view public health legislation was not a wrongful exercise of government authority to help the individual who really ought to be left to help himself, but a right and proper adjustment of a situation so beyond the control of the individual as to make self-help an impossible and unrealistic ideal. It is interesting to note, however, that Chadwick's main argument for public health reform avoided this kind of theoretical argument by stressing time and time again that reform was cheaper than putting up with dirt and disease.

Some recent historians have concentrated on what they consider to be the practical realities of the situation rather than the theoretical controversies of the time. For them, government intervention began when some intolerable evil became public knowledge, such as the ill-treatment of children in the factories or mines. This led to legislation, ultimately with the appointment of inspectors to see that the Acts were carried out. This in turn meant the development of a new centralized government department, and the realization that the original problem could not be solved at a stroke, but that it would need continual attention and further legislation for it to be kept under control. By this time parliament would have accepted the reality of the problem and become prepared to take the advice of experts such as inspectors, and to pass additional acts. Thus, from the appointment of inspectors onwards, a kind of administrative momentum would be created which made continued government intervention inevitable.

Clearly it would be impossible to sum up this subject in a single sentence, but this discussion should go some way at least to show that government intervention into working and living conditions was a complex business, owing much to the initiative of individual reformers, and to the skills with which they were able to combat the individualism of the age. Subsequently, of course, the growth of a central bureaucracy was all-important, though in the case of public health reform, this did not take place till the 1870s. From the working-class point of view, the motives behind intervention were immaterial—the important thing was that it had happened, with far-reaching consequences in the second half of the century which will be described and discussed in Chapter VII.

Chapter V
Government Intervention: Schools and Churches

Schools for the Working Classes

At the beginning of the nineteenth century there existed a number of schools for the working classes, but in no sense was there any system of schools, and as a result of the *laissez faire* beliefs discussed in the last chapter, there seemed little prospect of any government help for working-class education. The most important kind of school for children of the labouring classes was the charity school. These were usually financed by local subscription, and were founded in the seventeenth and eighteenth centuries, sometimes as residential schools, but more often as day schools. By 1800, there were 179 charity schools in and around London alone, though they were mostly small. The qualifications for entry into one school of this kind in the West Midlands were:

> First—that they be the sons of poor but honest parents who through poverty or otherwise would not else probably be educated and provided for as is here intended.
> Second—that no boys be sent who are maintained by the parish or whose parents have at any time received alms from it.
> Third—that they be free from any contagious diseases, or infecting bodily sores, or lameness as cripples.
> Fourth—that they be not under seven, nor above the age of eleven years, and that their ages be taken and certified from the parish register.

These boys were subsequently apprenticed at the age of 14, and whilst they were in the school they wore the traditional 'blue coat' uniform of the apprentice. Such schools were often known as 'blue coat schools'. The aims of charity schools were clear—to provide basic instruction in Christian beliefs and in reading and writing, so that the children were prepared for a simple and industrious life in trade or industry.

Another well-known type of school of the time was the Sunday School which originated in the Gloucester area for children working in the local pin factories. These schools concentrated on Bible teaching, and on teaching the children to read so that they might learn from the

Bible. Some Sunday schools taught writing as well. Samuel Bamford, the well-known Radical quoted in Chapter III, recorded that when he went to Sunday school in Middleton in Lancashire:

> I had not gone there long when I was set to writing. I soon mastered the rudimental lines, and quitting 'pot-hooks and ladles', as they were called, I commenced writing 'long-hand'. For the real old Arminian Methodists . . . thought it no desecration of the Sabbath to enable the rising generation on that day to write the word of God as well as to read it.

In addition to the charity schools and the Sunday schools, there were also trade schools, in which children were taught simple trades, their work being sold so as to make the school self-supporting. Such schools had only a limited success, since they were disliked by manufacturers, and also by many parents, who preferred their children to be out at work and earning a wage.

Lastly there were Dame Schools and Common Day Schools. Like all the other schools just described, they too were provided on a voluntary basis, but they also charged fees. Dame schools were often run by elderly females, or by old men who were unqualified for any other employment. Some of these schools were well-run, but the majority were not, the so-called school being really no more than a class of children taught by the dame in her living-room in the intervals between bouts of housework or serving in the shop. The Common Day schools, for older children, were as bad, the master often again being a man who had been unsuccessful in his trade, or who had been disabled in it. An inspector described one such master, in a school of 43 children aged five to 14, in a room about 12 feet square. The master had taken off his coat because of the heat in the room:

> In this undress he was the better able to wield the three canes, two of which, like the weapons of an old soldier, hung conspiciously on the wall, while the third was on the table ready for service.

The master claimed that he generally reasoned with the children, but they were 'abrupt and rash in their tempers', so that at times (as he put it) he had recourse to a little severity.

It is clear that the schooling available to the working classes in the early nineteenth century was of a very limited variety, yet this is not surprising in view of the strength of *laissez faire* beliefs and the very narrow conception of the proper functions of government. It would be wrong to suppose that there was a general hostility to giving any education at all to the working classes, but it was certainly believed that only a very elementary kind of education should be made available to them. Nowhere in the country, of course, was education compulsory, and many could see little point in schooling for children who went out to work as soon as they were big enough. There was also a widespread middle-class belief that too much education would make the working classes discontented with their lot, which would lead to insubordination and political unrest. This view was strengthened after the outbreak of war against France in 1793, when it was feared that revolutionary ideas would take root in this country. One journal, *The Anti-Jacobin*, called Sunday schools 'nurseries of fanaticism', while in 1800 the Bishop of Rochester declared dramatically that

> schools of Jacobinical rebellion . . . schools of atheism and disloyalty abound in this country; schools in the shape and disguise of Charity Schools and Sunday Schools.

No doubt these were extreme views, and not long after, public attitudes began to change. More and more it was realized that something would have to be done about the ever-increasing numbers of young children in the new industrial towns who were growing up out of reach of the churches or any other civilizing influence. Dame schools and Common Day schools could not possibly cope with such an increase. Further, with the spread of the radical popular press, it seemed essential to provide more schooling of a kind which would emphasize the importance of accepting one's proper station in life, and so to live in obedience to the will of God. As Hannah More put it in an address to villagers in the Mendips:

> The very ground you walk upon points out your daily labour. Excel in that, and an honest hogler [hog keeper] is as good in the eyes of the Almighty as an honest squire; therefore we wish to recommend you to do your duty in that state of life where God has placed and called you.

Given the belief that elementary education must always be given within a religious framework, the first move to provide more schools naturally came from the churches. The dissenters were first in the field, setting up the Royal Lancasterian Institution (later re-named the British and Foreign Schools Society) in 1808, while in 1811 the Church of England established the National Society for Promoting the Education of the Poor in the Principles of the Established Church. Of the two voluntary societies, the National Society was far stronger financially, and was rigidly Anglican in its teaching, while its rival was undenominational in approach. However, since they had to rely on voluntary subscriptions, both societies were concerned to provide education as cheaply as possible, and this was an important reason for their adopting the famous monitorial system. The version used by the British and Foreign Schools Society was devised by Joseph Lancaster, a Quaker who had opened his own school for poor children in London in 1798. The National Society used the system employed by Dr Andrew Bell, who had experimented with it in a school in Madras (National Schools were sometimes called Madras schools). The essence of the system is that the teacher would first teach the lesson to selected children (monitors) who would then teach it to their own group of between 10 and 20 children, who stood around the monitors. Cards of instructions were often used for this purpose. This method was cheap in that with the aid of the monitors a single master could teach a whole school of between 100 and 200 children at once. According to Lancaster:

> . . . every lesson placed on a card will serve for twelve or twenty boys at once: and when that twelve or twenty have repeated the whole lesson, as many times over as there are boys in the circle, they are dismissed to their spelling on the slate, and another like number of boys may study the same lesson in succession: indeed, *two hundred boys* may all repeat their lesson from *one* card, in the space of *three hours*.

Lancaster emphasised the great saving in paper and books that this meant—his children used chalk and slates, while Bell's children used sand trays.

The great feature of the monitorial system was its undeniable cheapness, because it employed the unpaid labour of the best children to teach the rest. Monitors might be given some additional tuition after hours, and in some schools were encouraged by awards of merit badges, or even awards of ½d or more a week. The curriculum, of course, concentrated very narrowly on reading, writing, and arithmetic, with the reading based on the Bible. The drawbacks to the system are obvious: the monitors spent much of their time teaching others, often imperfectly, when they should have been learning themselves. Moreover, learning was made more difficult by the noise of the class—there might be as many as the equivalent of six or seven present-day classes all engaged in oral work in one large room. Nevertheless, the monitorial system was very widely adopted, even spreading to the public schools and the grammar schools.

In the 20 years following the establishment of the voluntary societies, interest continued unabated in the subject of education for the working classes. In 1816 the Whig reformer, Henry Brougham, secured the appointment of a Select Committee into the Education of the Poor which reported in 1818 that only about 7 per cent of the total population of England and Wales were attending day schools, and this without reference to the length of attendance, which might be for only a few months, or even weeks. In 1820 Brougham introduced a bill by which schools should be financed out of the rates, and the teachers should be members of the Church of England. The hostility of the dissenters soon put paid to the bill.

However, in 1830 the Whigs at last returned to power and after a great struggle passed the Reform Act in 1832. The way now lay open for further and much needed reforms, not least in the realm of education. Precedents were already at hand for state support for education in the form of the annual grant made since 1815 to the Society for Promoting the Education of the Poor in Ireland (the Kildare Place Society), and in the decision in 1831 to set up a non-sectarian national educational system in Ireland. Thus in 1833 the Whig government decided that:

> a sum not exceeding £20 000 be granted to His Majesty, to be issued in aid of private subscriptions for the erection of school houses for the education of the children of the poorer classes in Great Britain to the 31st day of March, 1834.

This first annual grant to education was to be divided between the two voluntary societies and, it will be noted, was to be for buildings only, not equipment or staff.

In this way the first government grant to education in England and Wales was made, and the grant was undoubtedly a landmark in the history of education in this country. Nevertheless, the grant was in itself quite small—in the same year £50 000 was voted for the repair of the royal stables—and it was necessary for the societies to find half the cost of any new building themselves before applying for government assistance, thus preserving the voluntary principle. A further point is that the grant strengthened the hold of the societies over the education of the working classes, Anglicans and dissenters alike being very opposed to the state establishing its own system of schools independent of the societies. Others still rejected state interference on political principle, such as J. S. Mill who wrote as late as 1859:

> A general state education is merely a contrivance for moulding people to be exactly like each other, and as the mould in which it casts them is that which pleases the predominant power in the government, it establishes a despotism over the mind, leading by natural tendency to one over the body.

By 1839 the annual grant had been raised to £30 000, and it was decided to set up a special committee of the Privy Council to administer the grant, hitherto paid direct from the Treasury to the societies. It was also proposed to appoint government inspectors for schools, and to establish a model school and a training college to supply teachers to all types of school. Grants might also be available to schools other than church schools. The National Society, supported by the Church of England, attacked these proposals very bitterly, and the government had to withdraw most of them. Its one positive gain was the establishment of the Committee of the Privy Council. Over inspectors they had to compromise. Inspectors could be appointed, but only with the approval of the diocesan authorities. So the Church of England was triumphant. Four years later in 1843 when Graham sought to introduce his factory Bill with a clause specifying three hours education daily, there were loud protests from the dissenters, who thought the Anglicans would gain an unfair advantage. As a result, Graham had to drop his Bill. In the same year, the British and Foreign Schools Society obtained an undertaking from the government that no inspectors of their schools should be appointed without the society's consent. In this way, both the voluntary societies were successful in keeping the government at arm's length, and preserving their hold over the schools of the working classes. No wonder Graham once remarked:

> Religion, the Keystone of Education, is in this country the bar to progress.

Yet all was not lost to the government in 1839 and 1843. The setting up of the Committee of the Privy Council was a real step forward, especially as its first Secretary, Dr James Kay (the Kay of the Fever Reports, later to be Sir James Kay Shuttleworth) proved to be excellent. In 1843 the annual grant became available for furniture and apparatus as well as for buildings, and money was also granted to help build denominational training colleges. Meanwhile, the appointing of government inspectors turned out to be another great gain. There were only two at first—the Rev. John Allen and H. S. Tremenheere—but by 1852 there were 23 of them, with two assistant inspectors. They had to tread very warily in the face of hostility from both societies who in the early years of the Inspectorate would sometimes refuse a grant for a particular school rather than submit it to inspection. The Minute laying down their duties was worded very tactfully:

> Inspectors, authorized by HM in Council, will be appointed from time to time to visit schools to be henceforth aided by public money. The Inspectors will not interfere with the religious instruction, or discipline, or management of the school, it being their object to collect facts and information and report the results of their inspection to the Committee of Council.

Anyone reading the Reports of these Inspectors will be made aware of their earnest application to their work. They had to travel vast distances in the early days because their areas for inspection were so large, yet the impression given is of a very thorough and impartial reporting of what they saw. It soon became painfully apparent from

75

their Reports in the early 1840s that many of the church schools, whether Anglican or Free Church, were grossly unsatisfactory. Buildings were often quite inadequate, dark, damp, and ill-ventilated. Mr Allen reported on one school which simply consisted of a room about 10 feet by 12 feet behind a shop in which there were two dozen or so children left with nothing to do while the teacher was in the shop. British and Foreign Schools Society schools were sometimes in the basement of chapels, being very ill-lit and badly ventilated. HMI the Rev. F. Watkins reported that he had seen

> the steam covering the windows, and perspiration streaming down the children's faces . . .

The atmosphere of schoolrooms was sometimes poisoned by the rank odours of the privies. Even if the buildings were satisfactory the teachers themselves were not necessarily able to write:

> In one school . . . the Mistress (a good worker) was unable to write or to detect the most gross errors in spelling, and a large portion of the children were sitting wholly unoccupied.

It was clear by the 1840s that an enormous amount remained to be done to render the schools more satisfactory, and especially to improve the teachers themselves, since the monitorial sytem had its obvious weaknesses. In 1846, therefore, Kay Shuttleworth drafted minutes of the Committee of Council for a new scheme of teacher-training which were accepted by the Whig government, and led to immensely important changes. Henceforth a pupil-teacher scheme was to be instituted in selected schools. Monitors would be replaced by children of 13 years or more who would be apprenticed to the master for five years. They would be examined by HM Inspectors annually, and grants paid to both apprentice and master; they would also enter for national examinations set by the HMIs and the Principals of the denominational training colleges, and the best pupil-teachers would be awarded Queen's Scholarships to the training colleges. Those who failed to win scholarships might still gain Certificates of Merit which entitled the school where they taught to a special annual grant towards their salaries.

Not only was this the beginning of a properly organized system for training teachers but it also provided a new career for the working-class boy or girl with educational aspirations. Once the pupil-teacher system got under way, then a working class boy with academic ability might look forward to a secure career of a respectable nature. His salary would be £90 a year, with a house rent-free, and additional payments if he had pupil–teachers; in a school of 150 children, he could have six apprentices, and for teaching them he would receive £21. However, this new career was not intended to be on a par with middle-class occupations, or to give a status comparable to that of a solicitor, doctor, or clergyman. As Kay Shuttleworth said:

> It cannot be expected that members of the middle class of society will to any great extent choose the vocation of teachers of the poor . . .

But he went on to express the hope that his scheme would

> render the profession of schoolmaster popular among the poor, and to offer to their children the most powerful incentives to learning.

Educational Changes in Perspective

By the mid-nineteenth century it is clear that important advances had been made in the education of the working classes. With all its faults, the adoption of the monitorial system was evidence of a desire to improve working-class education, and the voluntary societies did much to put the new aims into practice. The beginnings of state aid to the societies was obviously of vital importance, and so was the institution of the pupil–teacher system. Indeed, by the late 1840s there was a much wider acceptance of the idea that it was right and proper for the government to encourage the development of schools for the working classes. The *Edinburgh Review*, for example, put forward the opinion that:

> The State has a *right* to see that children are so brought up that they are able to fulfil their social obligations towards their fellow citizens . . .

The *Quarterly Review* agreed with this point of view, declaring that:

> Sooner or later, popular education must be an affair of the state . . .

Nevertheless, the strength of these views must not be exaggerated. A kind of uneasy partnership existed between the state and the church societies from 1833 onwards, with the societies very much the senior partner. They succeeded in maintaining their control over elementary education for another 20 years or so. The National Society as the larger of the two societies received 80 per cent of all grants between 1839 and 1850.

It must also be recognized that by the standards of today, working-class education in 1850 still had far to go. The idea persisted that education should consist of the minimum amount of instruction to keep the working classes contented and reconciled to their lowly station in life. Moreover, this education was to be directed to the poorest classes rather than the skilled workers; it will be noted that Kay Shuttleworth referred to 'teachers of the poor'. It would be many years before it was accepted that the working-class boy or girl had a right to secondary and higher education if he or she could proft by it. On the contrary, at the time elementary education in elementary schools was all that was envisaged. This is not surprising, given the hierarchical nature of Victorian society and the social conservatism of the time which emphasised the need for social stability rather than social change. So, enough was to be done to preserve existing class relationships, but no more. Comments made by the Rev. James Fraser in 1861 make it clear how limited educational aims really were:

> Even if it were possible, I doubt whether it would be desirable, with a view to the real interests of the peasant boy to keep him at school till he was 14 or 15 years of age. But it is not possible. We must make up our minds to see the last of him, so far as the day school is concerned, at 10 or 11.

He went on to sketch out the essential elements of an education for such a boy—the ability to spell correctly, to read a common narrative (for example, in a newspaper), to write a letter home, to add up a shop bill, to have some knowledge of the whereabouts of foreign counties; and underlying all, to know enough of the Scriptures to understand a plain sermon and to know his duty towards his Maker and fellow man.

It is highly unlikely that many children reached even this standard in the schools of the 1850s. Many of them were still housed in unsuitable buildings with brick or stone floors, poor lighting, ventilation and heating, without playgrounds or proper lavatories. It took time for the new, trained teachers to come into the schools, and much of the teaching was still very poor. There was the further point that education was not as yet compulsory, nor was it free—the church schools still charged fees of a few pence a week. This helps to explain why by no means all children attended school. In 1854 Horace Mann calculated that only about one-ninth (11 per cent) of the total population was attending school instead of the one-sixth (16·8 per cent) which he thought should be in attendance between the ages of five and 12. Further, merely having a name on a register was no guarantee of attendance. At a conference in 1857 it was stated that of two million children at school, 42 per cent attended for less than a year, and only 22 per cent for between one and two years.

The fact is that in the industrial areas many parents were indifferent to the educational needs of their children. In the Black Country, according to HMI the Rev. J. P. Norris:

apathy, irregularity of attendance, the early age at which they leave . . . are all traceable in a great measure to this one source.

HMI Tremenheere did not agree entirely with this view, but thought the problem was more that the parents did not understand what education really signified. Most of them took the children away as soon as they could make out simple words, put down a few figures, do the simplest rules of arithmetic, and write little more than their names. Parents would urge schoolmasters to 'finish their boys quickly' so that they could leave school. He thought it was hard to know how to surmount the barrier of the parents' ignorance of the true worth of education because it requires a certain degree of education to know the advantage of education. Tremenheere was also aware of one basic objection of parents to sending their children to school: this was the loss of earnings due to their not being at home working in the family workshop—there were no restrictions on the employment of children in such workshops till the Workshops Act, 1867. Combined with this objection was the belief that schooling brought very little benefit, since some of the best-paid men had no education other than that of the workshop, pit, or forge. People who read and kept books, it was thought, were not necessarily better-off than those who did not. Learning in fact could be a drawback—in the words of the Black Country saying:

> The father went to the pit and made a fortune, his son went to school and lost it.

Only the passing of the Workshops Act in 1867 and the coming of compulsory education later on could bring a change in attitudes of this kind.

Religion and the Working Classes

The importance of religion has already received a certain amount of attention in this chapter, but at the beginning of the century the Church of England had still to shake off the laxity of the previous century. Indeed, this laxity continued even into the 1820s and 1830s, in spite of the fact that the increase in population led Parliament to vote £1 m in 1818 and a further half million pounds in 1824 for the building of new churches. Many parsons still held several livings at once, and candidates for Holy Orders were selected in a haphazard manner, for example, being interviewed by the bishop when he was shaving, or waiting to go in to bat. The one active branch of the Anglican church was that of the Evangelicals whose ranks included such notable reformers as Wilberforce and Shaftesbury. The Church of England was therefore not likely to make much of an appeal to the working classes in the early decades of the century, though agricultural labourers might find the squire wanting to know why they were not in church on a Sunday. In the towns they were more likely to worship at a chapel than a church, and more particularly at a Wesleyan Methodist chapel than the chapels of the Congregationalists, Baptists, or Unitarians, all of which were attended more by the middle classes than the working classes. Above all others, the Primitive Methodists (dating from 1810) attracted working-class support, the simplicity and directness of their teaching—their preachers were sometimes called 'ranters'—making a powerful appeal. In the 1830s another break-away movement from the Wesleyan Methodists also gained the support of the working classes —the New Connexion. Lastly, Roman Catholic churches, although less numerous than those of other denominations, had many working-class men and women in their congregations.

How far the working classes actually attended chapel or church in the first half of the nineteenth century is unknown, but historians have argued that dissenting or nonconformist belief had a profound social influence over many working-class people. One older view has been that with its emphasis on hard work and individual achievement Methodism in particular supplied a social discipline which encouraged the working classes to go on working and doing their duty to God and their fellow men, however harsh their environment. In other words, Methodism made for social conformity, and damped down any tendency to political action; put in an extreme form, Methodism saved England from revolution. A more recent view is that it was only *after* the failure of working-class leaders to gain political reform after 1815 that they turned in despair to nonconformity, so that religious observance became a kind of consolation after political defeat. Yet a third view is that dissenting religion helped the working classes to establish a separate class identity. Since they had their own chapels, especially in the new towns, this allowed them to break away from the Church of England where they were dependent upon the middle classes and to acquire skills of leadership and organization. Thus, sectarian religion was the midwife of class. All three theories are interesting, but basically speculative and incapable of proof in any conclusive manner until more historical evidence becomes available on which to base a firm judgement.

When in 1851 the national census was taken, it was decided to hold a religious census on the same day. This was the first, and up to the present day, the only national census of its kind. It seemed an opportune moment to make such an enquiry, for both the Church of England and the nonconformist churches had been building churches and chapels for some time in order to keep pace with the growing population. There was the further point that the Church of England had been drastically reformed by the Whigs in the mid-1830s, and the Church had also been greatly agitated by a movement aiming to reform its doctrine and rituals known as the Oxford Movement. This began in Oxford in the 1830s and in a succession of tracts stressed the essential continuity of the Church of England with the original Church of Rome. This aroused suspicions that supporters of the movement (often called Tractarians) were too friendly to the Roman Catholic Church and its rituals. In fact one of its most prominent members, John Newman, was converted to Roman Catholicism in 1845, later becoming a Cardinal. Dr Arnold voiced the feelings of many in a candid comment:

> I look upon a RC as an enemy in his uniform. I look upon a Tractarian as an enemy in disguise.

The Church of England was thus very different from what it had been earlier in the century.

The results of the census came as a great shock to middle-class opinion. In spite of the common belief that England was a deeply religious country, the figures revealed that after all allowance had been made for those unable to attend church because they were too young, or too old, or sick, or at work, only one in two had actually attended a place of worship on Census Sunday. Worse than this, it was evident that attendance was especially low in the largest industrial towns; in London the figure was only about one in three. Since London and the bigger towns contained large numbers of working people, it is clear that the majority of non-attenders must have been working class. The organizer of the census, Horace Mann, drew the conclusion that

> the masses of our working population . . . are never or but seldom seen in our religious congregations.

He went on to comment on attendance in the towns and cities:

> more especially in cities and large towns is it observable how absolutely insignificant a portion of the congregation is composed of artisans.

Yet this view was not entirely novel. Other middle-class observers had made similar remarks before 1851, and in particular Engels had made some famous observations on this subject in 1844:

> All bourgeois writers are agreed that the workers have no religion and do not go to church. Exceptions to this are the Irish, a few of the older workers, and those wage-earners who have one foot in the middle-class camp—overlookers, foremen, and so on. Among the mass of the working-class population, however, one nearly always finds an utter

indifference to religion. . . . The mere cry, 'He's a parson', is often enough to force a clergyman off the platform at a public meeting.

On the face of it, the evidence seems clear enough; and other contemporary statements appear to support it—for example, it was said in 1843 that not one family in 20 of artisans attended church or chapel in Sheffield; while in 1860 Lord Shaftesbury said that not 2 per cent of the working men in London attended church. Modern authorities have accepted these views, one remarking that the labouring class were generally outside all the religious institutions, and another that 'popular abstinence from worship' was an inherited custom among the working classes. It is not difficult to provide justification for these statements. For many working people the Church of England was very much the church of the employers, and their own social inferiority would be emphasized by the practice of charging pew rents, so that working-class worshippers would often be segregated into the free pews at the back or sides (pew rents were also levied in nonconformist chapels, even in those of the Primitive Methodists, but they were usually smaller than in the Church of England, and the number of free seats greater). The poorest of the working classes might not have a decent suit or dress in which to attend church, and illiteracy might make the use of prayer book or hymn book impossible. These reasons help to explain why there might be considerable barriers to the attendance of working people at church or chapel.

Nevertheless, the case can be pushed too far. Contemporary opinion might well have been right about London, Sheffield, and other large cities, but it still remains true that nationally one in two did actually attend divine service, and at least four-fifths of the nation may be adjudged working class in 1851. If working-class attendance was poor in the great towns and cities, it was much better in the countryside, and in the smaller industrial town or village. A recent study of West

	Free	Sittings Other	Total	Morning	Attendance Afternoon	Evening
Church of England	750	250	1000	228		
New Connexion	100	106	206	45	150	250
(2 chapels)	50	320	370	150	200	250
Unitarian	200		200			25
Primitive Methodist	120	130	250	50	200	250
Congregationalist	200	200	400	60	150	100
Wesleyan Methodist	200	300	500	80	120	310
	1620	1306	2926	613	820	1185

Midland nailers in industrial villages in the Black Country has shown their attendance (largely at Primitive and New Connexion chapels) to be about the national average—that is, one in two. The figures for the area are shown in the Table.

It is clear from these figures for an almost exclusively working-class area that attendance was very good in several of these chapels, and there is no doubt that some worshippers attended twice or even three times (this was common enough, and to allow for this and obtain the approximate number of attendants, it is usual to take two-thirds of the total attendances).

It would be wrong, therefore, to take contemporary (or even more recent) views on the failure of the working classes to attend church or chapel on 30 March 1851 too literally. It seems that the Victorians were so shocked at the national figures, and by the situation in the new towns, that they took little comfort from what was happening in the countryside or in the industrial areas which had expanded less rapidly. This is the key, of course. Where towns had expanded very quickly, church and chapel could not always keep pace, and in any case a massive immigrant population might not wish to resume the church-going forced on them in their native villages. But where immigration was on a more modest scale, and the Methodists could provide suitable services, then it was more likely that the working classes would attend chapel.

Lastly, it is obvious that the attendance figures would not have included all occasional attenders, especially those who attended only at Easter and Christmas. Others might not go even then, but would have some idea of Christian beliefs because they had attended Sunday schools, or had been taught some scraps of Biblical knowledge by their parents. The Anglican parson in the nailing villages mentioned above did not have a large congregation but was a vigorous and admired local figure. He exercised a strong influence over his parishoners, taking the men to the savings bank on a Saturday night, advising them on getting married, and even getting them to bathe in the local river from time to time. He kept open house to his flock, and after the cholera epidemic of 1848–9 he was presented with a purse of 100 guineas for his work among the poor. Yet he died leaving his wife and family unprovided for.

The nonconformist chapel itself might be a social centre with its choir practices, musical evenings, tea gatherings, mutual improvement societies, and so on. The activities of the famous Carr's Lane Chapel in Birmingham in 1859 are quite astonishing. Its minister described them as follows:

We are not one whit better than some others. . . . We have now an organization for the London Missionary Society, which raises as its regular contribution nearly £500 per annum. . . . For the Colonial

Missionary Society we raise, annually, £70. For our Sunday and day schools, which comprehend nearly 2 000 children, we raise £200. We support two town missionaries, at a cost of £200. Our ladies conduct a working society for orphan mission schools . . . they sustain also a Dorcas Society for the poor of the town; a Maternal Society, for visiting the sick poor. . . . Our Village Preachers' Society, which employs 12 or 14 lay agents, costs us scarcely anything. . . . We have a Young Men's Brotherly Society . . . we also have night schools for young men and women . . . and Bible classes . . .

All this was, of course, exceptional, but it seems unwise to suppose that the majority of the working classes were quite ignorant of the basic tenets of Christian belief in the middle years of the nineteenth century. Even if they were vague or misinformed on fundamental beliefs—and one shocked commissioner did encounter a child in 1862 who thought Christ was a wicked man—it is a reasonable assumption that most working men and women knew better than this. As for the institutional aspects of religion, they could hardly be avoided. The churches and chapels, many in new red brick, were there as a tangible reminder, and so were the graveyards which were the resting place of so many children who died before reaching adulthood. National days of prayer during cholera epidemics again drew attention to spiritual needs, and so did the weekly day of rest and the oppressive Sabbatarianism which closed all shops and all places of entertainment. Even for the most impoverished sections of the working classes, therefore, religion could scarcely be an entirely unknown quantity, in spite of what Engels had to say; and for the regular chapel-goers Sunday must often have been among the busiest days of the week.

Chapter VI
The Problem of Poverty

The Old Poor Law

The relieving of poverty was no new thing in the early nineteenth century. In medieval times it was taken for granted that it was everyone's Christian duty to help the sick and needy, and this was one of the accepted duties of the medieval church and of the guilds. However, poverty was so widespread and the majority of the population lived so much on the edge of starvation that it was extreme poverty or destitution which was relieved, rather than poverty in itself; and it was not until the Tudor period that the state took any part in giving relief. The sixteenth century witnessed both an increase in population and an expansion of trade and industry. The consequences were a greater number of unemployed when trade was slack, and the appearance of the sturdy rogue or vagabond who roamed from town to town, causing alarm and disorder:

Hark, hark! The dogs do bark—the beggars are coming to town . . .

and the old nursery rhyme ends:

Some gave them white bread, some gave them brown,
And some gave them a good horse-whip, and sent them out of town.

In fact, horse-whipping and severe punishment proved no answer to the problem of the unemployed vagrant, so that by the end of the sixteenth century the Tudor government was forced to change its earlier harsh attitude, and to pass two Acts in 1597 and 1601 which were to be the basis of the old Poor Law for nearly two and a half centuries.

Under the Elizabethan poor law legislation the care of the poor was entrusted to unpaid parish Overseers of the Poor who were under the general supervision of the local Justices of the Peace. Relief was paid for by a poor rate levied on householders in each parish. The paupers themselves were divided into four categories—the able-bodied unemployed, who in return for relief (either in money or kind) were set to work in workhouses; the sick and aged, who were relieved in poor-houses (almshouses) or in their own homes; the children, who were apprenticed, often to husbandry; and the sturdy beggars, who were to be punished in a house of correction (commonly the same building as the workhouse). Later in the seventeenth century and after the Restoration the Act of Settlement was passed in 1662. This Act attempted to stop poor people from going from parish to parish in search of the most generous relief. JPs were empowered within 40 days of any person coming into a parish and appearing likely to become chargeable to poor relief

> to remove and convey such person or persons to such parish where he or they were last legally settled either as a native householder, sojourner apprentice, or servant for the space of 40 days at the least unless he or they give sufficient security for the discharge of the said parish to be allowed by the said Justices.

In this way, each parish was supposed to look after its own poor, and strangers were removed, by force if necessary, to the parish where they last had legal settlement. This Act often led to distressing scenes when paupers were removed, especially pregnant women, lest both they and their offspring became chargeable to the parish. It used to be thought that the Act also restricted the mobility of labour, but in practice labourers looking for work could obtain settlement certificates from their own parishes, certifying that the overseers there would take financial responsibility if in fact the labourer had to apply for poor relief.

The Elizabethan Acts and the 1662 Act thus provided a framework within which the poor were aided for the rest of the seventeenth century and the eighteenth century. In addition, of course, the obligation of the individual, particularly the middle-class person, to help the poor had not ceased, and the setting up of the charity schools bears witness to the continuing of private charity. As far as the local system of poor relief was concerned, it took many different forms, depending upon conditions in each parish and on the particular ways in which the overseers chose to spend the proceeds from the poor rate. The governments of the day usually refrained from interference, and the only two poor law Acts of the eighteenth century of any importance merely reflected existing trends. The first, Knatchbull's Act of 1722, is to be seen in the light of the current move towards giving relief in workhouses designed to serve the needs of several parishes. It encouraged the setting up of workhouses and the withdrawing of relief from anyone who refused to enter them. The second, Gilbert's Act, 1782, allowed parishes to combine to establish a common workhouse without the need for a special local Act, and at the same time for the local magistrates to appoint a board of guardians, to be supervised by a person called a visitor. Further the earlier rule about having to enter a workhouse to gain relief was relaxed.

Such was the position when the long wars against France began in 1793. By 1795 a combination of poor harvests, rising prices, and real wages falling to starvation levels stirred the Berkshire magistrates to action. Meeting at the Pelican Inn in the village of Speenhamland, near Reading, they resolved not to regulate wages but to

> very earnestly recommend Farmers and others throughout the county to increase the pay of their labourers in proportion to the present price of provisions.

they went onto draw up a scale of allowances in support of wages, the amount paid to depend on the price of bread. Thus:

> When the Gallon Loaf of Second Flour, weighing 8 lb 11 oz shall cost 1s. Then every poor and industrious man shall have for his own support 3s weekly, either produced by his own or his family's labour, or an allowance from the poor rates, and for the support of his wife and every other of his family 1s 6d.

When the gallon loaf cost 1s 4d, the man was to receive 4s and every member of his family 1s 10d, and so on in proportion.

Because of the widespread distress among the agricultural labourers in the southern counties—and it must be remembered that the rise in population was making cheap labour ever more abundant at this time—the so-called Speenhamland system spread to many parts of agricultural England. The idea of supplementing wages was not a new idea, but in the circumstances of the time it now became very common. Other methods also came into use for helping the village labourer. In some parishes the 'roundsman' system was employed, that is, the labourers were sent 'on the rounds', going from one farmhouse to another looking for work, and being paid by the parish unless the farmers chose to employ them. In other parishes, the 'labour rate' was used, whereby each occupier was assessed at a certain amount, and a price put on the labour of each labourer. The occupier could either pay the rate or provide employment. If he paid less than the fixed price of the labourer, the difference would be paid to the parish. The farmer could choose his labourers, so that there was a certain element of competition for the services of the best men. Probably only about one parish in five used this method, and even fewer used the 'roundsman' system. Still another method occasionally resorted to was that of putting the labour of the unemployed up for auction. This was done in Kent in the late 1820s, with the best being paid 12/- a week, any paid less getting the difference made up from the poor rates.

By the end of the French Wars in 1815 there was mounting disquiet over the way in which the cost of Poor Law rates had risen during the wars, and Malthus's attacks on the Poor Law gained wide support. According to Malthus, the Poor Law system removed all initiative and degraded the independent labourer, while the Law of Settlement, even in its amended form, with its 'persecution of men whose families were liable to become chargeable, and of poor women who are near lying-in' was 'a most disgraceful and disgusting tyranny.' As things became no better, in the depression following 1815, a Select Committee on the Poor Laws was appointed whose Report published in 1817 echoed many of Malthus's criticisms. The Report also recommended administrative reforms which were put into effect by Sturges Bourne's Act 1819: parishes could appoint small committees to examine the granting of relief, and also appoint salaried assistant overseers. By 1828 nearly one in five of all parishes had adopted this Act.

Yet the cost of the Poor Law remained disturbingly high even though it fell somewhat after peaking in the year 1818–19 at £8·9 m. In 1824 another Select Committee was appointed, this time on labourers' wages, with particular reference to the subsidizing of wages. Its Report again found fault with a number of features of the Poor Law, especially the Roundsman system, and the paying of allowances for each child (a variant of the Speenhamland system) which was prevalent in the southern counties. It also reported that wages were higher in the North of England than in the South, where they had reached extraordinarily low levels:

> In the Wingham division in Kent alone, it appears, that the lowest wages paid were in one parish, sixpence; in four, eight pence; in eleven, one shilling and six pence; in four, two shillings; and in the greater number, one shilling per day.

Although the cost of poor relief had dropped below £6 m by 1822, it began to rise again after 1826 and by 1831 was again above £7 m. By this time there were very strong feelings that the Poor Law must be reformed. It seemed clear that something had gone wrong with the system. On the one hand, it had become very expensive, while on the other it appeared that it was demoralizing the agricultural labourers, particularly in the South. Moreover, it was frequently alleged that it was wrong in principle, because it sapped the spirit of independence and self-help. Malthus argued that 'any great interference with the affairs of other people is a species of tyranny', and declared

> I feel little doubt in my own mind that if the poor laws had never existed, though there might have been a few more instances of very severe distress, yet that the aggregate mass of happiness among the common people would have been much greater than it is at present.

Other objections came from those like Ricardo who believed that only a certain proportion of the national wealth was available for wages, and that the more that was spent from national resources on poor relief, the less was available for wages. Still others thought that what was really wanted was a deterrent workhouse. The Rev. J. T. Becher introduced a scheme in Nottinghamshire whereby 49 parishes joined together to set up an incorporated workhouse under Gilbert's Act, and to give relief only in the workhouse where 'every tenderness towards the infirm, the aged, and the guiltless' would be insured, but 'wholesome restraint upon the idle, the profligate, and the refractory' would be imposed. Becher claimed to have reduced expenditure at Southwell from over £2000 in 1821 to £551 in 1828. With so much criticism of the Poor Law in the air, it is not surprising that when the Swing Riots occurred in Kent in 1830 (agricultural riots caused principally by the introduction of the threshing machine in what we have seen to have been an area of very low wages) it was decided that reform could wait no longer. In February 1832 a Royal Commission on the Poor Laws was appointed.

The Poor Law Commission and the New Poor Law

The Commission was faced with the immense task of discovering how the Poor Law was being administered throughout the 15 000 parishes of England and Wales. Twenty-six assistant commissioners were sent out who visited about 3000 townships and parishes, and reported on what they saw. In addition, questionnaires were sent out to the parishes, replies being received from just over 10 per cent of them, covering in all about 20 per cent of the population of England and Wales. The Report which followed was written by Nassau Senior and Edwin Chadwick and was published in 1834. Its recommendations were generally accepted, and it was followed promptly by the passing of the Poor Law Amendment Act, 1834.

The Report was predictably hostile to the Speenhamland system. It criticized it strongly for allowing a disgraceful situation to develop. Wages were being reduced to nominal sums, and the workman told to obtain a supplement from the Poor Box. No workman, however industrious, could get more than the scale indicated, and the man with savings was penalized since relief was given only to paupers. Bastardy was encouraged, since the parish would pay for all children, legitimate or illegitimate. In fact, women with bastards were eligible wives. Financial corruption was common, for overseers were usually unpaid, and would give grants to the labourers of their own customers. Above all else, the Report emphasized that all motives of effort and ambition were being removed:

the most worthless were sure of something, while the prudent, the industrious, and the sober . . . obtained only something.

This slashing attack on the allowance system was combined with positive recommendations for reform. They show very clearly both the influence of the belief in individualism in general, and the effect of contemporary arguments about making the workhouse a deterrent, in particular. At the root of the recommendations is the principle that the person relieved must not be made more comfortable than the worst-paid labourer in work. In the words of the Report:

> his situation on the whole shall not be made really or apparently so eligible as the sitution of the independent labourer of the lowest class.

To do otherwise—and this is what had been happening, according to the Commissioners—would mean that the poorly paid

> are under the strongest inducements to quit the less eligible class of labourers and enter the more eligible class of paupers.

This was obviously wrong:

> Every penny bestowed that tends to render the condition of the pauper more eligible than that of the independent labourer is a bounty on indolence and vice. We have found that as the poor rates are at present administered, they operate as bounties of this description, to the amount of several millions annually.

The first major recommendations therefore followed:

> First, that except as to medical attendance, and subject to the exception respecting apprenticeship hereinafter stated, all relief whatever to able-bodied persons or to their families, otherwise than in well-regulated workhouses . . . shall be declared unlawful, and shall cease, in manner and at periods hereafter specified.

The Report goes on to say that pauperized labourers were 'not the authors of the abusive system', and that they were not to be blamed for it, so that the new system should be introduced gradually. As to the administration of the reformed system, it should remain in the hands of the locally appointed officers, subject to a 'comparatively small and cheap agency' which could assist them and impose uniformity:

We recommend therefore the appointment of a central board to control the administration of the poor laws, with such assistant commissioners as may be found requisite; and that the commissioners be empowered and directed to frame and enforce regulations for the government of work-houses, and as to the nature and amount of relief to be given, and the labour to be exacted in them . . .

Now there can be no doubt that there was considerable hostility to the allowance system even before the investigation began. Sidney and Beatrice Webb, writing in the 1920s their great work on the history of the Poor Law, reached the conclusion that the Report was heavily biassed against the old Poor Law system. Another historian, Professor R. H. Tawney, in 1926 described the Report as being 'brilliant, influential, and wildly unhistorical'—unhistorical in that it ignored the economic causes of such widespread distress, simply assuming that it was all the fault of the individual who was being pampered by an over-indulgent system. A more recent scholar, Professor Mark Blaug, has been even more critical, calling the Report 'wildly unstatistical'. According to Blaug, the Report is in no way based firmly on the great mass of evidence provided. The Report asserts that allowances were becoming more widespread, while Blaug argues that the evidence shows that on the contrary they were dying out, being confined to only 18 counties, mostly in the Midlands and the South. They had certainly been common enough during the Napoleonic Wars, but the criticisms of the Parliamentary Committees in 1817 and 1824 had caused many overseers to discontinue them. Moreover, Blaug considers that far from the Speenhamland system driving wages down, they were already very low before being supplemented in order to save labourers and their families from starving. Lastly, Blaug has shown that the Commission confused grants in aid of wages with family allowances. The latter were quite common, but were usually paid only for the third, fourth, or fifth child, so that the Malthusian view that allowances encouraged the poor to have large families was shown to be somewhat ill-founded. All in all, Blaug's findings confirm the suspicions that the Commissioners paid little attention to the detailed evidence presented, being content to rely on the general reports of the Assistant Commissioners, and on their own preconceptions—all very reprehensible, of course, but under-standable in the light of public opinion at the time.

However, much more research will be necessary before Professor Blaug's views are finally confirmed, and whether they are or not, the fact remains that the Report was certainly influential; and to quote Tawney further, the Report was to be 'one of the pillars of the social policy of the nineteenth century'. The Poor Law Amendment Act, 1834, followed the Report very closely in setting up new administrative machinery. Three Poor Law Commissioners were to be appointed with power over all local Poor Law authorities. In the interests of greater efficiency, unions of parishes were to be formed, generally centred on a market town and covering a radius of 10 miles. Within each union a Board of Guardians was to be elected by the ratepayers, the number of votes being up to six as occupier, and six as owner—12 votes in all as a maximum. There were to be salaried officials to help the Guardians, and the Boards were to be regulated by Orders issued by the Commissioners—General Orders (applicable to all unions, and subject to the approval of the Home Secretary); and Special Orders (applicable to individual unions only). There was nothing in the Act about the Workhouse Test—that is, giving relief only in the workhouse, and not as outdoor relief—or the Less Eligibility Rule for conditions in the workhouse, but it was taken for granted that these principles would be applied. Nor did the act give the Commissioners power to force the Guardians to build new workhouses. The Act was to last for five years only, during which time it was confidently expected that poor rates would fall.

The Act was a triumph for the new utilitarian thinking. An old institution—the old Poor Law—had been put to the test and had been found wanting, being replaced by a New Poor Law which combined central control from London with the maximum opportunity for the individual to practise self-help. The incentive to do so was that life on poor relief was to be inferior to life in the lowest paid job. Further, local control remained in the hands of the very people who had to pay the poor rates, so that it was in their interests to run the new system as economically as possible. The whole system therefore conformed to the basic principles of Benthamism—central supervision in the interests of uniformity, individualism, and efficiency.

The Enforcement of the Act

In the southern counties the Act was enforced without much difficulty, thanks to three good harvests and the beginning of the construction of the railways which provided a new source of employment. In the North it was quite otherwise. The out-door allowance system was far less widespread here, and had been employed only for certain depressed out-workers such as handloom weavers, or to meet sudden cases of short-time working, or unemployment due to a mill closing down. The Old Poor Law in Lancashire was quite well-organized with well-regulated workhouses and salaried officials. Consequently there was mass opposition to the new law from the working classes and from some of the middle classes. Public protest meetings were held in South Lancashire and the West Riding, and there was rioting in Bradford, requiring soldiers to be brought in from Leeds. Riots also occurred in Huddersfield, Dewsbury and Todmorden.

In parliament, the Tories at first supported the Act but turned against it when the advantages were realized of attacking the Whig manufacturers on the grounds that they only wanted the Act because it might provide more labour for them. There was opposition in the House of Commons from John Walter, the editor of *The Times*, Thomas Wakeley, editor of *The Lancet*, Disraeli, and John Fielden. Indeed, the leaders of the Ten Hour Movement—Fielden, Ferrand, Bull, Stephens, and Oastler—used the Short Time Committees to oppose the law, afterwards founding the Anti-Poor Law Association. The language of Oastler was as strong as ever. The title of a speech published by him in 1838 is

> Damnation! Eternal Damnation to the fiend-begotten, 'coarser food' New Poor Law.

The preface to the speech is extraordinarily violent:

> CHRISTIAN READER
> Be not alarmed at the sound of the Title. I cannot *bless* that which GOD and NATURE CURSE. The Bible being true, the Poor Law Amendment Act is false! The Bible contains the will of God—this accursed Act of Parliament embodies the will of Lucifer. It is the Sceptre of Belial, establishing its sway in the land of Bibles!! DAMNATION; ETERNAL DAMNATION TO THE ACCURSED FIEND!

In the same year Stephens, sounding a similar note, told a Newcastle audience with reference to the separation of man and wife in the new workhouses:

> Newcastle ought to be and should be one blaze of fire, with only one way to put it out, and that with the blood of all who supported this abominable measure . . . and let every man with a torch in one hand and a dagger in the other, put to death any and all who attempted to sever man and wife.

But in fact it was not long before working-class support in the North for the Anti-Poor Law Movement was transferred to Chartism, especially as the hated Bastilles (as the new workhouses were called) took a long time to appear, and in some places the Old Poor Law continued for many years as it had always done without Speenhamland, for the most part, and with low poor rates. In 1858 workhouses in the Rochdale Union were still being described as 'a refuge for the destitute', and 'more in the nature of almhouses than workhouses'.

Meanwhile all was not well with the central administration of the New Poor Law. The three Commissioners appointed to run the new organization from their Headquarters in Somerset House were Thomas Frankland Lewis, a member of the select Committee of 1817; George Nicholls, who had been associated with Becher's poor law reforms at Southwell, and was a great believer in a deterrent workhouse; and John Shaw-Lefevre, whose patron was Lord Althorp. Chadwick, who had had so much to do with the original Report, found to his chagrin that he was to be only Secretary to the Commission, and not a Commissioner. He soon quarrelled with Frankland Lewis, and relationships between the Commissioners and their Secretary remained strained. Progress was slow in the North, as we have seen, not only because of local opposition but because where new Boards of Guardians were elected, they were often the same men as before, and were disinclined to change their ways. In any case, where unions had already been formed before 1834 under Gilbert's Act, or by a special local Act, they could not be dissolved without their own consent. Again, relations between the Commissioners and the Assistant Commissioners, who had to supervise directly the Boards of Guardians, were not happy, especially after 1842 when their number was reduced from 12 to nine, and they were heavily overworked. Chadwick often took their side against the Commissioners, who were much disliked in the provinces and nicknamed the 'Bashaws of Somerset House'. Further, the severe depression of the early 1840s compelled the Commissioners to accept the fact that it was impossible to prohibit all out-door relief, for the simple reason that the workhouses were not big enough to take in all applicants for relief in times of mass local unemployment. They were therefore forced to issue an outdoor Labour Test Order in 1842 allowing outdoor relief to all able-bodied men in return for a task of work; this was commonly of an unpleasant kind, such as breaking stones.

A climax in the affairs of the Commission was reached as a result of the Andover scandal in 1845–6. A riot took place in the Andover workhouse when the inmates, set to grind bones from the local butchers, began to fight over the scraps of meat still adhering to the bones. The result was the appointment in 1846 of a Parliamentary Select Committee of Enquiry into the administration of the Andover workhouse, and this led to a number of exchanges about the conduct of business at Somerset House. Chadwick criticized the Commissioners for irregularity of proceedings; Frankland Lewis criticized Chadwick:

Am I right in supposing that on the whole you thought Mr Chadwick a dangerous man?—I think if I had trusted the business of the office to Mr Chadwick's guidance and management, he would have got me into innumerable difficulties.

That is no answer to my question?—Well, then, if you will have it, you must. Mr Chadwick was an able man, but I thought him as unscrupulous and dangerous an officer as I ever saw within the walls of an office.

After these revelations it was inevitable that the administration should be reformed. In 1847 the Poor Law Commission was replaced by a Poor Law Board of which certain members of the government were ex-officio members—the Lord President, the Lord Privy Seal, the Chancellor of the Exchequer, and the Home Secretary.

It is time to attempt an overall assessment of the Poor Law Amendment Act. There can be no doubt that reform was long overdue of a system which in the southern counties was often inefficient and sometimes corrupt. Few would today defend the Labour Rate, the Roundsman system, or putting the hire of labourers up to auction. These were mere expedients which failed to tackle the problem of poverty at the roots. Again, the allowance system, though humane in its intentions, no doubt did lessen incentive and self-respect, to some extent. Certainly the new system supplied the need for a larger administrative unit; there were about 600 unions instead of 15 000 parishes, and central control provided a much greater degree of uniformity and efficiency. At the same time there were many who saw a supreme virtue in the new system in that it reduced costs. In 1834 the cost of poor relief per head was 9s. By 1854 this had been reduced to 6s.

Against these views it might be argued that the 1834 Act was based on mistaken beliefs. The Speenhamland system was *not* widespread by the 1830s and in any case was dying out. Wages were *not* driven down on all sides by wage supplements, nor were larger families encouraged by them. It was all very well to encourage labourers to look for work and to strengthen the incentive to do so by withdrawing all out-door relief, but this could be very hard on the individual when there was simply no work available. This was to apply the doctrine of self-help in a very harsh fashion. In any case, the Report concentrated narrowly on the agricultural labourer, and had no solution to offer to the problem of mass industrial unemployment. In consequence it proved impossible to abolish all out-door relief, as we have seen. In 1846, of 1·33 m paupers, only 199 000 were in the workhouse—that is, about 85 per cent were on out-door relief. Of the total pauper host, only about 25 per cent were able-bodied, and of these, about 78 per cent were on out-door relief.

Above all, critics of the New Poor Law were hostile to the new Union Workhouse. In order to fulfil the condition of 'less eligibility' the diet had to be meagre, and often consisted largely of oatmeal. It was never intended, of course, to apply the rule to inmates other than the able-bodied adults, but it must have been difficult to prevent the old, the sick, the insane, and the children being affected by it. Another disagreeable feature of the new workhouse was the way in which all classes of pauper were herded together in the general mixed workhouse, in spite of earlier plans to keep them in separate institutions. Of course, men and women were accommodated separately, but this meant man and wife (and children) were kept apart. They were also subjected to prison-like discipline, with solitary confinement for breaches of the rules. No doubt there was a good deal of propaganda against the new workhouse in the early days, much of it of a sensational nature and entirely untrue. Some workhouses in fact were run on humane lines, and provided conditions far superior to life outside on out-door relief. Nevertheless, the Victorian workhouse became both feared and hated by the working classes as it symbolized degradation and loss of self-respect.

This last point was well brought out by Hippolyte Taine, the French thinker, who visited England in the early 1860s. He praised a Manchester workhouse:

> The building is spacious, perfectly clean, well-kept; it has large courts, gardens are attached to it, looks upon fields and stately trees . . .

and went on to describe the care given the different categories of paupers, and the diet provided:

> We were astounded; this was a palace compared with the kennels in which the poor dwell.

Yet according to Taine when an unemployed man is confronted by the Workhouse Test, nine out of 10 decline. Taine went on to explain why:

> I am informed that they prefer their home and freedom at any price, that they cannot bear being shut up and subject to discipline. They prefer to be free and to starve. . . . The workhouse is regarded as a prison; the poor consider it a point of honour not to go there. Perhaps it must be admitted that the system of administration is foolishly despotic and worrying, that is the fault of every administrative system; the human being becomes a machine; he is treated as if he were devoid of feeling, and insulted quite unconsciously.

If the final comment is that the New Poor Law was too harsh, then it must be said that it was the spirit of the age to emphasize self-help, and the problems of urban unemployment were not yet understood. Even today the problem of how much assistance the welfare state should give to those in need is still a subject of controversy. It must not be forgotten that Victorian aid to the poor still went on outside the poor law system, which would be the last resort for the respectable working man. Because the Poor Law necessarily occupies the centre of the stage, it is easy to overlook this important point. In times of depression in the industrial towns it was the common practice to set up soup kitchens, distribute free loaves of bread, and blankets in winter. Manufacturers' Relief Committees were also common, while the London Manufacturers' Committee, set up in the 1820s, received government support. It was particularly important in distributing cash relief on a national scale in the severe depression of the early 1840s. By the 1860s the annual spending of private charities in London has been estimated as being between £5·5 m and £7 m. Since London accounted for less than a tenth of the total population, the national figure for charitable spending must have been much more than this, and should be compared with the £5·8 m spent nationally on Poor Relief in 1861.

Nor should it be forgotten that the spirit of self-help was found among the working classes as well as the middle class. Those who could save, often did so. Small weekly savings would go into local 'sick and draw' clubs, usually organized in public houses. According to the 1817 Select Committee on the Poor Laws:

> The number of persons belonging to friendly societies appears to be for the past three years nearly $8\frac{1}{2}$ in the 100 of the resident population.

This figure must have increased substantially in the following decades as national friendly societies developed such as the Manchester Unity of Odd Fellows, and the Ancient Order of Foresters. By the mid-century the numbers in all kinds of friendly societies outnumbered those in trade unions several times over. After all, it was only to be expected that in the absence of social security services of the modern type the working classes would try to give themselves some protection against misfortune. Naturally enough, all depended on the opportunity (and willingness) to save. For the unskilled town labourer and the agricultural labourer their wages were too small to permit saving, and in times of need they had no reserves and had perforce to turn to charity and the Poor Law authorities.

The Standard of Living

At this point it is convenient to turn to the vexed subject of the standard of living of the working classes as a whole during the period 1815 to 1850. Were they better off as a result of the coming of industrialization? Or was it that the harsh working and living conditions brought about a decline in their standard of living, at least before the coming of mid-Victorian prosperity in the 1850s and 1860s? Historians of an older generation such as J. L. and Barbara Hammond, writing earlier in this century, had no doubt that things got worse for working people as the Industrial Revolution developed. It seemed obvious that this must be so in the light of the evidence in the Reports of Royal Commissions, eye-witness reports, and so on. Moreover, the Hammonds believed that this was the penalty that was paid for the development of unrestricted industrial capitalism; employers and landlords were simply allowed to make large profits out of the sufferings of ordinary men, women and children in the factories and down the mines.

It was not until the period between the wars that any doubts were raised about these views, and it was Sir John Clapham who first pointed out that the wages figures available, taken in conjunction with N. J. Silberling's price index, seemed to show an increase in real wages for industrial workers of about 60 per cent between 1790 and 1850. This surprising conclusion was to be followed by other arguments which seemed to put the coming of the Industrial Revolution into a new perspective, such as the fact that child labour was widespread before the factory system was established; that some of the evidence given before the various factory enquiries was biased; that conditions were often harsh in domestic industry; that the factory system provided more regular hours and employment than the domestic system; and that sanitary conditions were as foul in the older, non-industrial towns and cities as in the newer factory towns. These views were propounded by a number of historians, and particularly by one of Clapham's disciples, T. S. Ashton, who contributed to an important statement of the anti-Hammond viewpoint published in 1954 and entitled significantly *Capitalism and the Historians*.

From this point onwards battle was joined between those who take the side of the Hammonds—called for convenience, the pessimist school of thought—and those who follow Clapham and Ashton, the optimist school of thought. The terms 'optimist' and 'pessimist' were used in this connection by Professor Hobsbawm, himself a leading pessimist, though Professor Perkin has used the words 'meliorist' and 'deteriorationist'; while another pessimist historian, Edward Thompson, refers to the 'immiseration' of the working classes. The arguments of both schools have been expressed at length in a number of learned articles and books, and understandably enough the greatest area of controversy was at first over real wages.

It is obvious that if only it were possible to trace accurately the course of real wages for different kinds of occupations over a long enough period then we would have a substantial indication, at least, of what was happening to the standard of living, simply because real wages are a large element in estimating anyone's standard of living. In fact, it has proved impossible to do this. Some wage rates are known in some trades but wage rates are very different from actual *earnings* which might include additions for overtime, or reductions for short-time working. Only wages books would show this, but few have survived. If we do not know the extent of short-time working or actual unemployment, it becomes extremely difficult, if not impossible, to calculate a man's take-home pay over any length of time. Again, instead of weekly wages, in some occupations piece rates were paid, and once more there is the problem of how much was earned by the end of the week. To take a specific instance: in Black Country mining a certain quantity of coal had to be cut per shift (a 'stint'), and was paid for at a certain rate; but stronger miners would cut a stint and a half or even more, which would put up their earnings; but they might decide not to work on a Monday (St Monday) which would bring them down again. Earnings might be reduced by field insurance (i.e. insurance against injury or death) or by truck (payment in kind), or they might be in effect increased by beer allowances or a monthly coal allowance. If all this is not enough to show the difficulty of determining actual earnings, there is the great problem of ascertaining changes in the cost of food, rent, and so on, so as to calculate real wages. The cost of food and clothing varied from place to place and from one year to the next, and although Ashton was a follower of Clapham, he was forced to reject Silberling's cost of living index as being unreliable. For all these reasons, both optimists and pessimists have abandoned the attempt to prove their case by relying on real wages figures alone, and have turned to other aspects.

Among these, food consumption has received considerable attention, especially by Professor Hobsbawm. The figures for tea, coffee, sugar and beer in Customs and Excise Returns have been examined, but without conclusive results, since changing rates of duty and variations in price make it difficult to interpret the significance of changes in the quantities consumed. Efforts to draw conclusions on the basis of the consumption of bread and potatoes have similarly proved fruitless. The sale of beasts at Smithfield, London, has also come under review by Hobsbawm in an effort to discover whether more meat was being consumed, but since changes in the weight of the animals could not be ascertained, and since in any case London is not a typical industrial town, this project also ended in failure.

Another earlier line of investigation, followed up this time by Dr Hartwell, the leading optimist, was to attempt to trace changes in *per capita* national income. Earlier calculations seemed to show that income per head increased by 85 per cent between 1801 and 1851, but these figures have been challenged, and even if they were accepted on all sides, there remains the further question of how the increase was distributed—evenly among all classes, or more to the middle and upper classes? Professor Perkin has concluded that in the first half of the nineteenth century there was a 'considerable shift in income distribution towards the rich and well-to-do.' Other topics investigated have included housing, but although some historians have shown that not all new working-class housing was jerry-built, and that (as we saw in Chapter III), better-constructed houses were available in some towns for the better-paid skilled workers, the evidence as yet is too fragmentary to be of much use. Another recent feature of the controversy has been the undertaking of detailed studies of working-class standards of living in Bath and Glasgow, while two historians have begun to extend the study of the subject to the Black Country in the *second* half of the nineteenth century.

It is clear so far that attempts to prove a case one way or the other by purely *quantitative* methods—that is, by measuring changes in wages, prices, consumption levels, and so on—have hardly been successful.

For this reason, both optimists and pessimists have tended to shift their ground and to fall back on *qualitative* approaches. Hartwell has emphasized the social gains for the working classes as seen in the growth of friendly societies, schools, cooperative societies, trade unions, and the restrictions placed on child labour by the factory acts. Thompson, on the other hand, though conceding that there was 'over the period 1790–1840 . . . a slight improvement in average material standards', sweeps away all arguments over real wages by asserting that 'people may consume more goods and become less happy or less free at the same time'. The heart of his argument is that the Industrial Revolution with its ruthless work-discipline in a grim urban environment destroyed an older and more civilized mode of life. Many years previously the Hammonds touched on the same point when they contrasted the life of domestic workers who could at least take time off of their own choosing with the life of a spinner working in a temperature of 80 to 84 degrees and subject to the fines described in Chapter I.

The debate remains open, and indeed is likely to stay open for the forseeable future, since the problem to be solved is how historians are to evaluate a whole new way of life—that is, the new life of the urban industrial worker. Moreover, that way of life would vary from one industrial area to another, so that the life-style of a worker in a large cotton mill in Lancashire might be appreciably different from the life-style of a foundry worker in the Midlands. It may be that more regional studies are necessary before any further progress can be made. It might even be argued that no firm conclusions will ever be reached in this controversy because of the ideological passions of the historians who have participated in it, ranging from an outright rejection of industrial capitalism as an economic system to an equally strong acceptance and advocacy of private enterprise and individual profit. Nevertheless, the argument has at least led to a narrowing of the period in dispute to the 1820s and 1830s, for it is agreed by optimist and pessimist alike that the period of the French Wars and of the immediate post-war years was one of declining standards, whilst some kind of improvement certainly took place from the mid-forties onwards. Lastly, it might be observed that no one who has examined the evidence on this subject could possibly fail to realize that the pursuit of historical truth is a complex and many-sided task.

Section II
Equipoise and After 1850–1900

The 1850s and the 1860s saw a steady growth in the economy with stable or rising prices, an unprecedented increase in international trade, a continuing shift of manpower from agriculture to industry, and (in the 1860s) improved real wages. In these mid-century years Britain truly became the first industrial nation, and deserved the title of the 'Workshop of the World'. Prosperity peaked in the years 1870–73, but thereafter the pace of expansion slackened. Though exports continued to increase in volume, prices fell, and corn growers on less suitable soils faced heavy competition from imported North American wheat. These developments caused some alarm and led to the period 1873–96 being termed 'The Great Depression'. In reality, the depression was most noticeable in the form of lower rates of interest and profits, and seems to have been due principally to a failure to innovate in the face of increasing foreign competition. Unemployment became serious in certain areas, but real wages actually improved as prices fell. By the end of the century, the depression had lifted, but competition from America and Germany remained acute. Germany especially was well ahead of Britain in the invention and development of the petrol and diesel engines, in electrical engineering, and in the chemical industry.

Chapter VII
Further Reform of Working and Living Conditions

The Course of Reform

After the excitements of the first half of the nineteenth century—the struggle over the Ten Hours Bill, the opposition to the new Poor Law, the attempts at public health reform, and above all, the massive Chartist campaigns—the middle decades of the nineteenth century seem strangely calm and unremarkable. Indeed, one historian has called these years 'the age of equipoise'—a period when Victorian society, having survived the earlier strains of industrialization, seemed uncertain as to what ought to happen next. Things seemed to be somehow in a state of balance, awaiting some new development. However, there is no real mystery about this lull in social reform. It was caused in part by the onset of mid-Victorian prosperity, so that social reform no longer seemed quite so urgent, and partly by a period of coalition governments which lacked strong policies. Moreover, the leading politician of the day was Lord Palmerston, Prime Minister from 1855 to 1858, and again from 1859 till his death in 1865. When asked in 1864 what was to be his policy in domestic affairs, he replied:

> Oh, there is really nothing to be done. We cannot go on adding to the Statute Book *ad infinitum*. Perhaps we may have a little law reform; but we cannot go on legislating for ever.

This is not to say, of course, that no reforms at all were passed in the 1850s and 1860s, but certainly a fresh spate of reforms did not begin until Gladstone began his first ministry in 1868, to be succeeded by Disraeli in 1874. Thereafter social reform continued as an increasingly accepted feature of government policy, made necessary by the new industrialized society which had evolved during the century. Some ministries were more distinguished than others for the reforms passed—for example, Disraeli's ministry from 1874 to 1880—but the continuing need for more legislation in the fields of working and living conditions, and in other aspects of working-class life such as education, made social reform the rule in any ministry rather than the exception.

Working Conditions

It will be remembered that the reform in working conditions which had taken place by the 1850s had owed much to indignation at conditions in the new textile factories. The consequence was that although hours in such places had been limited for women, young persons, and children between the age of nine and 13, the working hours in all other places of employment were still quite unregulated; and these were the vast majority of workplaces, of course. The task confronting reformers was therefore to extend textile factory legislation to all other places of work so as to provide protection for the masses of children, young persons and women still working extremely long hours.

A start was made in the early 1860s with two Acts regulating hours for children in occupations associated with spinning and weaving—the Bleach and Dye Works Act, 1860, and the Lace Act, 1861. In the next year the second Children's Employment Commission was appointed which published seven reports over the next few years containing a mass of information on children at work. The reader of these reports might well think that employers generally were still completely indifferent to the arguments against long working hours for children—arguments which had been voiced time and time again earlier in the century. A 12 hour day was still very common for small children, with time off for meals. Thus, in the mills and forges of South Staffordshire boys of eight years of age were employed as scrap carriers or door drawers (operating the doors of furnaces) on 12 hour shifts, with an hour and a half off for meals. Hours might be longer than this. As noted in Chapter I, a boy in a Black Country skinworks, for instance, aged 13, usually worked from 6 am to 7 pm, but sometimes started at 5 am and worked till 8 pm.

Some of the worst conditions seem to have been in the brickyards where children were known to have started work as early as four years old, and where the girls were said to become degraded:

> The evil of the system of employing young girls at this work consists in its binding them from their infancy, as a general rule, to the most degraded lot in after life. They become rough, foul-mouthed boys before nature has taught them that they are women. Clad in a few dirty rags, their bare legs exposed far above the knees, their hair and faces covered with mud, they learn to treat with contempt all feelings of modesty and decency.

An Inspector reported in the same vein in 1864. He considered that in the brickyards the degradation of the female character was most complete:

> I have seen females of all ages . . . undistinguishable from men, excepting by the occasional peeping out of an earring, sparsely clad, up to the bare knees in clay splashes, and evidently without a vestige of womanly delicacy . . .

But perhaps the most striking evidence given before the Children's Employment Commission was that relating to conditions in pottery works and in match factories. In the former, the red lead used in the glazing process had a deadly effect:

> Few dippers continue many years at their work without suffering from painter's colic or paralysis; many become crippled at an early age.

Similarly in the match factories the poisonous fumes from the phosphorus attacked the jaws and lungs of the workers. One overlooker at Bryant & May's in London testified as follows:

> Has known many bad from the work. One lost his jaw. 'You could take his chin (showing) and shove it all in his mouth.' Has known several die from the 'phosphorus on their innards'. Has known eighteen or twenty lose their jaws.

The result of these revelations was that even before the Commission had published its final Report, Parliament passed the Factory Act, 1864, regulating hours and conditions in a number of industries including pottery and match manufacture. In 1867 Parliament went further and introduced the Workshop Regulation Act which for the first time defined a workshop and limited hours for women and children; there were to be no children under eight, children from eight to 13 could work only half-time, and women and young persons (13 to 18) were to work a maximum of 12 hours. The Act was unsatisfactory in its details, but it was at least a start on the enormous task of regulating the work of the great numbers outside the factories, many of them still working in domestic workshops. The greatest problem, of course, was enforcement.

At first, local inspectors were appointed, in spite of the fact that this system had proved altogether unsatisfactory under the early Factory Acts. However, in 1871 the factory inspectors took over the inspection of workshops as well, though it was to be some time before anything like an efficient system of inspection was achieved. Here again, sheer numbers were a problem; one inspector in the Black Country alleged in 1876 that he had 10 000 workshops in his district, with an average of three and a half persons in each. There was the further difficulty that not all domestic workshops were open to inspection—for example, a workshop containing only a man and his wife with no other workers did not come under the Act, and according to an inspector as late as 1889, it was not usual to proceed against a man for overworking his wife. Nevertheless, with all its imperfections, the 1867 Workshops Act was a great step forward, for it at last brought the majority of workers within the scope of regulation.

Meanwhile, the Factory Act, 1867 redefined factories so as to bring in other large places of work such as ironworks and glasshouses, and fixed hours of work therein, generally permitting only part-time work (and no night work) for children up to the age of 11 or 12. According to one inspector, half-time boys were 'practically expelled' from the forges because they could not work at night. The 1871 Factory Act made the age at which girls might start work in the brickyards as high as 16, while the Coal Mines Regulation Act, 1872, put up the age for boys underground to 12, with a maximum of 54 hours a week under the age of 16. Nor was agriculture forgotten in all this legislation; the last Report of the Children's Employment Commission published in 1867 drew attention to the practice in some agricultural counties in Eastern England of employing women and children in gangs. These gangs worked long hours in the fields under so-called gang-masters. Undoubtedly the conditions of labour were very harsh, and the gang-masters were often slave-drivers. By the Agricultural Gangs Act, 1868, all gang-masters were to be licenced by JPs, no boy or girl under eight was to be employed, and a licenced gang-mistress was necessary when women and girls were included in the gang.

Thus, by the 1870s important advances had been made in the regulation of working conditions, though the law was now becoming very complicated, with one set of rules for factories and another for workshops. In 1876 yet another Commission was set up to enquire into the working of the Factories and Workshops Acts, and this was followed in 1878 by the Factories and Workshops Act which attempted to consolidate the law and to iron out inconsistencies. Thereafter attention shifted to the sweated trades—that is, those trades often carried on in domestic workshops or actually in the home, where hours were notoriously long and wages low. A Select Committee of the House of Lords was appointed in 1888 to report on the Sweating System, as it was called, and it reported on a number of trades, including nailmaking, bootmaking, and tailoring. In 1892 another Royal Commission was established, this time on Labour Conditions generally, which provided valuable information on both sweated and non-sweated trades. At the turn of the century the Factories and Workshops Act, 1901, consolidated the law still further.

Meanwhile in the major industries a new practice had grown up which had a further influence on the limiting of hours. This was the setting up of Wages Boards or Trades Boards on which both employers and work people were represented. In the course of determining wages, working hours had also to be taken into consideration, and this was particularly important when there was still no Act of Parliament restricting the working hours of men. The Nottingham Hosiery Board dated from the 1860s, while the Midlands Iron and Steel Board came into informal existence in 1872, being re-constituted more formally in 1876. In 1892 its operative Secretary, giving evidence before the Royal Commission on Labour, remarked that he had been in all the strikes before 1872

> till I was sick of striking and therefore was prepared for any machinery and to take any trouble which would prevent their possibility.

The Midlands Mining Wages Board also began informally in 1874, having an official existence from 1883 onwards. The last two boards adopted a procedure whereby it was aimed to avoid disputes over wages by constructing sliding scales—wages would be adjusted periodically according to the selling price of the product, whether coal or iron and steel. In addition, in the Birmingham area, the 'alliance system' was utilized from time to time. Under this arrangement employers would fix wages and employ only union labour, while the workmen would all join the union and work only for employers in the alliance. In this way it was hoped to avoid competitive wage-cutting by employers.

In all these ways working conditions were improved in the second half of the nineteenth century, and a great mass of information was built up on all aspects of labour. A valuable contribution to this body of knowledge was made by the Reports of the Mines Inspectors and the Inspectors of Factories and Workshops which became more and more detailed as the century advanced. If one explanation of the early opposition to the Factory Acts was simple ignorance of conditions in the factories, there could be no such excuse by 1900. Early in the twentieth century two further advances must be noted: in 1908 there was passed at last the first Act regulating the hours of work of men—the Eight Hours Act, fixing the working day for miners (in 1912 there was even an attempt to fix minimum mining wages, district by district, but the Act was not entirely satisfactory). Then in 1909 the Sweated Industries Act was passed, made necessary by the continued sweating of workers in certain trades. Jack London described some of these trades in the East End of London in his book, *People of the Abyss* (1903). He quotes a shoemaker who explains what happened when there was a rush of work:

> An' then we work twelve, thirteen and fourteen hours a day, just as fast as we can. An' you should see us sweat! Just running from us! If you could see us, it'd dazzle your eyes—tacks flyin' out of mouth like from a machine.

The 1909 Act required wages boards to be set up in specified sweated industries such as tailoring, so that even these industries, which were notoriously difficult to control, now came under increasing supervision. This legislation is dealt with again in a different context in Chapter XII.

It remains to survey the length and character of the working week at the end of the nineteenth century. The working day for the adult male was still long by the standards of today—usually about 11 hours, including meals—but it had shortened somewhat since the 1850s. Although the working week was still a six-day week, Saturday labour was less than before, and only a half-day was worked in many trades from the 1870s onwards. It was about this time that the working man acquired four days statutory holiday with the passing of the Bank Holiday Acts in 1871 and 1875. By the end of the century a week's holiday a year was not unknown, though as might be expected it was much more likely to be enjoyed by skilled workers rather than unskilled workers. It must be remembered, of course, that as described in Chapter II some unskilled workers still took a working holiday in the fields at harvest time. Then again, the development of the railways in the second half of the century made the cheap-day excursion possible, particularly the trip to the seaside.

As for conditions at work, regulations grew increasingly complex in an effort to make work safer. The Coal Mines Acts provide a good illustration here. By 1911 the safety regulations were very extensive. Among other requirements, all managers had to be trained and certificated, all shafts had to have guides, cages, overhead covers and signalling systems, winding machinery had to be of a specified type, the use of explosives was closely controlled, and so were all haulage systems underground. The 1911 Act added further regulations covering many different matters, e.g. the fixing of hours for engine men, the provision of baths and facilities for drying clothes at the bigger pits, and the searching of men for matches and other forbidden articles. Accidents still happened, of course, and the rules were not always obeyed, but the contrast with the 1850s is very striking.

At other places of work the employer found himself under increasing pressure to make his premises safe. The Employers Liability Act, 1880 and the Workman's Compensation Act, 1906 required the employer to pay compensation to any workman suffering injury or disease resulting from unsafe or unhealthy working conditions. Even a cursory glance at the Factory Inspectors Reports at the turn of the century will show the extent of regulations regarding the use of extractor fans, electrical equipment, and dangerous acids as in galvanizing. There can be no doubt that conditions at work were much safer than they had been 50 years earlier.

There is one further point, too, which needs to be made. The worker in 1900 was much less likely to be forced to work excessive hours than his predecessor in 1850, simply because standards had been established as to what constituted a fair day's work; the Factory Acts, the Wages

Boards, and the spread of trade unionism had seen to this. Workers might still be dismissed on the spot in a way unthinkable at the present day, but industrial relations had become much more complex, and the ordinary workman, particularly the unskilled or semi-skilled, had much greater protection than he had in 1850 when he was virtually defenceless against an employer who was determined to exploit his labour. Lastly, it will have been noticed that the regulation of working conditions became very widespread in the second half of the nineteenth century, yet in this subject attention is usually focused on the first half of the century rather than the second. This is understandable enough in view of the human interest to be found in the story of the Factory Reform Movement. Nevertheless, that movement was only the beginning of the story, and important though it was in setting precedents and establishing principles, the great mass of the working population were more affected by the legislation of the second half of the century than by the pioneering acts earlier on.

Living Conditions

It will be recalled that by 1850 only one important Public Health Act had been passed, and that was largely permissive. In view of the fact that no large scale public health legislation was undertaken for more than 20 years after the 1848 Act, it might be thought that little progress was made in the 1850s and 1860s. This is not really so, partly because significant advances took place on the basis of local initiative, and partly because some of the apparently minor Acts which were passed were actually of considerable importance.

In 1848 Dr John Simon was appointed Medical Officer of Health to the City of London and immediately began to hammer home what he called the 'national prevalence of sanitary neglect'. He proved to be the natural successor to Chadwick, becoming Medical Officer to the Privy Council when the Board of Health was dissolved in 1858, and eventually Chief Medical Officer to the new Local Government Board in 1871. In his Annual Reports to the City Corporation he constantly drew attention to such insanitary evils as overcrowding:

> Instances are innumerable in which a single room is occupied by a whole family—whatever may be its number, and whatever the ages and sexes of the children; birth and death go on side by side; where the mother in travail, or the child with smallpox, or the corpse waiting internment, has no separation from the rest . . .

Simon's reforming influence within the City contributed to reform in London beyond the City Boundaries. The Metropolitan Local Management Act, 1855 set up a Board of Works for London which by 1865 had established two major sewerage schemes, one North of the Thames and one to the South. Meanwhile, efforts were made in London to provide model dwellings for the working classes by such bodies as the Peabody Trust, Sir Sydney Waterlow's Improved Industrial Dwellings Company, and the Artisans' Labourers' and General Dwellings Company. The Peabody Trust's dwellings in Shoreditch were described as follows in 1866:

> Though there is nothing picturesque in these buildings the architect has done wonders for the health and comfort of the residents. . . . The closets are numerous, private and convenient, light and spacious; the lavatories (washrooms) are ample and accessible . . .

Model dwellings, in fact, became a subject of public interest in the middle decades of the century, Prince Albert designing a dwelling which went on show at the Great Exhibition, and a number of books were written on the subject.

In addition to these attempts to encourage better quality building, it became common practice to draw up bye-laws for the construction of new streets and houses. In some parts it appears that sets of model regulations were adopted, specifying for example, the amount of free space at the rear of the building, how rooms were to be ventilated, and so on:

> Every building to be erected and used as a dwelling house shall have in the rear, or at the side thereof, an open space exclusively belonging thereto, to the extent at least of 150 square feet. . . . Every habitable room shall have at least one window, and the total area of the window or windows, clear of the sash frame, shall be at the least one tenth of the area of every such room, and the top of one at least of such windows shall be not less than 7' 6" above the floor . . .

Thus, something seems to have been done locally in order to improve the quality of new building before the 1870s, while a succession of Nuisance Acts in 1848, 1855, 1860, and 1863 set up nuisance authorities for the removal of public nuisances such as dung heaps or cesspools. The Common Lodging Houses Acts of 1851 and 1853 provided for the police to inspect and if necessary close down lodging houses, some of which were no more than cheap and disreputable doss-houses in which the bed would be a bundle of dirty straw. The worst kind were graphically described in a contemporary account:

> Nothing can be worse to the health than these places, without ventilation, cleanliness, or decency, and with forty people's breath perhaps mingling together in one foul choking steam of stench.

109

One other act, the Sanitation Act, 1866 was potentially the most important of all, for it made more widely available the powers previously given by the 1848 Act, and made the powers mandatory rather than permissive. Unfortunately the drafting of the act was defective, so that it was less effective than had been hoped.

By the end of the 1860s, however, the time had come to survey the position after the advances of the past two decades, and in 1869 the Royal Sanitary Commission was appointed. In spite of all the reforms which had taken place, there were still massive problems of bad housing and the lack of water closets and piped water supplies. The root causes of the difficulties were the continued permissiveness of the law, its great complexity, and the extraordinary variety of local authorities with public health duties—there were local boards of health, municipal authorities, improvement commissioners, burial boards, drainage boards, highway boards, poor law unions, vestries—the list seems endless. It is no wonder that the Commission recommended in its Report published in 1871 that the administration of the Sanitary Law should be made 'uniform, universal, and imperative'. In addition the Report emphasized that if a civilized social life was to be maintained, proper drainage and water supplies were essential, together with the removal of nuisances, the provision of burial facilities, the eradication of preventable disease, and the inspection and banning of unwholesome food.

As a result the Local Government Board was set up in 1871, taking over the administration of both public health and poor law. In the following year the Public Health Act divided the country into sanitary districts, each to have a sanitary authority, either a municipal corporation (in the towns), or a local board (in other well-populated areas), or a Board of Guardians (in rural areas). Each sanitary authority was to have a Medical Officer, and an Inspector of Nuisances. In this way, new central and local authorities were established. There remained the task of reforming the law itself, and this was undertaken in the most important Public Health Act, 1875, which specified the duties of the new authorities. This Act provided a large-scale codification of the existing law which was to constitute the basis of the law of public health until 1936. Also in 1875 there was passed the first of Cross's Housing Acts (Cross was the Home Secretary of the time). This was not the first housing Act—Torren's Act, 1866, gave local authorities powers to force slum landlords to improve their property, but its effect was only limited. Cross's 1875 Act was the first to give local authorities power to demolish slum property, and it was followed by a second Cross Act and a second Torrens Act in 1879 (both amended in 1882).

It is clear that the legislation of the 1870s marks the abandonment of the old kind of individualism and the beginning of the more modern, collectivist approach to public health. At last it was accepted that—to adapt the famous remarks of *The Times* in 1848—the nation really could not afford any longer to take its chance on cholera and the rest, but must submit to being bullied into good health. In plain words, compulsion had to be applied, and ratepayers had to pay up. This often proved expensive, and it was perhaps fortunate that the beginning of this major period of reform saw England at the peak of industrial and commercial prosperity. The greatest source of expense was the installation of deep drainage and connection of houses to the new drains or sewers. An essential part of this procedure was the replacement of earth privies by water closets, and the provision of piped water to flush the closets. In the last quarter of the nineteenth century these major tasks were tackled in all the urban areas, though in some parts they were not completed even by 1914. Nevertheless, up and down the country, authorities obtained estimates from sanitary engineers for deep drainage of their towns. A typical proposal for a small town to be connected to a district system went into technical details before estimating costs:

> The proposed sewers are all intended to be made with earthenware pipes from 12 to 9 inches in diameter. . . . When sewers are properly constructed, of such size as to occasionally run half-full, no deposit can take place in the sewer, and the liability to obstruction is reduced to a minimum. It is not generally understood that a 9 inch pipe running two-thirds full with a fall of one foot in 400 feet would discharge nearly 300 000 gallons of sewage in one day . . .
>
> The total cost of the works proposed, as shewn on the accompanying Plans and Sections, we estimate at £4915. . . . This sum borrowed for 30 years at $3\frac{3}{4}$ per cent would require for repayment and interest an annual sum of about £275, equal to a general district rate of about $2\frac{3}{4}d$ in the £.

This deep drainage probably constitutes the biggest single sanitary achievement of Victorian England, although surprisingly little attention has been paid to it in the history books. In getting rid of the earth privy and the night soil men it revolutionized urban sanitation, banishing nauseating sights and smells from the towns, and having a powerful effect on the spread of disease and on mortality rates. Urban life today would be unthinkable, of course, without deep drainage, yet it is taken for granted and there is too little awareness of the sanitary revolution which brought it about.

If the battle for deep drainage was largely won by 1914, the same cannot be said of the attempts to get rid of the slums. Here the problems were of a different order. Respect for private property was so deeply entrenched that local authorities were slow to take advantage of the earlier Housing Acts, and even when they did demolish slum property they usually left the site to be developed for working-class housing by private builders. The result was that although slum clearance certainly took place in Glasgow, Edinburgh and Liverpool from the 1860s, and in London and Birmingham from the 1870s (Birmingham's scheme is particularly famous, owing much to the Lord

Mayor of the time, Joseph Chamberlain, who claimed that in 1873 to 1876 the city was 'parked, paved, assized, marketed, gas-and-watered, and *improved*), re-housing was not systematically undertaken. Indeed, in London the clearances resulting from the 1875 Housing Act led to much suffering among dispossessed tenants. Moreover, there was so much poor quality housing in the larger towns and cities that housing was decaying faster than it could be demolished or replaced.

By the 1880s it was quite evident that not enough was being done. In London something like a crisis developed as a result of the operation of the Cross Acts which came on top of earlier extensive clearances in the 1860s for the new railway lines and stations, and other clearances for the building of government offices, office blocks, and warehouses. The working people who lost their housing could not afford to move out to the suburbs, for the railway companies failed to provide enough cheap workman's trains; yet when new accommodation was eventually provided for them the rents were often too high. As a consequence there was an actual increase in overcrowding, leading to the creation of new slums. This problem was dramatically highlighted by a pamphlet published by a Congregationalist minister, Arthur Mearns, in 1883, entitled *The Bitter Cry of Outcast London* in which he warned his readers that:

> . . . seething in the very centre of our great cities, concealed by the thinnest crust of civilization and decency, is a vast mass of moral corruption, of heartbreaking misery and absolute godlessness . . .

There followed a description of housing conditions in London in terms typical of the Reports of the 1840s:

> courts reeking with poisonous and malodorous gases arising from accumulations of sewage and refuse scattered in all directions . . . dark and filthy passages swarming with vermin . . . walls and ceilings are black with the accretions of filth which have gathered upon them through years of neglect . . .

His pamphlet caused a considerable stir, and there were some who thought the situation was so serious that it might lead to political demonstrations. Cardinal Newman considered that 'some day this crater will overwhelm London . . .' while George Sims wrote that:

> It has now got into a condition in which it cannot be left. This mighty mob of famished, diseased and filthy helots is getting dangerous, physically, morally, politically dangerous.

It may be that their fears were exaggerated, but a Royal Commission on Housing was appointed in 1885, its members including both the Prince of Wales and Cardinal Manning. Its Report confirmed that the state of the worst housing was very bad, but it offered no remedy beyond the more energetic enforcement of the existing legislation.

In 1890 a further Housing of the Working Classes Act was passed, permitting local authorities to build working-class housing themselves, thus at last breaking away from the idea that re-housing must be left to private enterprise or model dwelling companies. Local councils could now begin to provide municipal housing in the form of council houses and council flats, though many were hesitant about this use of local authority power, still preferring to leave it to private builders. In 1909 the last of the pre-war housing Acts was passed, the Town and Country Planning Act, a somewhat mild Act concerned with town planning rather than directly with housing. It allowed local authorities to make additional regulations regarding both streets and buildings, and to condemn poor quality housing.

The housing situation in 1914 is not easy to sum up, for conditions varied considerably from one town to another. In the big cities the slums were still there, though now diminished by slum clearance schemes. As already noted, one problem here was that as slum buildings were removed, other buildings began to decay and to slip into the slum category, so that the process of urban renewal seemed to have no end. Since council house building was as yet very limited in scale, there was a housing shortage in a number of places as the slums were cleared. Birmingham is an example of this. In this city in 1913 there were still 200 000 persons housed in 43 366 back-to-back houses. Over 42 000 dwellings were without a separate water supply or sink. In other smaller towns where the number of slum houses was much more limited, the council could make good progress in repairing older houses and installing taps, sinks, and water closets. Any new houses built had to conform, of course, to local building regulations, and hence were usually of a reasonable quality. Yet these same bye-laws made difficulties for some builders; they found it a problem to build houses to the required standard (which involved more expense) and still make a profit out of the rent of 3s or 4s a week which was all the labourer could afford. This is an additional reason why there was a noticeable shortage of houses at cheap enough rents in a number of towns, including Crewe, Sheffield and Nottingham.

Nevertheless, by 1914 public health services had improved greatly compared with the 1870s. Not only was the number of hospitals increasing, but important medical discoveries such as how disease is transmitted by germs, the need for antiseptics, and the use of anaesthetics, all transformed medical and surgical procedures. More attention was being given to the health of the individual. The need to encourage healthy exercise was acknowledged in the further provision of parks, recreation grounds, and swimming baths by local authorities. County councils began to employ health visitors (sometimes called 'mission-ers'), and in 1899 St Helens became the first town to provide free milk for needy mothers. Early in the new century there was considerable concern at the poor physical condition of some Boer War recruits, and in 1904 an Interdepartmental Committee on Physical Deterioration was set up. This Committee recommended the provision of school meals and also the medical inspection of school children. These recommendations were put into effect in the Education Acts of 1906 and 1907. Also in 1907 there was set up the first Infant Welfare Centre in London. Of greater importance than any other reforms of the times was the National Insurance Act, 1911 (to be discussed in detail in Chapter XII) which provided a contributory health insurance scheme for the working classes as a whole.

These developments before the First World War took time before they could have any appreciable effect on the health of the nation, but by 1914 the improvement brought about by deep drainage, piped water supplies, the removal of refuse, better housing, medical discoveries, and the health education of the individual, had become obvious. This can be seen in the fall in the death rates for England and Wales since the 1880s, and also in the Infant Mortality rates, that is, the deaths of infants under one year per 1000 live births. The fall in the infant rates after 1906 is especially significant in view of the development of Infant Welfare Centres and Health Visitors:

	Death Rates	Infant Mortality
1881–5	19·4	139
1886–90	18·9	145
1891–5	18·7	151
1896–1900	17·7	136
1901–5	16·1	138
1906–10	14·7	117
1911–14	13·9	110

Nevertheless, welfare services of the modern kind were only just beginning, and there was much still to be done. The 1911 insurance scheme covered only the person insured, not his family, so that doctor's bills would have to be paid for them as before. Nor were the hospitals free. With the exception of the poor law infirmaries, they were still run on a voluntary basis. Many of the working classes were still living in bad housing condtions as the Birmingham figures for 1913 show very clearly, and Birmingham was by no means the city with the worst housing in the country. The struggle for improved living conditions therefore had to be resumed after the First World War had ended in 1918.

Leisure Activities

Many of the leisure activities described in Chapter II continued in the second half of the century—cultural activities such as lectures and readings, and less cultured pursuits such as the popular theatrical shows, trips and jaunts, and drinking in the local public house. In addition to these forms of amusement, several new developments in working-class leisure pursuits may be discerned from the mid-century onwards.

One of the most important of these was the growth of professional sport and of the modern mass audience which follows it. It must be remembered that in the second half of the nineteenth century, the typical working man was a town dweller rather than a countryman. With the shortening of the working week, the urban working man had his Saturday afternoons free and could support a local team. Already by 1860 football was beginning to be organized on a national basis; in 1863 the Football Association was founded, basing the rules of the game on the rules followed by Cambridge undergraduates. In 1871 the first Cup Competition was held, and the first real international match was played between England and Scotland in 1872. By 1885, professionalism—the employment of paid players—was officially recognized by the Football Association. In 1897 there was an attendance of 65 000 at the Cup Final held on the Crystal Palace ground.

In this way association football became the favourite sport of the working man. Rugby football also developed its own organization—the Rugby Union was founded in 1871—but remained a middle-class sport except in Wales. Cricket also became more of a spectator sport, charging for entrance, and developing on a county basis; but the players themselves remained a curious mixture of well-to-do amateurs and paid professionals—Gentlemen and Players were the terms used at the time. W. G. Grace made the game very popular in the 1870s and 1880s, and the first Test Match was played against a visiting Australian team (who won) in 1878. New middle-class games also achieved prominence at this time such as golf and lawn tennis, but they were out of reach for the working classes.

The one entirely new sport which did attract working-class support was cycling. Although penny-farthings, cycles with very large front wheels and small back wheels, date from much earlier on, it was not until the 1880s that the bicycle was transformed by the development of the modern frame with two equal-sized wheels, and the invention of the pneumatic tyre. Henceforth the bicycle provided a new form of transport, in the first place for the middle-class young gentleman who could not afford a horse, and then for the working man. Not only was the bicycle a new and cheap way of getting to work, but it led to the formation of over 2000 cycling clubs which organized cycling tours. In this way the young and energetic working man could take advantage of another means of getting out of the towns and cities and into the fresh air of the countryside. It is estimated that there were more than $1\frac{1}{2}$ m cyclists in the mid-1890s.

It remains true, however, that football was the one sport to become overwhelmingly a working-class game. The working classes played it, either as paid professionals in the great national sides, or as amateurs in local teams; and the working classes provided the mass support in their many thousands on a Saturday afternoon. Working-class support for cricket was much more limited, though it, too, had its working-class supporters and its local teams. It is perhaps not surprising that crowded urban conditions produced team games played before mass audiences. Yet it must be noted how much the two main team games owed to middle-class encouragement and regulation. Both received a powerful boost in the reformed public schools of the mid-century, and middle- and upper-class influence was strong in the drawing up of rules by the Football Association and the Marylebone Cricket Club. Annual cricket matches and fetes might be held under noble patronage. Lord Stamford, president of the MCC, used to arrange one such game every year at Enville Hall, his family seat, where *The Illustrated London News* claimed the ground was the best in the world, 'smooth and even as a billiard table'. According to the paper, the event was:

> an annual gift from a noble lord to the toiling thousands of the Black Country.

The spirit in which both football and cricket was played was very different from the barbarous spirit of the cock-pit. Emphasis was laid on good sportsmanship—a mixture of courage, self-discipline, and chivalrous respect for one's opponents. It is not too much to say that cricket, especially, was played with something approaching moral fervour, and by the end of the century 'It isn't cricket' was used quite seriously by the middle classes to describe milder forms of unworthy conduct; though probably the working man would usually think the phrase too affected to use himself.

Another major development in urban entertainment was the music hall. It seems to have first begun in London as a place where customers might eat and drink while being entertained by a succession of artistes. By 1868 there were 39 music halls in London, nine in Birmingham, and eight in Manchester and Leeds. Over the country as a whole, and excluding London, the number amounted to about 300. By the end of the century the music hall had become a well-established popular institution, though by then food and drink were no longer provided in the body of the hall. The great stars of the time—Marie Lloyd, Albert Chevalier, Dan Leno, Gus Elen—acquired a national reputation with comic songs which often took aspects of working-class life as their subject, and treated them with a wry and sometimes sardonic humour. Thus, Gus Elen sang about the cramped housing in the East End of

London:

> Oh! It really is a werry pretty garden,
> And Chingford to the eastward could be seen;
> Wiv a ladder and some glasses
> You could see the 'Ackney Marshes
> If it wasn't for the 'ouses in between . . .

A third development of a different kind was that of the popular press. The national press was well-established at the mid-century, of course, with *The Times* pre-eminent, and although the 60s and 70s saw the rise of *The Daily Telegraph* and important provincial papers such as the *Manchester Guardian*, yet as late as the 1880s there was still no daily paper for the thoughtful working-class reader. The only newspapers catering directly for the working classes were the more lurid Sunday papers such as *Lloyd's*, *Reynold's*, and the *Illustrated Police News*. In the 1880s, however, it was increasingly realized that the existing daily press was too dull for the large numbers of the working classes now subject to compulsory education in the board and church schools. George Newnes began to cater for a mass lower middle-class and upper working-class readership with his weekly *Tit Bits* in 1881 (very different from today's publication), while Alfred Harmsworth (later Lord Northcliffe) published another weekly, *Answers*, in 1896, then a new daily, *The Daily Mail*, in 1896. This new daily newspaper was by no means sensational in appearance, but it no longer assumed that all readers were interested almost entirely in political news; instead it concentrated on personalities rather than principles, and laid great stress on the latest news. It was deliberately aimed at the skilled working man and the successful business man who lacked secondary education. It began the popular press of the present day with its emphasis on news as entertainment, and it dominated newspaper circulations for the next 30 years. It was followed by *The Daily Express* (founded in 1900) and a new picture paper, originally intended for women readers, *The Daily Mirror*, in 1905. None of these popular papers was remotely like the popular press of today, but they were its forerunners in their efforts to seek a new readership among the newly literate.

So much for the major new developments; for the rest, as we have already noted, many activities went on as they had done earlier in the century. In the home, there was still reading, card-playing, or drinking, with a piano in the front parlour of the more affluent, or even one of the new gramophones. Outside there might be a patch of garden to dig, or a yard in which pets such as rabbits or racing pigeons could be kept. Public entertainment towards the end of the century began to include the cinema—there were 4500 of them by 1917—but the music hall was still the working man's theatre. By 1914 more public amenities were available such as public libraries (often helped by a grant from the

Scottish-American philanthropist, Andrew Carnegie), and public parks in which a band would often play on Sundays. As strict Sabbatarianism declined towards the end of the century, so Sunday became less a day for the chapel and more a day of relaxation on which trips and outings might take place. Railway excursions were increasingly popular, and it was the railways which made possible the growth of seaside resorts like Blackpool and Margate, where the better-off working-class family might now take a week's holiday. For merely local trips, the new urban electric trams could take families to the town's boundries and within reach of the fields and moors. Yet for many working men, the popular place of relaxation was what it has always been throughout the century—the public house, still open all day long and till late at night. By the end of the century, the number of public houses was as large as ever—about one for every 300 of the population.

As compared with the mid-century, leisure activities just before the First World War were more varied and more numerous. Nevertheless, leisure had significance only for those in regular employment with steady wages. For the one-third of the urban working classes below the poverty line, and the more so for the 'submerged tenth' to be described in Chapter X, many of the leisure activities just described had no meaning. They lived a life apart, constituting the greatest social problem of the age.

Chapter VIII
Schools, Churches and Chapels after 1850

Educational Developments in the 1850s and 60s

Although there was still no state system of schools in England in the mid-nineteenth century, and although education for the working classes was still neither compulsory nor free, important progress was being made in providing elementary education. The annual grant by the government to the church societies had grown from the original £20 000 to over half a million pounds by 1857. The sheer cost of education to the government was becoming a matter for concern, and in 1853 Lord Russell introduced a Bill to permit towns of over 5000 inhabitants to raise an education rate to assist their church schools. The usual religious jealousies caused the bill to be rejected, but in 1858 it was decided to carry out a thorough survey of the state of elementary education and a Royal Commission was appointed headed by the Duke of Newcastle. Its terms of reference were:

> To enquire into the present state of popular education in England, and to consider and report what measures, if any, are required for the extension of sound and cheap elementary education to all classes of people.

The Newcastle Commission issued its report in 1862. On the whole, the Commissioners were not dissatisfied with the results of their investigations. They calculated that just under one in eight was attending school in 1858, and they had failed to come across any large numbers of children who did not attend school at some time in their lives. However, they too were concerned at the cost of education, and followed up Russell's earlier suggestion by proposing that a county education rate should be levied, administered by a county education board. Moreover, they were critical of the failure of many teachers to concentrate sufficiently on the 3 R's, wasting their time on less essential subjects, so that money was not being spent to the best advantage:

> . . . the junior classes in the schools, comprehending the great majority of the children, do not learn, or learn imperfectly, the most necessary part of what they come to learn—reading, writing, and arithmetic.

The solution in their view was to make the proposed grant out of the rates depend on a satisfactory performance of every child in annual examinations carried out by a special county inspector. Thus, two objectives would be achieved—the efficient teaching of the 3 R's, and economy in the spending of the taxpayer's money.

Whether the commissioners were justified in their criticisms of the teachers in an open question. What is certain is that they were convinced that teachers preferred subject-teaching to 3R work which the teachers found difficult and boring. In their view, a way had to be found of compelling the teachers to concentrate on this work rather than on the frills. The consequence was that although the idea of the county education rate was dropped, the Vice-President of the Committee of Council, Robert Lowe, drew up a Revised Code of regulations in 1862 which made payment of the annual grant from the government depend on the kind of examination proposed by the Commissioners, but now to be conducted by a Government Inspector. In this way there was introduced a new system of Payment by Results, its main emphasis being on regular attendance and satisfactory examination performance. As the regulations put it:

> The managers of schools may claim 1d per scholar for every attendance after the first 100, at the morning or afternoon meeting. One third part of the sum thus claimable is forfeited if the scholar fails to satisfy the inspector in reading, one third if in writing, and one third if in arithmetic respectively.

Children under six were exempted from the new scheme, but those over six were grouped into standards, moving up a standard every year, and not being re-examined in any standard which had been failed.

The only immediate benefits of Payment by Results was a considerable saving in money; whereas the annual grant in 1862 was £840 000, by 1864 it had been reduced to £705 000. It is hard to know whether there were any beneficial educational results. In theory, of course, the standard of children's work should have improved very markedly. In practice, it is difficult to assess whether this did in fact happen, because the new system produced so much strain in the schools. All turned on attendance, and on success in the examinations. As a consequence, great emphasis was placed on regular attendance at school, and the children had to be bullied or cajoled into coming to school, even if they were ill. Teachers would be greatly upset when attendance was low owing to a local epidemic in winter, or to harvesting in summer. The need for a good performance in the examination resulted in children being relentlessly drilled, little time being left for anything else. The examination day itself was one of great tension, with the teacher often in a highly nervous condition (for his salary depended on the result) and the children correspondingly overwrought. The majority of the inspectors were opposed to the new system, but had no alternative but to implement it. The greatest blame should probably be attached to Robert Lowe, a man with little sympathy for the working classes, whose concern appeared to be less with good teaching than with a kind of mechanical instruction at the cheapest possible cost: hence his famous promise to the House of Commons:

> . . . if it is not cheap it shall be efficient; if it is not efficient, it shall be cheap.

In the event, it was cheap, but was educationally very inefficient.

The second half of the century therefore opened with something of a set-back for working-class education, almost as if the middle classes had suddenly become aware of the implications of the increasing education grant and were determined to limit educational developments to simple basic instruction. Payment by Results cast long shadows over the schools for the following 30 years, although the 1862 Code was modified from time to time as in 1871, when grants were made for examination success in two subjects other than the 3 R's; and again in 1875 grants were made for class proficiency in class subjects, instead of attainment by individual children. By the mid-1890s Payment by Results had almost been abandoned, and in 1898 inspectors were told that they

> should not include any of the processes heretofor employed in formal examination.

The Education Act 1870

Meanwhile, the need for more school accommodation for the ever-increasing population had to be met in some way or another, and it was obvious that the church societies, even with government grants, could not go on building schools indefinitely. The result was the Education Act of 1870, sometimes called Forster's Act after W. E. Forster, the Vice-President of the Committee of Council who introduced the measure. Historians have argued over the causes of this Act, and in some ways it is surprising that an Act of such importance should be passed so soon after the restrictive Code of 1862. However, it must be remembered that the sheer pressure of numbers made it imperative that more schools should be provided. A National Education League was founded in 1869, campaigning for compulsory, free and secular education to be available in schools paid for out of the rates; and although this might seem at first to invite opposition from the church societies, always concerned to preserve their near-monopoly of working-class education, in fact they were prepared to compromise. The British and Foreign Schools Society knew that they could never provide enough schools for all nonconformist children, particularly in rural areas where their numbers might be very small, so that a new system of secular schools might be to their advantage. Similarly the National Society began to face the fact that as a voluntary society their funds were limited, and that schools paid for out of the rates were becoming inevitable, even though they naturally disliked the idea that such schools would not be under their control. So when the Liberals led by Gladstone won the election of 1868, Forster drew up the Education Bill. It is also significant that of the two parties, the Liberal Party attracted strong nonconformist support, while Forster himself was a Quaker by upbringing.

These seem to be the main reasons why the Education Bill was introduced in 1870, though older historians have emphasized other causes which may have had an effect. One of these is the Reform Act 1867, which gave the vote to working-class male householders in the towns. Robert Lowe's slighting remark on the passing of this Act was that 'we must educate our masters', but it is not true that the newly-enfranchised workmen in the towns made any very significant difference to the voting in the 1868 election. It is unlikely that the 1867 Act had much effect on the thinking of Forster or the Cabinet in 1870; so that the suggestion that the Act was passed either to meet a working-class demand for education or to make sure that voters were fit to vote must remain somewhat dubious. The same can be said of the other older explanation for the 1870 Act, that Prussia had a state system of education, and her military successes against Austria in 1866 and against France in 1870–1 proved the case for state education. Once more, the immediate problems of the church societies in the late 1860s are a much more likely reason than this.

In fact, Forster's bill proved to be a skilful compromise between the extremes of greatly extending the provision of church schools, on the one hand, and replacing them completely by state schools, on the other. His bill aimed to 'provide for public elementary education in England and Wales', and to do this he proposed to supply schools where church schools did not exist. As he put it, he planned to

> supplement the present voluntary system—that is, . . . fill up its gaps at least cost of public money, with least loss of voluntary cooperation, and with most aid from the parents.

In practice this meant that where a new school was necessary, and the church societies would not, or could not, supply the deficiency, then a school board was to be set up by the local ratepayers who would have authority to levy an educational rate and build and maintain the necessary school or schools. These new board schools would thus supplement the existing system, and be paid for out of the rates, but they would also be given annual grants by the government. Attendance at these schools was not compulsory, but the Act allowed school boards to make by-laws for attendance between five and 13 if they wished, with exemption between 10 and 13 if required. Nor were the schools to be free—it was laid down that

> every child attending a school provided by any school board shall pay such weekly fees as may be prescribed by the school board

but these fees were not to exceed 9d per week. Lastly, the delicate question of religious instruction was covered by the famous Cowper–Temple clause in the Act, which provided that there should be taught 'no religious catechism or religious formulary which is distinctive of any particular denomination'—that is, that religious teaching should be undenominational. There was the further safeguard for the parent that he could withdraw his child from religious instruction if he so wished.

Thus the way was opened for a very considerable expansion of the school system for the working classes. The 1870 Act really signalled the beginning of a state system of schools in this country, yet it was not done by abolishing the church schools. Indeed, the church societies were given a period of six months in which to make up deficiencies in the provision of schools, and numerous new church schools went up in this period before government grants ceased: 3003 applications for building grants were made in the last five months of 1870 compared with 226 for the whole of 1869. Meanwhile the Education Department carried out a nation-wide enquiry into the provision of schools. This was not an easy task, and in particular in the thinly populated rural districts it was difficult to find anyone sufficiently well-educated to be a member of a school board, should it be necessary to set up a new school. As one HMI put it:

> If a school were ordered it would probably be built and managed by a school board; and in Anglesey the members of the board would be five men whose opinion on a pig might be accepted, if the pig belonged to a perfect stranger, but on school matters the pig's opinions would be equally valuable.

In the cities, of course, it was quite otherwise. In London the Board was under the chairmanship of Baron Lawrence, who had recently been

Viceroy of India, while Joseph Chamberlain was prominent on the Birmingham School Board.

The work of electing school boards went on throughout the 1870s and even into the 1880s as deficiencies were revealed. How quickly any one board would come into existence would depend very much on the nature of the local opposition to it. In some places supporters of the Church of England were very hostile, disputing the figures for the deficiency of school places issued by the Education Department. In York it took four years (1888–92) before a board was set up. Even when a school board was elected, the religious beliefs of the candidates would be well-known and they would attract votes accordingly. Anglican parsons elected would sometimes obstruct the business of the board in order to give advantages to local National schools, or invoke clause 25 of the Act which permitted boards to pay the fees of poor pupils in church schools as well as in board schools. In 1876 these powers were transferred to the Boards of Guardians. Some school boards had the difficult task of establishing schools in the roughest of city areas where the societies had made no attempt to build schools. They might also take over church schools which the societies had no desire to continue. Their work had an important democratic significance, for at last elementary education was no longer dominated by the church societies. Moreover, it was not unusual to find a working man a member of a school board, and membership was also open to women.

Two issues became of increasing importance in the first 20 years of the school boards. The first was that of compulsory attendance. Even before the passing of the Act, this had been a matter of some controversy. The Factory Act, 1833 had provided for two hours compulsory education a day, but there were many who opposed the idea of full-time compulsion. The Newcastle Commission had investigated compulsory education in Prussia and had decided against it:

> Any universal compulsory system appears to us neither attainable nor desirable . . . we also found that the result of this system, as seen in Prussia, do not appear to be so much superior to those which had been already attained among ourselves by voluntary efforts . . . .

The principle at stake, of course, was whether it was right to interfere so drastically with parental rights, especially when fees were charged in schools, and where child labour was still so common.

However, the extension in the 1860s of the Factory Acts to employment in workshops and other workplaces meant that the children were generally prevented from starting work under the age of 10. Should they not therefore be sent to school? As we have seen, the 1870 Act left it to each school board to decide for itself. In 1876 Lord Sandon's Act set up school attendance committees for areas without school boards with the authority to compel attendance just like a school board if they so wished; and the same Act declared that it was the duty of parents to send their children to school between the ages of five and 10. This was not direct compulsion, but getting near it. In the same year the Royal Commission on the Factory Acts reported in favour of compulsory attendance, while schools which had problems in getting good attendance began to see how compulsion would help to maintain their grant. Yet authorities seemed reluctant to introduce compulsion locally—by 1880 only 450 of the 2000 or so school boards and 20 of the 190 school attendance committees had opted for it. Finally, in 1880 Gladstone's Education Act made the attendance clauses of the 1870 Act obligatory on all local authorities—that is, attendance between the ages of five and 13 with exemptions from the age of 10.

The settling of this matter raised the second issue in an acute form—that of free schooling. Compulsory attendance would eventually bring into the schools the children of the very poorest parents. Was it right to charge these parents fees? Must there be wholesale remission of fees for them? The situation was made worse when the voluntary schools (i.e. the church schools) deliberately charged high fees in order to keep out the riff-raff and retain the children of the more religious working classes who, it was thought, were not the poorest, since they benefited from 'habits of temperance, industry, and steadiness'. Quite apart from this, there was the problem of whether to remit fees when even respectable parents were thrown out of work by a local trade depression. Finally, Lord Salisbury's Act in 1891 eased the situation by allowing a new government grant to compensate schools which abolished fees; parents were also given the right to demand free places. In effect then, school fees were abolished, though some voluntary schools went on charging them as long as parents were prepared to go on paying them.

By the mid-1880s it was decided that another general survey of the state of elementary education should be undertaken, and so the Cross Commission was appointed, reporting in 1888. Its recommendations brought about important changes in the system of Payment by Results, which was heavily criticized. The majority of the Commission wanted it 'modified and relaxed', while the minority wanted it abolished altogether. In the 1890 Code the system of grants was so drastically modified that it was clear that Payment by Results was soon to be brought to an end. The commission also criticized the pupil–teacher system and recommended the setting-up of non-residential training colleges, and of day-colleges attached to university colleges. The Code of 1890 permitted the establishment of the latter.

On two further matters discussed by the Commission no action was taken for the time being, though their comments have significance for the future. With regard to the voluntary schools, the majority thought they should receive some assistance from the rates, while the minority were opposed to this. The other matter was that of the higher grade schools which some school boards had been developing for children who stayed on to receive some specialized teaching beyond what would normally be considered elementary education. These schools obtained extra grants from the Department of Science and Art at South Kensington for success in public examinations such as those of the Royal Society of Arts. To some extent they offered competition to fee-paying secondary schools, most of which were old endowed grammar schools attended by middle-class children. The Cross Commission was dubious about this development:

> We cannot therefore regard as completely satisfactory the present position of the class of schools to which we have referred. On the one hand they are obliged to adapt their curriculum in such a way as to bring them within the requirements of the Education Acts and of the Code in order that they may obtain Government grants; whilst, on the other hand, their object is to provide a much higher education than is ordinarily understood by the word 'elementary'.

The nub of the matter was that the 1870 Act had never defined 'elementary education' so that it was not at all clear what the ratepayers' money might properly be spent on. But for the time being neither this point nor that relating to paying for the church schools out of the rates was carried any further.

In the next year 1889 the Technical Instruction Act was passed. The Act was the result of increasing uneasiness at the way in which our industrial rivals were developing technical education and were competing with us more and more strongly in world markets. Yet the only encouragement to technical education in this country so far was the system of grants operated by the Department of Science and Art which has just been referred to. The setting up of the new county councils in 1888 supplied an excellent opportunity to create a new educational authority to assist technical education. The Act therefore gave the county councils authority to levy a penny rate for technical education, and also to raise money by loan for new school buildings.

The Demand for Secondary Education

The 1890s opened with secondary education as the major subject of educational controversy. There was no doubt that working-class education could no longer be confined to simple instruction in the 3 R's. Already there were cases of working-class children actually going to University, and although these cases were highly exceptional, they were a pointer to the future. In 1894 the Bryce Commission was appointed to report on secondary education. Its report, published in 1895, brought out very well the confused state of secondary education which was being provided in three different types of school: higher grade elementary schools under the direct control of the Education Department, a new government department established in 1856; technical schools run by the county councils under the Science and Art Department; and grammar schools, mostly under the supervision of the Charity Commissioners because of their charitable endowments.

Clearly administrative reform was necessary which would not only unify control but also make possible the joint planning of secondary and primary education. Moreover, reform was urgent if what the Report called 'the want of . . . coherence and correlation' was not to have serious results as each authority became more entrenched:

> The existing authorities and agencies whose want of cooperation we lament, are each of them getting more accustomed to the exercise of their present powers and less disposed to surrender them . . .

The Commission therefore recommended the formation of a new central educational authority presided over by a minister which would be responsible for both elementary and secondary education. Further, the new local educational authority should be the county council (or county borough council) with an education committee responsible for all secondary education, including the higher grade schools.

The first recommendation was carried out with comparative ease. In 1899 the Board of Education was established on the basis of a merger of the Education Department and the Department of Science and Art. The new Board was headed by a President and retained all the powers of the bodies it had replaced, together with the educational functions of the Charity Commissioners. The second recommendation, for the setting up of new secondary education authorities, was not so easy to carry out without controversy.

The fact is that the whole subject of secondary education for the working classes had now become a matter for heated discussion. In the first place, there was argument about the extent to which working-class boys and girls would really profit by education beyond the elementary stage. Although there was much talk about an 'educational ladder' leading to higher education, in fact many were privately very dubious about this, as is shown in the tone of a question put to a witness before the Cross Commission:

> Do you think that in the long run we do any real good to a clever boy belonging to the working classes if we give him an exhibition to the University, and lift him out of his own social station, and put him in one which is not congenial to him?—If it is not congenial to him, you have clearly done him mischief.

Secondly, by the end of the century the position of the church schools had become much weaker. It is true that the voluntary schools were still more numerous than the board schools in 1900—nearly 14 500 compared with nearly 5700, with roughly two and a half million in voluntary schools and nearly two million in board schools—but the voluntary schools were in an increasingly bad condition due to a shortage of funds. Church attendance was declining, and the Church of England authorities resented the superior financial resources of the board schools. Nothing had been done to implement the majority recommendation of the Cross Commission that church schools should be assisted from the rates. In 1895 the two archbishops led an impressive deputation to the Prime Minister and argued the case for increased financial aid to the church schools; but an Education Bill designed to provide this and to appoint new local education authorities failed to pass in the following year, mainly because of the opposition of school board and nonconformist interests.

Thirdly, the criticism of the privileged position of the board schools was not without political undertones. For the Labour Movement, school boards were democratic institutions, freely elected by the people, and providing schools for the people, independently of the Church of England, which was regarded as an essentially conservative body and part of the upper-class Establishment. Given these beliefs, politically-minded supporters of the school boards were very sensitive to attacks which they believed (not without some foundation) to be based on political ideas different from their own.

Unfortunately for the school boards, they found themselves in a vulnerable position. It is true that they had achieved great things in elementary education, and were extending their activities in secondary education; by 1894 there were 60 higher grade schools outside London, and by 1900 the London School Board had 79. Nevertheless, the latter Board in particular made enemies by the vigour of its policy, its rapid expansion of higher grade schools and evening schools, and the sheer cost to the rates of its services. Further, at the other end of the scale, some school boards were too small to be efficient—there were 151 boards with less than 250 inhabitants in their districts—and new local authority bodies had now come into existence, not only the county councils but also since 1895 the urban district councils and the rural district councils. Worst of all, the legality of the use of ratepayers' money for higher grade schools and for evening schools for adults was highly questionable. It was certainly difficult to see this as 'elementary education'.

The crisis came in 1899 when it was arranged for a complaint to be made by a ratepayer to the district auditor, Cockerton, against the London School Board's use of ratepayers' money on education other than elementary education. When the auditor disallowed the expenditure on higher grade schools, the School Board appealed to the High Court on the grounds that the 1870 Act had not clearly defined 'elementary education' or what 'child' meant in terms of age; and further, that higher grade education had continued unchecked for years without official disapproval. All this was in vain. In the opinion of one of the judges:

> We must ask what and to whom did the Acts of 1870 and later authorize the School Boards to teach at the expense of the rates. It is clearly stated that children are to be given elementary education, and this cannot be held to cover teaching foreign languages and advanced science to adults.

The Court decided that the use of school rates to finance higher grade schools and evening continuation schools must stop. In other words, the London School Board must discontinue these schools since it would be impossible to run them on the Science and Art grants alone.

The Education Act, 1902

The decision was a great victory for the enemies of the school boards. For the time being, the boards were allowed to continue running the higher grade schools pending the introduction of a new education Bill, but in reality the boards were doomed. The Education Act, 1902, swept them away, replacing them by county and county borough councils who were made responsible for both secondary and elementary education, except that in the smaller boroughs and urban areas the borough councils and urban district councils were made the authority for elementary education only. The board schools themselves continued to exist but, so to speak, under new management, and became known as council schools. The church schools also continued, but now they were to get aid for maintenance out of the rates, while in return the local education authority would appoint up to one-third of the managers. Lastly, the county and county borough councils had to survey the need for secondary education in their areas and make appropriate provision, including the building of new schools when necessary.

The 1902 Education Act was a bitter disappointment to the supporters of the school boards. Although it had always seemed possible that they might lose the higher grade schools, this did not mean that the boards themselves must necessarily disappear. Yet the re-organization of local government had provided new councils which could conveniently take over the work of the boards. The critics of the Act still thought the new councils no substitute for the old boards. A. J. Mundella, who had been Vice President of the old Committee of Council in Gladstone's second ministry in the 1880s, said that the school boards were 'the most democratic education authorities we possess', and that the Act

> eliminated the effective democratic element by destroying the directly elected School Boards and substituting nominated committees.

Whether this is true or not, Sir John Gorst, the last Vice President, was an enemy of the school boards and disliked their democratic aspect. Curiously enough, he received strong support from Sidney Webb, the Fabian socialist, who might have been expected to support democratically elected bodies, but who favoured the local councils, presumably because he was influenced by his experience as chairman of the London County Council's Technical Education Board.

The most determined opponents of the new Act were the nonconformists, who objected strongly to the church schools gaining assistance from the rates—something which the Education Act of 1870 had carefully avoided. This putting of the Church on the rates aroused passionate protests, especially in Wales, where protesters actually went as far as to go to prison rather than give financial support to Church of England schools.

Yet the new administrative machinery worked well. At last it was possible for both secondary and elementary schools to come under unified control, and secondary education certainly benefited. The county education committees found it necessary to provide more secondary schools (county schools) at which a proportion of places were free and could be filled by winners of scholarships from the elementary schools. In this way a ladder was provided from the elementary school to the university. Admittedly it was a very narrow ladder, and even if a working-class pupil obtained a place at a university there remained the problem of the cost of fees and residence. There is also the fact that secondary education for the working-class boy or girl was still thought of as somewhat exceptional, instead of a necessary stage in the education of all children, academically minded or otherwise. The consequence was that the new county secondary schools were run on traditional grammar school lines, ignoring the technical and scientific strengths of the old higher grade schools. Thus, the elementary or council school was still regarded as the basic type of school for the working classes, and only a minority went on to a school of the conventional academic kind where the majority of places were paid for. The new educational opportunities for the working classes were real enough, but they were very limited in nature.

What is undeniable, of course, is that the education of working-class children changed radically between the mid-nineteenth century and the coming of World War I in 1914. Education had become compulsory between the ages of five and 13 and the age of exemption was raised from 10 to 11 in 1893, and to 12 in 1899. It had also become free with very minor exceptions between the same age limits from 1891 onwards. These developments alone meant a dramatic fall in illiteracy, so that by the end of the century the literacy rate for both men and women stood at 97 per cent. Working-class education had still far to go in 1914, but the door was slowly opening onto wider prospects.

Churches and Chapels

If working-class attendance at school increased substantially in the second half of the nineteenth century, the same cannot be said of attendance at church or chapel. It will be remembered that the 1851 Religious Census revealed that only one in two went to church or chapel on Census Sunday and that in some areas such as London and the larger towns and cities working-class attendance was very limited indeed. Although the experiment of holding a national religious census was not repeated, there can be no doubt that religious observance among all classes declined still further after 1851, particularly from the 1880s onwards.

The reasons for this decline are various. Most historians would lay emphasis on the increasing rationalism of the second half of the century which threw doubt on the literal truth of the Bible. Lyell had already published his *Principles of Geology* in 1830–3, while Darwin's *Origin of Species* dates from 1859, and his *The Descent of Man* from 1871. Such books denied not the essential truth of Christianity but the Bible versions of the creation of the Earth and of Man which were central beliefs of much Victorian religious teaching. Associated with this was a growing rejection of other aspects of orthodox theology such as the belief in Hell and the need for personal salvation which to many now seemed at odds with the idea of a kind and loving God. These changes in ideas, naturally enough, did not directly affect working-class thinking, but they began to take effect on the middle and upper classes just at the time when the upper classes had begun to indulge more frankly in the open pursuit of pleasure and luxurious living. Here the Prince of Wales took the lead, openly holding dinner parties on Sunday evenings at Marlborough House, and arriving late with his guests at church at Sandringham but in time for a sermon which by arrangement would last only 10 minutes.

The consequences of this loss of earlier beliefs showed themselves in the gradual abandonment of family prayers in middle- and upper-class families, in a greater freedom of discussion in the press, and in the relaxing of the strict keeping of the Sabbath. In the 1890s the museums and art galleries of London were opened to the public on Sunday afternoons, and bands were permitted to play in the parks. The National Sunday League arranged cheap railway excursions on Sundays. Above all else, the change in attitude was to be seen in a falling away of attendance at church and chapel. A series of surveys in 1882 of regular attenders in some of the major cities showed the following percentages of attenders to population in the cities concerned:

Sheffield	23	Southampton	38
Nottingham	24	Hull	41
Liverpool	26	Portsmouth	41
Bristol	31	Bath	52

About 37 per cent of these attenders were members of the Church of England as compared with about 50 per cent in 1851; the nonconformists appeared to be holding their own, while the Roman Catholics were gaining ground.

London, of course, was an exceptional case because of its sheer size and complexity. Here a census carried out for 1902–3 by the *Daily News* showed a marked fall in attendance, with a striking fall among the upper and middle classes. Overall attendance was 22·0 per cent of the adult population (allowing for those attending twice, only 19 per cent). Percentage attendances in some working-class areas were remarkably small: for example:

	Church of England	Nonconformist
Fulham	5·7	4·2
West Ham	5·4	10·4
Poplar	5·4	6·8
Stepney	4·2	6·3

A recent calculation has estimated the percentage attendances based upon the classification employed by Charles Booth in his religious survey of London made in the years 1897–1900. They are as follows:

The Poor	11·7	Middle Class	22·7
Working class (unskilled)	13·2	Wealthy Suburbs	36·8
Upper Working Class	16·1	West End	33·8
Lower Middle Class	18·2		

These figures show that the poorest working classes in London rarely attended church or chapel, and when they did attend it was more likely to be chapel rather than church. It is no wonder that in 1894 the vicar of St Giles, Camberwell (a working-class area) lamented the fact that

> less come to church than did ten or even four years ago. The tendency seems to be in this direction increasingly.

Naturally, strenuous attempts were made to bring the working classes back into church (though many of them had never attended there in the first place). Revivalist campaigns were common, and included the famous visit of the Americans Sankey and Moody in 1873. Missions were set up, and in 1878 the Salvation Army was founded by the Rev. William Booth, with its citadels and barracks in the large towns, after 13 years of mission work by him in the East End of

London. In 1875 the Pleasant Sunday Afternoon Movement was founded in a West Bromwich congregational chapel and spread to other towns, the first London branch being set up in 1888, and a national organization by 1905. In 1913 there were said to be 329 branches and 55 931 members in London alone. This movement concentrated on providing music, discussion, and informal Christian teaching.

Another movement, that of the Labour Church, was founded in Manchester in 1891 and was designed to develop the religious ideas of brotherhood associated with the Labour Movement. Under the title of the Brotherhood Church it spread to the Congregationalists, and by 1907 there were some 30 Labour Churches. However, by 1912 it had become more political in nature than religious, and its Statement of Principles of that year omitted all references to God. By this time the Labour Church was more a meeting place for socialists than for religious worship.

It is clear that at the outbreak of the First World War in 1914 these movements had been unsuccessful in stemming the drift from attendance at church or chapel; the working classes as a whole were still failing to attend in any substantial numbers. No doubt all those forces which were diminishing middle- and upper-class attendance took effect to some extent, while in addition the need to conform to social convention by going to church which had formerly operated on many of the skilled working classes was no longer as strong as before. Social activities were now available which rivalled those of the chapel—cricket and football clubs, cycling clubs, Sunday League concerts and excursions—while opportunities were increasing in the Labour Movement for active working men who wished to reform society and make the world a better place.

This is not to say, of course, that the working classes as a whole were becoming totally remote from the teachings of church and chapel. There were still more children in church schools than in board schools at the turn of the century, and Sunday Schools were still well-attended, many parents believing that they provided worthwhile moral education. Most parents still took children to be baptised, and were married in church and were buried by the church. Probably most adults believed in a Christian God of some sort, but did not think it necessary to attend regularly a place of worship, though they might still go at Christmas. But it remains true that by 1914 there were many empty places in the churches and chapels. As one West Midland newspaper put it in 1913, congregations at most if not all places of worship had a tendency to decrease, and churches dedicated 40 years previously were much too large to hold the meagre congregations; this was not due to indifferent ministers, but

nevertheless it would seem for some reason the church is out of sympathy with the masses, and that its services are but poorly attended . . .

In the previous year in the same locality a vigorous Anglican minister delivered a sermon entitled, 'Is Religion played out?' Attitudes had indeed changed over the previous half-century.

Chapter IX
Changing Attitudes to Poverty

The Workhouse System

In Chapter VI we saw how as a result of the Poor Law Amendment Act, 1834, a new poor law system was set up, based on the Union workhouse, and supervised from London by the Poor Law Commission until 1847, and thereafter by the Poor Law Board. Only one other major change took place in the administrative machinery before 1914, and that was in 1871 when the newly-created Local Government Board took over the running of both the poor law and public health services. This left the local administration virtually unchanged, so that it remained the responsibility of the Boards of Guardians to relieve poverty in response to local conditions, but within the spirit of the 'workhouse test' and 'less eligibility'. In practice, as was noted in Chapter VI, it proved impossible to apply the 'workhouse test' in all cases, and outdoor relief was frequently given, partly because it was impossible to find room within the workhouse for all seeking relief in times of trade depression, and partly because outdoor relief was cheaper; in London in 1862 it cost 4s 8d a week to maintain a pauper within the workhouse, but only 2s 3d on outdoor relief. The 'less eligibility' rule was a different matter, but here too the rule was limited in practice because increasingly the workhouses contained the old, the young, and the sick in body and mind to whom the rule did not apply.

Indeed, the story of the workhouse in the second half of the nineteenth century is the story of more and more specialized care given to the different classes of inmates. It is true that the workhouse was still a grim and forbidding place at the end of the century, but much more thought was being given by then to the needs of paupers. For example, earlier on the children had very little specialized attention, and it was some time before schools were provided for them. These schools were often very large, accommodating up to 2000 children, but some were smaller, and Charles Dickens reported favourably in his magazine *Household Words* on the Manchester Board's school at Swinton in 1850:

We went into the playground of the junior department, where more than 150 children were assembled. Some were enjoying themselves in the sunshine, some were playing at marbles, others were frisking cheerfully. These children ranged from four to seven years of age . . .

By the 1870s the belief was growing that children should be removed from the workhouse altogether, and some kind of family life provided for them as far as that was possible. One way of doing this was to board out children with working-class families, a practice already adopted successfully in Scotland. Another approach was that of the Sheffield Guardians in 1893 who employed the 'scattered homes' system, whereby the board acquired houses in different parts of the city, and set up family units in each house under the supervision of foster parents. A third method was the 'cottage homes' system. A report in 1908 described the cottage homes at Sidcup, run by the Greenwich Union:

> These children have a most beautiful park of 58½ acres. At its entrance is a charming Cottage Receiving Home. Dotted over the park are homes and cottages designed to house from 15 to 53 children. Each cottage is a self-contained household presided over by a foster-mother and father, the latter being one of the industrial trainers for the boys. Inside the cottage everything is designed on the most natural home lines, and thus the artificiality of institution life is avoided . . .

Naturally enough, not all cottage home estates were as good as Sidcup, which had its own school, gymnasium, swimming bath, and workshops. Further, even by 1914 not all children had been placed in separate homes. In 1906 there were still nearly 22 000 children resident in the workhouse. Nevertheless, there had been very noticeable improvements since Dickens was moved to write in the 1840s of Oliver Twist's experiences in the Union workhouse.

The same kind of improvement was to be seen in the care of the sick. Earlier on no special care whatever seems to have been given to sick paupers in the average workhouse, and sometimes they were not even segregated from other inmates. Nurses were often untrained paupers. An inspector investigating a complaint about conditions in the Huddersfield Union workhouse in 1848 reported that:

> . . . the hospital was extremely filthy, the floors were filthy. I don't think they had been washed down throughout the hospital from the time of its being opened; marks of uncleanliness presented themselves nearly everywhere; cobwebs hung from the ceilings; the coverings of the beds were very deficient—mere rags some of them; some of the blankets would hardly hold together if you shook them . . .

Little or nothing was done for the mentally sick who were left to wander about if harmless, or locked up if violent.

Reform began in the 1860s, following the investigation in 1866 of the conditions of sick paupers in London workhouses by the famous medical journal, the *Lancet*. A succession of reports by the investigators appeared in the journal, and so shocked public opinion that in 1868 the Poor Law Board was compelled to issue instructions on the equipment of sick wards, and the need to employ trained nurses. Meanwhile, authority was given in 1862 for separate wards for lunatics in work-house infirmaries, while the Metropolitan Poor Act, 1867 permitted the setting up of separate asylums for the insane or sick in London. By the end of the century, many boards of guardians in the large towns had established their own separate infirmaries which became the general hospitals for the working classes of the area.

As for the aged, they were often given outdoor relief, but if they were forced to enter the House, they suffered in the earlier part of the period from the separation of man from wife. From the 1880s, however, a more humane policy was adopted, and married couples over 60 were allowed to have separate bedrooms. By the 1890s it was realised that sheer loss of earning capacity due to old age brought many couples into the workhouse, and that old age pensions would be one way of avoiding this. Although the Royal Commission on the Aged Poor, 1895, was against the idea of pensions, support was forthcoming from the Select Committee on the Aged Poor, 1899, and old age pensions were finally provided in 1908 of 5s 0d per week at the age of 70 (see Chapter XII for further details).

The last category of pauper to be considered is that of the able-bodied. In theory, there should have been few paupers of this description in the workhouses if the 'less eligibility' rule was taking effect, and this was so in practice. In any case, as pointed out earlier, in times of depression the workhouse would be too small to accommodate all the unemployed, so that outdoor relief would have to be given in return for a task of work. This situation remained unchanged throughout the second half of the nineteenth century, though with a gradual change in attitude towards the able-bodied unemployed man. In particular, the Lanca-shire cotton famine in the early 1860s, due to the American Civil War, caused mass unemployment among many working men and women who could not possibly be accused of being work-shy; so that the accepted belief that if a man was unemployed, then it was his own fault, was clearly shown to be wrong, in this instance at least.

This did not stop the new Local Government Board from trying to tighten up the rules relating to outdoor relief in the early 1870s. In a circular to poor law inspectors issued in December, 1871 it was observed that enquiries had shown

That outdoor relief is in many cases granted by the Guardians too readily and without sufficient enquiry, and that they give it also in numerous instances in which it would be more judicious to apply the workhouse test . . .

The prosperity of the time kept the numbers of able-bodied unemployed at a low level, but the onset of the Great Depression increased unemployment, and by the 1880s it was more than ever impossible to apply the workhouse test to all who sought relief. Once more it was clear that the workhouse system could do little to give positive help to the genuinely unemployed. Some attempt had been made to help the unemployed Lancashire textile workers by the Public Works (Manufacturing Districts) Act, 1863 which permitted local authorities to obtain government loans so as to support public work schemes, but the Act had proved a failure. Another attempt of a similar kind was made in 1886 by the Chamberlain Circular, sent out by Joseph Chamberlain, President of the Local Government Board. Its object was to encourage Boards of Guardians and other local authorities to provide work other than the customary task of work (usually stone-breaking or oakum-picking) which, as the Circular put it, 'presses hardly upon the skilled artisians'. The Circular went on to put the problem very clearly:

> What is required in the endeavour to relieve artisans and others who have hitherto avoided Poor Law Assistance, and who are temporarily deprived of employment, is—
> 1. Work which will not involve the stigma of pauperism;
> 2. Work which all can perform, whatever may have been their previous avocations;
> 3. Work which does not compete with that of other labourers at present in employment;
> And lastly, work which is not likely to interfere with the resumption of regular employment in their own trades by those who seek it.

The Circular makes it very evident that thinking about the unemployed had changed considerably since the 1830s. Some local authorities did provide some employment of the kind required, usually in the form of work on roads, but such schemes did not go very far, and for the ordinary working man they were still tainted with the humiliation of applying for poor relief. Moreover, applying to the Guardians still entailed disqualification from voting, a point of increased importance after the 1867 and 1884 Reform Acts had given the vote to working men householders in both the borough and county constituencies.

A last effort was made in the early 1900s to encourage public work schemes when the Local Government Board suggested the forming of joint distress committees in London on which Guardians, local authorities, and charitable organizations would be represented. These committees would then devise relief schemes of work as required. This was followed by the Unemployed Workmen Act, 1905 which established joint distress committees nationally, and gave them powers to provide work, set up employment exchanges, and assist the emigration of the unemployed. This act proved no more successful than earlier attempts at public work projects, and it was also criticized by those who thought it might remove initiative and make the unemployed rely too much on Poor Law assistance. However, the Liberal reforms passed just before World War I were to make a fresh attempt at relieving both unemployment and poverty and they will be described in Chapter XII.

Any survey of the relief of poverty through the Poor Law in the second half of the nineteenth century must lay emphasis on the increasingly humane way in which the different classes of paupers were treated. At the same time, two essential points must be stressed. The first is that the workhouse was still disliked by the working classes for whom it symbolized failure, heartbreak, and degradation. The humiliation of entering the House was still deeply felt, as it had always been intended that it should be felt. The 1834 Report deliberately advocated a deterrent Poor Law, and the use by Chamberlain of the term 'stigma of pauperism' is one result of that fact. The second point is that as the century progressed it became more and more apparent that the Poor Law system was the wrong instrument for solving the social problems of an industrial nation. Above all else, its approach to unemployment (a word which, it is significant to note, first came into use in the 1880s) was fundamentally wrong, for it was no use trying to frighten an unemployed industrial worker into finding work when there was no work available in the area. It is not surprising that the debate over the Poor Law came to a head in the early twentieth century, as we shall see later in this chapter.

Charitable Organizations

It was pointed out in Chapter VI that in addition to the Poor Law system, private charities were very numerous in Victorian England, and by the 1860s they were probably spending more on the poor than was being spent through the workhouse system. In London alone in 1861 there were some 640 charities, of which 144 had been founded in the 1850s. The City of London's parochial charities increased their income from about £67 000 in 1865 to about £100 000 10 years later. The City was exceptionally rich, of course, but some small cathedral cities might have surprisingly large funds. Lichfield, for example, had nearly £4000 available for distribution annually in a city of 8000 people. There is no doubt, therefore, that large sums of money were available locally, and reference was made in Chapter VI to special funds set up in times of trade depression in manufacturing areas. The most famous of these in the second half of the century was the Million Pound Fund set up in Lancashire during the cotton famine.

There were so many charities of so many different kinds that it is hard to classify them. Many were under the control of the churches. The nonconformists were strong in providing charities for particular groups, such as the Cabmen's Club Aid Society (1859), the Christian Excavators' Union (1877), the Railway Mission (1881) and the Christian Police Association (1883). Other charities were associated with well-known philanthropists who were often men and women of strong religious beliefs. Lord Shaftsbury is famous for the Shaftesbury Homes and the Ragged School Union (schools for the very poorest children), while Dr Barnardo opened his first home in 1878. Elizabeth Fry carried on the prison reform work begun by John Howard at the beginning of the century, and this led to the founding of the Howard Association for penal reform in 1866. In addition to these national bodies, there were innumerable local organizations for almshouses, dispensaries, and schools, together with many small charitable trusts for annual donations of food, clothing, or money.

So great was the quantity of charity available for the poor in the later Victorian period that the question naturally arises, why was there so much of it? And what was the response of the working classes to it? The most obvious answer to the first question is that the new industrial and urbanized society stood in great need of it, and that the religious and humanitarian feelings of the age responded to that need. No doubt less worthy motives also played a part: charitable activity helped to keep the working classes grateful and obedient, and less likely to cause political trouble. Further, participation in charitable work eased the conscience of the comfortably-off, gave opportunities for committee work and public service, and contributed to the image of respectability so important to the middle classes. At the same time it was a practical means whereby the moral improvement of the working classes could be undertaken, a favourite aim of the benevolent. But whatever the motives, the Victorian charitable impulse provided a massive system of relief alternative to, or it could be supplementary to, the Poor Law system.

The response of the working classes to help from charity took various forms. At one extreme, the skilled worker would be the least likely to seek it, and his feelings might well be of resentment and humiliation if he was forced to apply for it. At the other extreme, the unskilled labourer was probably resigned to applying for help, and some of this class might become professional scroungers, despised by those in regular work. Thomas Wright, himself a working man, wrote caustically in 1868 of

> . . . many of the casually employed classes, and of the poorer kinds of regular labourers, and others who are not poor, who habitually prey upon charity, ordinary or special. To these pauper-souled cormorants, the bread of charity has no bitterness, and they seek it with a shameless, lying perseverance.

Although it is commonly alleged that charitable help was often patronizing in nature, and that it fostered servility, in fact much would depend on the spirit in which it was offered, and on what terms. Presumably help given in a genuine spirit of Christian charity would be acceptable enough to many working people who took the hierarchical nature of society for granted, and who were quite prepared to be helped by those they regarded as their superiors. It is more likely to be the independent, skilled worker like Thomas Wright, who took pride in himself as a craftsman, who would find charity objectionable. Thus William Lovett, a cabinet maker and therefore a member of the aristocracy of labour, was of the opinion that

> Charity by diminishing the energies of self-dependence, creates a spirit of hypocrisy and servility.

It is probable that many of the poorest, faced with the choice between the workhouse and charitable help, would hardly pause to reflect on the philosophical niceties of the matter.

Whatever the reactions of the working classes as a whole to charity, there was an increasing middle-class concern in the 1860s at the indiscriminate way in which help was being given without cooperation between charities, and without any very clear objectives other than providing immediate relief. To remedy this state of affairs, the Charity Organization Society was established in 1869. It had two basic principles. The first was that charitable help should be given only after investigation of the individual case, so that only the worthy should be assisted. The second was that the principal purpose of charitable work should be to assist the poor to help themselves, so that they were able to be self-reliant in all the usual crises of family life—sickness, unemployment, bereavement—leaving charitable assistance for cases of exceptional misfortune. In the words of the Annual Report of the COS for 1876:

> The principle is, that it is good for the poor that they should meet all the ordinary contingencies of life, relying not upon public or private charity, but upon their own industry and thrift, and upon the powers of self-help that are to be developed by individual and collective effort.

In short, charity must aim at moral regeneration, or as C. S. Loch (secretary of the Society from 1875 to 1913) put it, 'We must use charity to create the power of self-help'.

In their advocacy of careful enquiry into the individual case—the building up of case-work, to use the modern term—the COS laid the foundations of social work today, even though the method itself was not entirely new. It had been used by Thomas Chalmers in Glasgow in the

1820s, by Bishop Blomfield and the Metropolitan Visiting and Relief Association in 1843, and by the Central Relief Society in Liverpool in the 1860s. Nevertheless, the COS became so influential that its system of enquiry and actual visiting of the poor became standard practice, and it set up its own scheme for training social workers in 1890. The approach did not exclude a sympathetic understanding of the problems of the poor, but it was intended to be rigorous, so as to do the maximum good and exclude the undeserving. As Loch said 'Charity . . . works through sympathy, it depends on science'. It is understandable, nevertheless, that this policy was not popular with many of the poor, who preferred less scientific and more old-fashioned treatment; and indeed for the very poorest earning low wages and frequently out of work, the COS insistence on self-help could hardly have made much sense.

Yet in spite of the increasing challenge to self-help made by collectivist thinking towards the end of the century, the better-off working classes still believed in self-help and in making provision for emergencies, especially sickness and death. This is shown by the increase in membership of friendly societies from 4·2 m members with funds of £22·7 m in 1891 to 6·2 m members with £48·2 m funds in 1909. For a payment of 6d per week, for example, the Manchester Unity of Odd Fellows gave benefits of 9s 0d per week for the first 12 months sickness, and 4s 6d per week thereafter, together with £9 at the death of a member, and £4 10s at the death of his wife. Most societies required subscriptions of between 4d and 9d per week, and some laid down a minimum wage level for subscribers.

For those who could not afford these subscriptions there existed a large number of unregistered, collecting societies which operated on a smaller scale with payments of 2d or 3d per week, providing smaller sums than the national societies as death benefit. Numbers in these societies were probably as great as in the registered friendly societies, that is, up to about 6 m, thus giving a total of about 12 m in some form of insurance scheme. Though the figures are far from precise and must be treated with caution, it is undeniable that a substantial proportion of the working classes took steps to protect themselves against misfortune and also, incidentally, against both the guardians and the COS, and other charities.

The Royal Commission on the Poor Laws 1905–9

As indicated earlier in this chapter, the debate over the Poor Law intensified in the early twentieth century, and led to the appointment of a Royal Commission in 1905. Significantly, this move came just after the passing of the Unemployed Workmen Act, and it is clear that concern over unemployment, and the inadequacy of the Poor Law to deal with it, was a major cause of the appointment. But there were other reasons why a general survey of the working of the Poor Law system was necessary.

Perhaps the most important of these reasons is the fact that in spite of all the reforms of the second half of the century, it could not be denied that povery still existed on a massive scale. Moreover, it became increasingly apparent that this poverty could not be explained away by the idleness or drunkenness of those who were very poor. The journalist Henry Mayhew shocked the middle classes with his articles on the London poor in the *Morning Chronicle*, afterwards incorporated into four large volumes in 1861–2, even though the books concentrated mostly on London street traders rather than the London working classes as a whole. Further shocks were administered by Mearn's *Bitter Cry of Outcast London*, 1883 (already mentioned in Chapter VII); and it was revelations of this kind, together with claims made in newspapers such as the *Pall Mall Gazette* that a quarter of London's inhabitants were living in poverty, which led Charles Booth, a member of the wealthy Liverpool shipowning family, to begin his own investigations into the London poor.

The result was Booth's monumental *Life and Labour of the People in London* in 17 volumes, published between 1889 and 1903, and based on the work of Booth and seven voluntary helpers. Booth's original intention was to disprove what he considered to be the exaggerated estimates of the extent of London poverty, yet early on he admitted that, if anything, the amount of poverty had been under-estimated. In his 1892 volume he gave figures for his eight classes of inhabitants in London (classes A to H) and indicated whether they were above or below his 'poverty line'—that is, a minimum income of between 18s and 21s a week for a man, wife and three children. The result was as follows:

				In
Class A (lowest)	37 610	or	0·9 per cent ⎫	Poverty
B (very poor)	316 834		7·5 ⎬	30·7
C and D (poor)	938 293		22·3 ⎭	per cent
E and F (working class,				In
comfortable)	2 166 503		51·5 ⎫	Comfort
G and H (middle class			⎬	69·3
and above)	749 930		17·8 ⎭	per cent
Inmates of	4 209 170		100·0	
Institutions	99 830			
	4 309 000			

Thus Booth showed that 30·7 per cent, or nearly one-third of the population of London, did not have an income sufficient to maintain the most frugal mode of life, while classes A and B, 8·4 per cent of the total, were living in abject poverty. Booth was no sentimentalist about these two classes. Of class A he wrote:

> Their life is the life of savages, with vicissitudes of extreme hardship and occasional excess. Their food is of the coarsest description, and their only luxury is drink . . .
>
> They render no useful service, they create no wealth; more often they destroy it. They degrade whatever they touch, and as individuals are perhaps incapable of improvement . . .

Booth's 8·4 per cent for his class A and class B may be compared with the estimate of about one-tenth of the total population claimed to be living in acute and wretched poverty by his namesake, William Booth in his book, *In Darkest England and the Way Out* (1890). William Booth, the founder of the Salvation Army (but no relation to Charles Booth), wrote movingly of this Submerged Tenth:

> Three million men, women, and children, a vast despairing multitude in a condition nominally free, but really enslaved.

Startling though Booth's figures were at the time, they were soon matched by another survey, this time of the poor in York, and published in 1901 under the title, *Poverty: A Study of Town Life*. Its author was Benjamin Seebohm Rowntree, the son of the York cocoa manufacturer, Joseph Rowntree. Taking up Booth's notion of an income level as an aid to defining poverty, he fixed his poverty line much more precisely at 21s 8d for a man, wife and three children, and went on to distinguish basic or 'primary' poverty from 'secondary' poverty. Primary poverty existed where income was simply insufficient to meet basic needs; secondary poverty, where income was sufficient, but misspent (through extravagence or otherwise) so as to produce poverty. His actual figures were:

		Proportion of total population of York
Persons in primary poverty	7230	9·91 per cent
Persons in secondary poverty	13072	17·93
	20302	27·84

It can be seen that Rowntree's figure of 27·84 per cent is close to Booth's 30·7 per cent. Rowntree also explained how poverty increased or diminished according to the stage of life of the individual worker (the 'poverty cycle'). For example, in childhood he might suffer poverty, but grow more prosperous when starting work, becoming impoverished again when he marries and has children. He might regain prosperity when his children started work and became self-supporting, but finally lapse into poverty yet again when he became too old to work. Rowntree then analysed the causes of primary poverty as follows:

Immediate cause	Totals affected	Percentage of all in Primary Poverty
Death of chief wage-earner	1130	15·63
Illness or old age of chief wage-earner	370	5·11
Chief wage-earner out of work	167	2·31
Irregularity of work	205	2·83
Largeness of family (more than 4 children)	1602	22·16
In regular work, but at low wages	3756	51·96

This was perhaps the clearest and most authoritative statement yet that poverty was not due in the main to drink or laziness, but to one or other of half a dozen causes. Of these, the most important, quite obviously, was low wages.

Shortly after Rowntree's survey, further concern was aroused by Sir Frederick Maurice's statement that 60 per cent of the recruits for the Boer War (1899–1902) were unfit for military service. In fact, this claim proved alarmist, and an enquiry reduced the figure to 34 per cent who had failed to meet the army's standards of height, weight, and eyesight. Nevertheless, a rejection rate of one in three was bad enough, and helped to strengthen the belief that the whole subject of the condition of the poor and their treatment must be investigated anew.

A third reason for the appointment of the Poor Law Commission was the growth of socialist thinking and the strengthening of the Labour Movement which occurred towards the end of the century. This will be considered in detail in the next chapter, but in short, beliefs in the need for a socialist reorganization of society had a powerful effect on middle class political thinking, and found expression in new political bodies such as the Fabian Society. At the same time the trade union movement was expanding with the spread of unionism to many unskilled workers, and socialists were prominent among the leaders of the new unions. Even among the left-wing liberals, who were certainly not socialists, there was a greater belief in the need for collectivism (that is, state intervention) to help the poorest section of the working classes for whom the classic liberal belief in individual freedom was a mere mockery. There is no doubt that Rowntree's 9·91 per cent in primary poverty had little freedom; as William Booth put it, they were 'really enslaved'. Thus, when Sir William Harcourt, Chancellor of the Exchequer in the Liberal government in 1894, remarked that 'We are all socialists now', he did not mean it literally, but rather that most politicians could see that there was a case for greater government action to help the poor; and this applied even to the Conservative Party, as evidenced by the Chamberlain Circular and the Unemployed Workmen Act in 1905.

All in all, there is an unmistakable, new kind of thinking about the poor at the turn of the century. Concern about the need to alleviate unemployment in the face of which the Poor Law seemed helpless, grave uneasiness at the extent of poverty revealed by the surveys, and a fresh willingness to contemplate an extension of state action, all form a background to the appointment of the Royal Commission in November 1905, and in fact help to explain the nature of its findings. The problem was now not so much what to do about pauperism, as it had been in 1834, but what to do about preventing the poverty which led to pauperism.

There were 20 members appointed to the Commission, including six members of the COS (an indication of its importance at the time); Beatrice Webb of the Fabian Society, niece of Charles Booth, who had helped him in the early stages of his survey; and Charles Booth himself. The results of their enquiries were not published till February 1909 and were based on a very thorough investigation, including visits to 200 unions and 400 institutions, running to 47 volumes in all. Because of the differences of opinion on the Commission it was necessary to publish two Reports—a Majority Report signed by the Chairman and 14 members, and a Minority Report signed by Mrs Webb, George Lansbury, well-known as the Poplar socialist councillor, Francis Chandler, a Manchester trade unionist and guardian, and the Rev. Russell Wakefield, Dean of Norwich.

Both Reports condemned the existing Poor Law system which lacked uniformity in the granting of relief, and provided services, for example, in education and health, now being provided by local councils, so that there was a wasteful duplication of services. They also criticized the continuance in some unions of the old mixed workhouse in which children had still not been removed to cottage homes, or lunatics to asylums. The main difference between the Reports lay in how the administrative machinery could be improved, the disagreement being rooted in ideological differences.

The signatories of the Majority Report wanted to abolish the Boards of Guardians and transfer their powers to the county councils who would set up Public Assistance Committees consisting of elected council members and coopted members. This idea may be compared with the transfer of power from the school boards to local authorities which occurred under the Education Act, 1902. There would also be Voluntary Aid Committees consisting of representatives of the local charities. These two kinds of committees would share the work of helping the poor, only the really destitute being passed to the Public Assistance Committee. The proposal shows clearly the influence of the COS, which had always seen the function of private charity in this way. The plan also allowed scope for the continued moral teaching of the poor, for signatories of the Majority Report still thought that poverty could be due to a considerable extent to the failings of the poor:

> . . . we feel strongly that the pauperism and distress we have described can never be successfully combated by administration and expenditure. The cause of distress are not only economic and industrial; in their origin and character they are largely moral. Government by itself cannot correct or remove such influences.

They went on in their Conclusions to stress the need for well-organized voluntary help:

> Great Britain is the home of voluntary effort, and its triumphs and successes constitute in themselves much of the history of the country.

Those signing the Minority Report took a different line. Significantly, the Report was written by Beatrice Webb and her husband, Sidney, who was not a member of the Commission. As such, it bore the marks of a much greater belief in state control, without the important place allotted to private charity by the Majority Report. Although the Minority Report agreed that the Boards of Guardians should be abolished, it argued that there was no place for Public Assistance Committees or Voluntary Aid Committees. Instead, it recommended the 'breaking up of the Poor Law'. The powers of the Destitution Authorities (the Webbs' name for the Guardians) should be transferred to committees of the county councils, the children being looked after by the education committee, the sick and aged by the health committee, and so on. Further, the able-bodied unemployed were to have special treatment. Because unemployment was a national not a local problem, the Report recommended:

> that the duty of so organizing the National Labour Market as to prevent or minimize unemployment should be placed upon a Minister responsible to Parliament, who may be designated the Minister for Labour.

This harked back to the complaints of the Poplar Board of Guardians, of which board Lansbury was a member, that it was unfair that impoverished areas such as Poplar with a very limited income from the poor rate, should have the heaviest financial burden, for such areas had the largest numbers of unemployed. It was further suggested that this proposal should be backed up by labour exchanges, public works schemes, and penal measures against the persistently idle. Even the Webbs still thought that means might have to be taken against the moral failings of a minority. As Beatrice Webb remarked in a letter in 1911:

> . . . destitution must be prevented and where necessary penalized as a public nuisance.

Thus there were substantial differences between the two Reports, the one keeping the basic structure of the Poor Law administration but transferring control to the county councils, at the same time retaining an important role for public charities; the other seeking to dismantle the Poor Law machinery completely, ignoring the charities and trusting to local and central organizations to provide a new social service. In the event, neither Report was implemented before 1914 and major reform did not come till 1929, when the Majority Report was put into effect.

The main reason for the government's failure to take action was probably that between 1909 and 1911 the Liberal government embarked on a series of reforms to help the poor and unemployed, and these reforms will be discussed in Chapter XII. The fact that the Commission had not been unanimous provided a good reason for not reforming the Poor Law system itself, but for taking action outside the system. It has also been argued that the violent propaganda campaign waged by the Webbs after 1909 in favour of the Minority Report may have done more harm than good. It antagonized both the Boards of Guardians and the more conservative officials at the Local Government Board, including the Minister in charge, John Burns. A private member's bill based on the Minority Report in 1910 failed to survive its second reading. The Conservatives were very suspicious of it, both on account of cost and its bureaucratic tendencies. According to Austin Chamberlain:

> The popular and *sound* objections to the minority scheme in its entirety are:
> 1. That it would cost about 50 millions!
> 2. That it establishes an intolerable bureaucratic tyranny.

So the Poor Law system based on the Union workhouse and the Boards of Guardians remained unchanged before the outbreak of the First World War in 1914. It is still true that attitudes to the poor had changed enormously since 1834. For example, the Majority Report concluded that:

> Our investigations prove the existence in our midst of a class whose condition and environment are a discredit, and a peril to the whole community. Each and every section of society has a common duty to perform in combating this evil . . .

As noted earlier, the Majority Report's recommendations were put into effect in 1929, and the Minority Report was implemented in 1948 when the workhouse system came to an end, and the Poor Law was at last broken up by the post-World War II Labour government.

Chapter X
The Growth of Modern Unionism

Model Unionism

When trade revived after the depression of the early 1840s, the trade union movement began to expand again, and a number of unions were founded or re-established, some of them on a national basis. In 1851 the Journeymen Steam Engine Makers, founded in Manchester in 1826, merged with other local societies to form the Amalgamated Society of Engineers. The new union had its headquarters in London, and employed a full-time, paid secretary. The subscription was relatively high—1s 0d a week—and so the union was able to provide good pension, sickness and death benefits. The emphasis was very much on skilled membership based on apprenticeship. The preface to their book of rules made it clear why the Society barred those who had not served an apprenticeship. They did so

> . . . knowing that such encroachments are productive of evil . . . and result in reducing the condition of the artisan to that of the unskilled labourer, and confer no permanent advantage on those admitted.

By the end of 1851 the union had nearly 12 000 members, and its success was such that the Webbs considered it to be a model for similar unions of skilled workers. Hence the prosperous period of the 1850s and 1860s was thought by the Webbs to constitute an important new era in the history of trade unionism. The characteristics of model unionism as compared with earlier unionism were, national organization, a skilled membership, high subscription rates, paid officials, and a disinclination to strike. Unions of this kind, according to the Webbs, were now prepared to accept industrial capitalism and to share its benefits with the employers, unlike the earlier, aggressive unions of the 1830s.

Now there can be no doubt that trade unions such as the ASE represent an important advance in trade unionism, and in organization they certainly have a modern look. However, more recent historians have sought to re-assess their significance. They point out that there was nothing radically new in their being on a national basis, since this had already been tried in the 1820s and 1830s. As for their skilled membership and high subscriptions, these were characteristics of the craft unions going back to the previous century. Further as regards avoiding strikes, this again had always been typical of the more prosperous society which tried to keep its funds for unemployment or sickness benefits, rather than spend them in strike pay. Thus, the Amalgamated Society of Carpenters, a so-called model union, merely continued this practice in not allowing any branch to strike without a careful investigation of the circumstances. A lengthy application form had to be filled up and submitted by the branch containing such questions as:

> What is the state of trade at present, and what reasons have you for anticipating that at the time when the notice expires the state of trade will be such as to induce your employers to concede the advance asked for?

However, if there was no other alternative, the craft unions of course would go on strike, as did the ASE itself in the early months of 1852. Model unions were by no means unduly pacific in attitude to employers, nor were they uncritical of the workings of capitalism.

For all these reasons it appears that the views of the Webbs require revision. One historian has suggested that 'what occurred . . . in the 50s and 60s was not the creation of a "New Model", but a strengthening of the old'. Another has even claimed that 'New Model unionism ranks as a piece of historical fiction'. Perhaps this is to go too far, but the evidence seems to show that model unionism was not in itself a new departure in membership, organization, or attitudes. What is important is that highly organized unions of skilled workers on a national scale became well established after 1850, sometimes after a number of false starts; the National Flint Glass Makers Society, for example, established itself on a permanent basis in 1851 after four earlier attempts.

Of course, it would be wrong to assume that all unions after 1850 automatically conformed to the pattern of the ASE. There were many unions still organized on a local or regional basis, and this was especially true of miners' unions, and unions in the cotton industry. Other trades in which model unionism played no part were those of metal manufacture, tailoring, cabinet-making and shoe-making. Nevertheless, the model unions pointed the way to the future development of the union movement, and certainly dominated the scene in the 1850s.

In 1859 unionism in London was confronted by a fresh challenge. A strike by masons employed by Messrs Trollope & Co, a large building firm, developed into a full-scale strike and a lock-out by other builders. On the one hand, the men demanded a reduction of working hours from 10 to nine a day; on the other, the employers refused to employ anyone who would not sign 'the document'—a promise not to be a member of a trade union. After a bitter six months' struggle, a compromise was reached whereby the men withdrew their demand for the nine-hour day, while the employers dropped 'the document'. An important consequence of the builders' strike was the formation of the London Trades Council in 1860. Trades Councils were not in themselves new. They had been set up before, sometimes on a temporary basis, as a means of organizing local support for workers out on strike. The London Trades Council was established to safeguard the interests of the London trade unions, and it soon began to concern itself with political as well as industrial matters, including electoral reform, labour legislation, and even international affairs such as the American Civil War.

By the mid-1860s trade unions had gained a greatly enhanced importance, and the prosperity of the sixties helps to explain why this came about. Although there were still many local and district societies, the model unions were the most prominent type of society, and in London the secretaries of four of these unions frequently consulted together. This group was termed the 'Junta' by the Webbs. It consisted of Robert Applegarth (Amalgamated Carpenters), William Allen (ASE), Edwin Coulson (Operative Bricklayers), and David Guile (Ironfounders), together with the secretary of the London Trades Council, George Odger. The Junta were able to exercise considerable influence over the Trades Council, though it has been argued that the Webbs tended to exaggerate the importance of the Junta. It is certainly true that they were frequently opposed on the Trades Council by representatives of smaller but more militant societies, and in particular by George Potter, the editor of the labour paper, the *Beehive*.

Nevertheless, it was the model unions which attracted most public attention, and they seemed the most respectable, in middle-class eyes. They were now strong enough to forbid what one society called the 'degrading and demoralizing' system of tramping, whereby an out-of-work member would tramp from one town to another in search of work, stopping overnight in the home of a fellow-member. Some unions produced papers or journals which printed articles and poetry of general literary interest, with editorials full of moral earnestness. The *Flint Glass Makers Magazine* told its members to 'get intelligence instead of alcohol', reminding them that:

> the name of glassmaker used to be synonymous with Ignorance and Drunkenness . . . it was thought that we could not do without being drunkards.

Sentiments such as these naturally made the unions more acceptable to employers, though this did not prevent a serious strike by the glassmakers in 1858–9 when an employer tried to increase the number of apprentices (thereby increasing the supply of labour) in opposition to the wishes of the unions. All the same, relations between employers and men were improving, and this is illustrated by the passing of the Master and Servant Act in 1867. Under the law of master and servant, a man could be imprisoned for breaking his contract with his employer, e.g. by leaving without notice. By the 1867 Act he might be imprisoned only for extreme or aggravated breach of contract—an improvement on the previous law, though not going as far as to abolish imprisonment for breach of contract altogether, as the unions would have liked.

However, the story of peaceful progress by the union movement was rudely interrupted in 1866 by the Sheffield Outrages of that year, and further by the Hornby v. Close case in 1867. The outrages in Sheffield took the form of acts of violence against blacklegs in the cutlery trade, including the blowing up of a workman's house in October, 1866. Now, the intimidation of blacklegs was nothing new, but the blowing up of a house was a different matter, leading in the first instance to some sensational press reports which blackened the name of trade unionism, and later to the appointment in February 1867 of a Royal Commission on the Sheffield Outrages and on trade unionism as a whole. In the same year in the case of Hornby v. Close the Boiler Makers Society sued the secretary of the Bradford branch for the return of £24 which he was withholding from the Society. As the Society had deposited its rules with the Registrar of Friendly Societies it had assumed that it was legally entitled to bring an action under the Friendly Society Act, 1855. In fact, the judges held that trade unions could not bring actions under the Act because although not positively illegal, they had no defined legal status and might still be considered to be in restraint of trade. Thus, the protection afforded by the repeal of the Combination Acts was now open to question. The trade union movement quite suddenly was facing a crisis.

For a time the crisis grew worse as the Royal Commission pursued its enquiries into the Sheffield Outrages. It transpired that acts of extreme violence, even including murder, had been committed by some trade unionists. The secretary of the Grinders Union, William Broadhead, confessed to paying £20 to a man for murdering an employer. Similar acts of violence had occurred in Manchester. Even sympathizers with the trade union cause were upset by these revelations. There were also disclosures of restrictive practices which put the unions in a bad light. Frederic Harrison, the one member of the Commission whom the TUs had been permitted to nominate, was very disturbed by these disclosures, writing privately that unless the unions could justify their practices, they would seem to be 'mere organs of class tyranny'.

What saved the day for the trade unions was the very skilful work of the Junta, now meeting weekly in London under the title of the Conference of Amalgamated Trades. They were successful in presenting evidence before the Commission which emphasized the entirely peaceful proceedings of the amalgamated unions with their large memberships and ample funds. Undoubtedly Applegarth, Allen and Coulson made an excellent impression on the Commission, and

Applegarth in particular produced a bland justification of picketing, somewhat remote, one might think, from reality:

> I *do* justify picketing . . . . I say that it is perfectly justifiable for men to appoint other men to wait at a shop door and to say to those who come, 'The men were dissatisfied with the terms upon which they were working at that place, and if you go in you will go in and undersell us; now we beg you that you will not do that'. That is as far as I would justify men in going. If they use threats or coerce or intimidate that is beyond the instructions . . .

At first the Junta did not have it all their own way, as George Potter and his followers were allowed to have a representative at the meetings of the Commission, but Potter was soon excluded for publicly attacking one of the Commissioners. Thus the Junta was left to represent the trade union movement as a whole. The final Report of the Commission owed much to the influence of Frederic Harrison, and of Thomas Hughes, the Christian Socialist, the other friend to the unions on the Commission. It recommended that trade unions should be given a clear legal status, and that they might register their rules with the Registrar of Friendly Societies, provided the rules did not permit restrictive practices, such as the limitation of the number of apprentices. Harrison and Hughes also prepared a Minority Report, which again stressed the essentially peaceful nature of unionism, claiming that with the exception of recent events in Sheffield and Manchester

> instances of actual attempts on life and limb rarely occur. The peculiarly atrocious crime of vitriol throwing, with which the former Reports are full, has not been mentioned here. Nothing has been heard of either incendiarism or machine breaking.

This Minority Report similarly advocated the legalization of unions but without the limitations suggested by the Majority Report.

These Reports certainly did much to allay the fears aroused originally by some of the evidence presented to the Commission, and it now remained for the government to prepare suitable legislation. Meanwhile an important move was made in 1868 when the Manchester Trades Council organized a Congress of Trade Unions so that matters of interest to the whole movement could be discussed. The intention was to provide a conference similar to that of the National Social Science Association which had shown interest in trade unions but was too middle-class in outlook to provide a suitable platform. The Manchester Congress was attended by only 34 delegates, most of them from trades councils, but none from the London Trades Council. Indeed, the London-based Junta's policy of conciliation came under attack at the

Congress; but at the second Congress in Birmingham in 1869 the 40 delegates present (now including representatives of the London Trades Council) gave general support to the policy. At the third Trades Union Congress in London in 1871, a Parliamentary Committee was appointed. Its purpose was to bring pressure on MPs to amend the government's trade union legislation which had been introduced in the previous month.

The new trade union Bill was in fact something of a disappointment. It is true that it put the legal position of trade unions beyond doubt. As the *Economist* put it:

> First it abolishes altogether the common law superstition that Trades Unions are not to be recognized by law because they are in 'restraint of trade'. This doctrine was invented by a very learned and acute judge at a time when Trades Unions were thought to be necessarily pernicious, and when also it was thought possible to put them down.

The Bill also made it possible for them to register with the Registrar of Friendly Societies. But at the same time the Junta's great emphasis on the essentially peaceful nature of trade unions led the government in effect to prohibit picketing, though this had previously been legalized in 1859. At this point the Junta decided to bring the Conference of Amalgamated Trades to an end, and to concentrate their efforts on the TUC Parliamentary Committee. Henceforth the Committee became the most powerful body in the movement, and the Junta no longer maintained its existence as a separate group.

Eventually the government was prevailed upon to put its proposals into two Bills which became the Trade Union Act (1871) containing the major and beneficial changes, and the Criminal Law Amendment Act (1871) prohibiting picketing. This left the trade unions free to concentrate on getting the second Act repealed. In the 1874 general election, the Parliamentary Committee asked candidates certain Test Questions on their attitudes to trade unions, and members were urged to vote for or against them on the basis of their replies. Two trade unionist candidates, both miners, were actually elected in this election—Alexander MacDonald at Stafford, and Thomas Burt at Morpeth. The new Conservative government appointed another Royal Commission, this time on the Labour Laws, but it was boycotted by the Parliamentary Committee, and it achieved very little.

Yet the campaign to get the Criminal Law Amendment Act repealed gained a surprising success when in 1875 the government introduced the Conspiracy and Protection of Property Act which legalized picketing again. It also redefined the legal position of trade unions so that, for example, striking could not come under the law of conspiracy. In the same year the Employers and Workmen Act replaced the 1867 Act so that imprisonment for breach of contract was abolished altogether, and

155

employers and workmen became equal partners in a contract of employment. After eight years of struggle, the trade unions had gained a stronger legal position than ever before, oddly enough with the assistance of a Conservative government led by Disraeli.

The legal gains of the mid-1870s were so great that there seemed no immediate need for any further legislation. The Parliamentary committee believed that the 'work of emancipation' was 'full and complete', and its secretary, George Howell, thought that the Committee could be disbanded. It is true that the trade union movement had made important steps forward, and that the prosperity of the early 1870s had expanded membership to well over a million. It must be emphasized, however, that although the Junta had been so successful, the amalgamated or model unions still represented only a minority of workers in a limited number of trades. Their members were still very concerned to keep out the less skilled and to restrict the number of apprentices. Other unions such as those in cotton and coal-mining admitted the relatively unskilled as well as the skilled, and were still strongly local or regional in character. Even when the Miners National Union was founded in 1863, the local constituent organizations still had a great deal of independence. In addition to such unions, prosperous conditions in the early 1870s encouraged the growth of unions among the semi-skilled and the unskilled: the Amalgamated Society of Railway Servants was established in 1871, the London gas workers formed a union in 1872, and the National Agricultural Labourers Union was also set up in the same year by Joseph Arch as the result of a memorable meeting addressed by him at Wellesbourne near Stratford on Avon, under the old chestnut tree:

> It was an extraordinary sight, and I shall never forget it, not to my dying day. I mounted an old pig stool, and in the flickering light of the lanterns I saw the earnest upturned faces of these poor brothers of mine—faces gaunt with hunger and pinched with want—all looking towards me and ready to listen to the words that would fall from my lips . . .

These developments make it clear enough that important as model unions were, they were by no means representative of trade unionism as a whole.

Before moving on to the events of the 1880s, some reference is necessary to the political activities of the unions in the 1860s and 70s. Although unions were concerned primarily with industrial matters, they played a part in the agitation for giving the vote to the working man in the mid-1860s. The Reform League was founded in 1865 with this as its aim, and its massive meetings drew public attention to the issue. It was supported by many of the London trade unionists. After the Reform Act was passed in 1867, the Labour Representation League was founded in 1869 for the election to Parliament of working-class candidates. Again, trade union leaders were active as members of the executive. Individual trade unions actually put up 13 candidates in the 1874 election, and we have already seen that two of them—MacDonald and Burt—were elected. Their aim was to represent the interests of Labour, but they took the Liberal Party whip, and became known as Lib-Labs. After the legal gains of the mid-70s, political pressure by the unions tended to slacken, but it is evident that they were no strangers to political action at this time, and the foundations were being laid for further political developments in the 1880s and 1890s.

The Revival of Socialism

Socialism was not new in England in the 1880s, of course. Earlier in the century Robert Owen was well known for his beliefs in socialist cooperation, and there were some socialist supporters of Chartism. In the middle years of the century, however, prosperity confined socialist thinking to a small minority of political groups, and although the first volume of Marx's great work *Capital* was published in 1867, it was not available in an English version till 1887. The trade union movement as a whole certainly was not strongly influenced by socialism before the 1880s. The majority of unionists were probably liberals, and the Lib-Lab alliance in parliament seemed a very suitable arrangement. Yet after 1880 socialist ideas began to gain influence in the movement, particularly among the younger trade unionist leaders, and this was to have important consequences for the future.

Socialism revived at this time for a number of reasons. The Great Depression (1873–96) seemed to show that industrial capitalism did not automatically bring increasing prosperity to all sectors of the working classes, even though the fall in prices meant increased real wages for those still in employment. Then again, progress in elementary education, and the conferring of the vote on most working men in the towns in 1867, and in the countryside in 1884, together led to a greater interest in political reform; and this was at a time when the Liberal Party's reforming zeal had been devoted by Gladstone to the cause of reform in Ireland, so that great social issues in England were being almost ignored. A most important factor was the middle-class awareness of the profits which industrialization had brought them while at the same time some of the working classes were still living in squalor. Guilt feelings about this (Beatrice Webb wrote about the middle-class 'collective or class consciousness' of sin) led some middle-class reformers in the direction of socialism, and help to explain the prominence of new socialist bodies with middle-class leaders in the 1880s.

One of the most important of these was the Social Democratic Federation (SDF) founded by H. M. Hyndman in 1884. In its original radical form of the Democratic Federation, founded 1881, it offered an alternative to Gladstone's liberal policies but it moved to the left and became fully socialist in outlook by 1884. Hyndman himself was a product of Eton and Cambridge, and unashamedly middle class in his manner and appearance. As a famous description has it:

> In the early years of open-air propaganda—for he took his turn regularly at out-door meetings as well as indoor—his essentially bourgeois appearance attracted much attention. The tall hat, the frock coat, and the long beard often drew the curious-minded who would not have spent time in listening to one in workman's attire.

His views were strongly Marxist in nature; he had been converted to Marxism—or to his own version of Marxism—by reading *Capital* in a French translation in 1881. The SDF was only a small society, but it had in its ranks a number of vigorous young socialists who were to gain prominence later, including Tom Mann and John Burns, both of the ASE. William Morris, the wealthy poet and art designer, one of the Pre-Raphaelite group, was also a member for a time before breaking away to form another group, the Socialist League, in December 1884.

The other famous socialist body of the 1880s was the Fabian Society, also founded in 1884. It soon numbered among its leaders such famous people as George Bernard Shaw, Sidney and Beatrice Webb, and Annie Besant, the well-known journalist and feminist. The Society took its name from the Roman general Fabius, who won his victories by a process of wearing down the enemy rather than by direct and full-scale attack. Similarly the Fabians believed in achieving socialism by gradually converting the major political parties to it by rational argument, and not by revolution. In this they differed from Hyndman and the SDF who were never very clear how the socialist state would be gained except that it would come, as Marx predicted, through revolution. Sidney Webb summed up the Fabian beliefs in the famous volume of *Fabian Essays*, published in 1889:

> Socialists as well as Individualists realize that important organic changes can only be (1) democratic, and thus acceptable to a majority of the people, and prepared for in the minds of all; (2) gradual, and thus causing no dislocation, however rapid may be the rate of progress; (3) not regarded as immoral by the mass of the people, and thus not subjectively demoralizing to them; and (4) in this country at any rate constitutional and peaceful.

Thus socialism would develop slowly and inevitably in a peaceful and democratic manner—the phrase 'inevitability of gradualism' sums it up well. It follows from their belief in the permeation of their ideas into the thinking of men of all parties that no new political party was required.

What was needed instead was a constant flow of rational argument designed 'to make thinking persons socialist', in the words of Beatrice Webb. This they provided in a great outpouring of pamphlets. How far their arguments really influenced either the Liberal or Conservative Party is a moot question, but the leaders were persons of social influence, well-known in London political and intellectual circles. Since their brand of socialism included not only the public ownership of the means of production, distribution and exchange, but also all forms of state enterprise, they could claim that socialism was already making headway in the provision of municipal services such as gas works, waterworks, tramways, and so on. This kind of socialism was soon nicknamed 'gas and water' socialism.

The Fabian Society and the Social Democratic Federation were to be the two outstanding socialist bodies of the 1880s, but their memberships were very small compared with the trade unions, and they had no direct connections with the unions. For their part, the unions viewed the Marxist ideas of the SDF with great suspicion, while the Fabians were regarded as a middle-class propaganda machine with nothing to offer in the industrial field. However, the next development in the trade union movement was certainly influenced by socialist thinking.

New Unionism

It is customary to date the extension of trade unionism to the largely unskilled workers ('new' unionism) from the late 1880s, but as we have already seen, this movement really began in the early 1870s. It was probably the Great Depression which held it back in the later 70s, only to revive again with a temporary lessening of depression towards the end of the next decade. Its causes lay deeper, however, than the alternation of boom and slump. Just as the spread of education and the extension of the franchise contributed to the spread of socialism, so the same forces increased the working-class sense of class unity, and a desire for bargaining strength. The further decline of the small master economy meant an increase in the size of many firms, and a greater concentration of workers in one works. Because of the fall in prices, the rise in real wages enabled some labourers to afford union subscriptions for the first time. For all these reasons, new unions developed, usually with low subscriptions to be used for strike pay rather than sickness or out-of-work benefits, and often led by vigorous young men influenced by socialist thinking.

The difference in thinking between these young leaders and that of the older unionists was remarkable. In 1886 Tom Mann wrote in a pamphlet that:

The true Unionist policy of *aggression* seems entirely lost sight of; in fact the average unionist of today is a man with a fossilized intellect, either hopelessly apathetic, or supporting a policy that plays directly into the hands of the capitalist exploiter.

The new unions were certainly more aggressive than the old in relationships with employers. In 1890 Mann and another leading believer in new unionism, Ben Tillett, spelt out the difference:

> In conclusion, we repeat that the real difference between the 'new' and the 'old' is, that those who belong to the latter and delight in being distinct from the policy endorsed by the 'new', do so because they do not recognize, as we do, that it is the work of *the trade unionist to stamp out poverty from the land*.

This was the new note sounded from the mid-1880s on. Leaders of the new unions were active in support of the unemployed, and in a march of unemployed men in London in January 1886, windows were smashed in Pall Mall, and Hyndman and Burns were arrested. In 1887 John Burns was again present at a radical meeting which the organizers tried to hold in Trafalgar Square, though the Square had been closed to them by the police. In the fighting which followed, many were injured, John Burns was arrested and sentenced to six weeks' imprisonment, and the whole affair afterwards nicknamed 'Bloody Sunday'.

In the next year 1888 the first strike involving new unionism took place in London, though new unions were already being formed outside London in the cotton trades, and also among seamen on Tyneside and elsewhere, led by Joseph Havelock Wilson. The London strike was by the match girls employed by Bryant & May. Their plight was exposed by Mrs Annie Besant in her socialist weekly *The Link*. She regarded their conditions of work as a form of white slavery, and launched a hard-hitting attack on their employers:

> But who cares for the fate of these white wage slaves? Born in slums, driven to work while still children, undersized because underfed, oppressed because helpless, flung aside as soon as worked out, who cares if they die or go on the streets, provided only that the Bryant & May shareholders get their 23 per cent . . .

With Mrs Besant's help, the strike was successful, and the match girls formed a new union of their own.

In March of the following year, another new union was formed in London among the gasworkers. Its organizer was another member of the SDF, an almost illiterate Irishman born in Birmingham, Will Thorne. He received considerable clerical help from Eleanor Marx, daughter of Karl Marx. Such was the strength of the union, the National Union of Gas Workers and General Labourers, Thorne was able to gain a substantial cut in hours by the South Metropolitan Gas Company without even calling the men out on strike.

Later in 1889 there occurred one of the most famous strikes of all—the London Docks Strike. Only a small minority of dock workers were already in unions—the skilled stevedores and watermen—together with a limited number of labourers in a new union founded in 1887 by Ben Tillett. Some labourers were extremely poor. According to the General Manager of the Millwall Docks:

> They are the most miserable of specimens; there are men who are reduced to the direst poverty, men with every disposition to work well, but without the strength to do it. There are men who come to work in our docks . . . who come on without having a bit of food in their stomachs, perhaps since the previous day; they have worked for an hour and have earned 5d; their hunger will not allow them to continue; they take the 5d in order that they might get food, perhaps the first food they have had in 24 hours.

Tillett's union of tea warehousemen was brought out on strike by him for the 'docker's tanner'—an increase from 5d to 6d per hour—and they were speedily joined by large numbers of other dockers. Tom Mann and John Burns were brought in to help organize the strike, and membership of Tillett's union went up by leaps and bounds. Regular marches of dockers took place through the City, and their good order and generally peaceful behaviour attracted much sympathy to the dockers' cause. Nevertheless, the strike began to falter after a fortnight or so, but the situation was saved by financial help amounting to £30 000 from Australian trade unionists. This made it unnecessary to proceed with the rather desperate proposal for calling a general strike, and the work of conciliation by Cardinal Manning brought the strike to an end after five weeks. The employers then gave in and conceded the 'docker's tanner'.

The year 1889 was therefore a year of triumph for new unionism. Tillett was able to set up a new union for dock workers called the Dock, Wharf, Riverside, and General Labourers Union, with 30 000 members by November. Wilson's Seamen's Union increased its membership to 65 000. The London gasworkers union established by Will Thorne became a national union, and included general labourers. The General Railway Workers Union was founded, for lower grades of railway workers. Not only was the number increasing of semi-skilled and unskilled trade unionists, but at the same time the influence of socialism was also growing stronger through the new unions. It found additional outlets, too, in the increasing number of trades councils. About 60 new trades councils were established, according to the

Webbs, in the years 1889–91. Thus, the trade union movement was more and more split in leadership between the veterans of the model unions and the young socialists of the new unions. In a well-known passage, Burns described their appearance at the 1890 TUC:

> Physically, the 'old' unionists were much bigger than the new. . . . A great number of them looked like respectable city gentlemen; wore very good coats, large watch chains, and high hats. . . . Among the new delegates not a single one wore a tall hat. They looked workmen; they were workmen. They were not such sticklers for formality or court procedure, but were guided more by common sense.

Yet it would be wrong to suppose that the older unions were quite overshadowed or even replaced by the new unions from 1889 onwards. In the first place, not all the new unions survived the return of depression in and after 1891. Labourers could not afford subscriptions when out of work, and their unions could not afford out-of-work benefits. Again, some employers counterattacked the new unions, particularly those of the dockers and sailors, and introduced blackleg labour when they could. The result was that strikes in the great ports were all defeated between 1890 and 1893. The only new unions to avoid collapse were those whose members had some skill and therefore some bargaining power. Such unions were not 'general' (i.e. catering for workers in different industries) at all, in spite of that word appearing in their title. Moreover, some of these unions began to provide benefits other than strike pay, thereby drawing closer to the model unions in nature. Recent historians, in fact, have emphasized the way in which new unions which originally did bring in new groups of workers and were general in organization, nevertheless in the course of time settled down to work amicably with the model or craft unions. The older unions for their part, gained in strength during the relatively prosperous years of 1889–91, and some of them increased their membership still further by recruiting less skilled workers. So the older unions kept well ahead of the new unions in sheer numbers. In 1900, for example, they outnumbered the new unions in membership by about 10 to one.

However, if the model unions still dominated the trade union movement in the 1890s, the political views of the new unions still had an important and permanent effect on trade unionism. This is seen in the arguments at the annual meeting of the TUC where in 1890 the new unions controlled about a quarter of the votes. In that year with the help of some of the older unions they were able to pass a number of socialist resolutions together with a resolution in favour of the eight-hour day. At this point Henry Broadhurst, the Liberal secretary of the Parliamentary Committee, resigned from office. He was replaced by another moderate, but by 1894 the new Secretary, Sam Woods, was much more sympathetic to the new unions.

Indeed, by 1894 the influence of the new unions was such that the moderate representatives on the Parliamentary Committee thought it necessary to strike back by changing the system of voting at Congress. Previously, voting was by individual, and as Trades Councils were represented separately from the unions and were often dominated by socialists, this was to the benefit of the new unions who thereby in some cases acquired double representation. The new rules stipulated that Trades Councils should no longer be represented, that union delegates should have one vote per thousand members, and that every delegate must either work at his trade or be a paid TU official. In this way socialist influence was reduced in the TUC for the time being; but in the meanwhile socialist thinking was gaining ground outside the ranks of the TUC.

The Independent Labour Party

In the early 1890s the system whereby Lib-Labs sat in the House of Commons to represent trade union interests continued unchanged. There were 11 of these Lib-Labs in the parliament which was dissolved in 1892. In the general election of that year, the number of trade union representatives increased to 13, but they included three men who for the first time claimed to stand as independents. Of these three, John Burns and Havelock Wilson soon reverted to Lib–Labbism; but the third, Keir Hardie, refused to cooperate with the Liberals, and argued for the creation of a separate labour party at the 1892 TUC. Of all the labour leaders mentioned so far, Keir Hardie was the most striking. Largely self-taught, he had worked down the mine in Lanarkshire until he was black-listed for his union and political activities. He had then become a journalist and union organizer, moving from liberalism to socialism, though never joining the SDF or ever becoming a Marxist; Marxism, he thought, 'did not touch one human sentiment or feeling'. His political beliefs were based on a deep ethical conviction that the social injustices of the capitalist system must be brought to an end. His arrival at the House of Commons to take up his seat in 1892 is famous. Instead of arriving in the customary sober attire, he deliberately dressed informally. According to Burns it was:

> the kind of thing you saw going to Epping Forest, an old deerstalker cap and knickers [trousers] of check, you could have played draughts on them.

His supporters accompanied him in a two-horse carriage, and included a cornet player. Of the three independents in 1892, it was left to Hardie to persevere with the idea of a labour party, having already formed a small independent body in Scotland in 1888, the Scottish Labour Party.

In fact, the time seemed to be ripe for the creation of a separate Labour Party in England, too, for a number of labour groups already existed up and down the country. In Bradford the situation appeared especially favourable. There were no less than 23 labour clubs in existence there, and socialist ideas were strong. Under Hardie's guidance a conference was held in Bradford in January 1893, attended by 120 delegates. They represented the labour clubs, the Scottish Labour Party, the SDF, the Fabians, and a small number of trade unions. A new political party was set up—the Independent Labour Party—independent, that is, of the Liberal Party, and clearly aiming at socialism. In Keir Hardie's words:

> The ILP starts from the assumption that the worker should be as free industrially and economically as he is supposed to be politically, and the instruments of production should be owned by the community . . .

Although the new party was set up with great enthusiasm, it had to face considerable disappointment early on. In the event, both the London Fabians and the SDF held aloof, and the Liberal Party was hostile for obvious reasons. Nor did the Parliamentary Committee of the TUC welcome the new party, since many of the members were satisfied with the existing Lib–Lab arrangements. The ILP was also short of money. Worst of all, every one of the 28 candidates put up in the 1895 election was defeated, including Hardie himself. The new party's influence was still too regional, and it had failed to gain national recognition. For the next two years the ILP made little progress, and a succession of events brought set-backs for the union movement as a whole.

Perhaps the most serious threat to the unions now came from certain employers who launched a second counter-attack against the growing power of the unions by forming their own employers' associations, such as the Engineering Employers Federation, founded 1894. This was followed by the establishment in 1898 of an Employers Parliamentary Committee, a clear rival to the TUC's Parliamentary Committee. Meanwhile, the use of blackleg labour increased with the creation in 1893 of the National Free Labour Association, led by William Collinson, though such labour could only be used when the men on strike were unskilled. In 1897 the most famous of the model unions, the ASE, was challenged by the engineering employers, who successfully locked the men out for six months between July 1897 and January 1898. Even more alarming, the case of Lyons v. Wilkins decided an employer named Lyons was within his rights in applying for an injunction to prevent a union from picketing his premises. All at once it seemed as if the rights of peaceful picketing had been lost.

Just before the end of the century, therefore, the trade unions once again found they had their backs to the wall. It seemed vital that they should take joint action. The first step was to create the General Federation of Trade Unions in January 1899, in order to provide a general strike fund. The response to this was very limited; only 44 unions joined, with less than a quarter of the membership of Congress. The second step was to strengthen the trade unions' political influence at Westminster so as to increase union pressure on the government. It had become patently obvious to many that the Lib–Lab system was not operating satisfactorily, so that more direct representation was necessary. The Liberal Party had suffered a disastrous defeat in the 1895 election, yet still would not adopt working-class candidates for parliament. If the Liberals would not help the unions, they must help themselves. The prospects were not unpromising, for it had already proved possible for Labour candidates to be successful in local government elections; by 1895 there were 600 local Labour councillors, and in 1898 West Ham Council had actually gained a labour majority. The moral seemed clear. The labour movement must be represented more directly in the Commons, and a conference had to be held of all interested parties to discuss ways and means of bringing this about—something Keir Hardie had been advocating since 1896.

The Labour Representation Committee

At the 1899 TUC it was soon apparent that the dislike of socialism felt by the older members of the model unions was outweighed by the determination of the TUC as a whole to get something done. The key resolution was put by James Holmes, representing the Amalgamated Society of Railway Servants which now contained a strong ILP element:

> That this Congress . . . with a view to securing a better representation of the interests of labour in the House of Commons, hereby instructs the Parliamentary Committee to invite the cooperation of all the cooperative, socialistic, trade union and other working organizations to jointly cooperate on lines mutually agreed upon in convening a special congress . . . to devise ways and means for securing the return of an increased number of labour MPs to the next parliament.

This rather laboriously worded motion was debated for three hours and passed by 546 000 votes to 434 000. The urgent need for action had caused a major change in attitude on the issue of political representation.

The special congress met at the Memorial Hall in Farringdon Street, London on 27 February 1900. It was attended by delegates from the socialist bodies including the ILP, the SDF, and the Fabian Society, together with representatives from a number of unions (mostly new unions) the membership of which amounted to less than half the total membership of the TUC. The conference proceeded to pass the key resolution moved by Keir Hardie in favour of forming

> . . . a distinct Labour group in Parliament, who shall have their whips, and agree upon their policy, which must embrace a readiness to cooperate with any party which for the time being may be engaged in promoting legislation in the direct interest of labour . . .

They then set up the Labour Representation Committee. On it there were two members of the ILP, two from the SDF, one from the Fabians, and seven from the unions. Thus, the socialist bodies were treated very favourably, being given five members to the unions' seven, which was grossly out of proportion to the memberships involved. The setting up of the LRC was a great achievement for Hardie, for this had been one of his principal objectives for some years past. The secretary of the new committee was to be James Ramsay MacDonald, and the expense of putting up candidates was to be borne by the trade unions and the societies concerned. In 1906, as we shall see in the next chapter, the LRC was to take on a new name—the Labour Party.

From this account of the origins of the LRC, and hence of the Labour Party, it should be clear that the new organization was by no means the result of a new burst of militancy on the part of the TUC. In fact, it was quite the contrary, and stemmed from the TUC's need to defend its members. Nor was it an inevitable consequence of the growth of unionism and socialism. Rather it was a practical response to a particular situation, the creation of a pressure group to achieve certain purposes which did not exclude continued cooperation with the Liberal Party—witness the reference in Hardie's resolution to a 'readiness to cooperate with any party . . .'. Of course, it may be argued that once the working classes had the vote, and as class consciousness grew towards the end of the century, a separate political party was bound to evolve in the end. But the Liberal Party was traditionally the party which attracted the majority of the working-class votes, and there is no particular reason why it should not have continued as the party of both the middle classes and the working classes. It was the Liberal Party's misfortune that at this time its local associations were often dominated by middle-class employers who were reluctant to meet the expense of putting up working-class candidates. Such candidates could contribute little to election costs, and had no private incomes to meet expenses if they were elected. So the Liberal Party, still divided and distracted over the issues of Home Rule, imperialism and the Boer War, missed the opportunity of consolidating and extending its electoral basis.

Who deserves the most credit for the founding of the Labour Party? Because of the odd turn which events took at the end of the century, it is difficult to answer this question. The trade union movement as a whole was divided over the issue and as we have seen, the older unions were actually against the move, even though some of them were coming under socialist influence: the secretary of the ASE, for example, from 1896 onwards was George Barnes, a member of the ILP. In these circumstances it would obviously be wrong to give all the credit to the unions, though it was the TUC which summoned the conference in 1900 (even then, the vote was only narrowly in favour of the resolution). Of the socialist bodies, the Fabians always held aloof from the unions, and they contributed little to the creation of the LRC. The SDF's contribution was also very limited, and in fact their delegates actually tried to force the 1900 conference to create, in the words of their resolution

> a distinct party—separate from the capitalist parties, based upon the recognition of the class war, and having for its ultimate object the socialization of the means of production, distribution, and exchange.

This was clearly far too extreme for the majority, and the resolution gained little support.

It was really Keir Hardie and his supporters in the ILP who could see that the way ahead was to set up a broadly based, national Labour Party, committed in very general terms to the cause of labour. Such an objective would gain far more support than any narrow, doctrinaire approach. Moreover, Hardie could see the possibilities in gaining financial support from the unions. It follows therefore that Hardie probably did more than any other person to bring about the creation of the LRC, and it was his faith in socialism which drove him on. Thus in the last analysis, it can be argued that socialist conviction was the dynamic force which produced the LRC, though it was the trade union movement which provided the practical opportunity for this to happen. It remains to be seen in the next chapter hqw the LRC became the Labour Party.

The Revival of Cooperation

Although the cooperative movement had made only limited progress earlier on, from the 1840s it expanded greatly on the basis of retail selling rather than the manufacture of goods. The beginnings of this expansion are usually held to date from the founding of the Rochdale Society of Equitable Pioneers in 1844. As its title may indicate, this society originally planned to carry out a number of projects designed to make the world a fairer place for the working classes: apart from establishing a retail store, they proposed to employ their own members in manufacturing, provide them with houses, settle others on estates which they intended to buy, set up a Temperance Hotel, and as soon as possible 'proceed to arrange the powers of production, distribution, education, and government'. Of all these impressive aims, it was the setting-up of the retail store which was successful and provided a pattern for similar stores elsewhere.

The Rochdale Society was founded by seven flannel weavers who opened their shop on the ground floor of a warehouse in Toad Lane, Rochdale on 21 December 1844. They concentrated on retailing from the beginning, and paid a dividend on purchases and on capital subscribed as well. The giving of a dividend on purchases was not a new idea, but it proved very popular as an easy means of saving, and helped to get the store well established. The venture was also assisted by the increasing prosperity of the late 1840s and 1850s, and by the emphasis on the sale of goods rather than the more ambitious undertaking of manufacture. Since the goods were sold at market price, the member receiving his dividend was in effect buying them more cheaply than elsewhere. Shops of the Toad Lane type supplied unadulterated food to their members, an important consideration at a time when foodstuffs were often adulterated, for example, by putting sand into brown sugar, or Plaster of Paris into confectionery. Such shops also became social centres for meeting friends when buying the weekly groceries and for having a good gossip. By 1851 there were as many as 130 societies of the same type as the society in Rochdale, with 15 000 members. Societies of this kind were given Friendly Society status in 1852, and could become limited liability companies in 1862.

By the 1860s the modern cooperative society movement was firmly established, and was strong enough to set up its own wholesale organization in England in 1863 as a buying agency—the Cooperative Wholesale Society. In this way the profits of the middle man were eliminated, and the CWS paid dividends on purchases by the stores, just as the retail stores paid dividends to their members. The CWS benefited from the prosperity of the 1860s as much as the retail branch of the movement. Its sales rose from £52 000 in 1864 to more than £1 500 000 in 1874. By this time the cooperative movement was strong enough to have started its own insurance scheme in 1867 and a deposit and loan department in 1871. In 1872 it began the manufacture of its own goods, commencing with the making of biscuits in the Manchester district, and later moving into boots and shoes, and then soap. By 1914 sales of the CWS to the retail shops amounted to £35 m, while the membership of the retail societies had reached three million, and their sales £88 m. By 1945 membership had grown further to nine million, and retail sales to £361 m.

There can be no doubt of the success of the cooperative movement in the second half of the nineteenth century and after. Especially in the North of England (but less so in London and the Midlands) it became an important part of working-class life. The combination of pure food and the dividend proved to be of great importance. But this success was purchased at the expense of the sacrifice of some of the earlier ideals.

Only very limited amounts were spent on education into the cooperative way of life, and the movement certainly failed to supplant the capitalist system of production and distribution. It is true that it began its own annual congresses in 1869, and eventually between the wars put up its own MPs who were virtually indistinguishable from Labour MPs. It had little political influence of its own, however, and became a manufacturer and retailer of goods within the capitalist system favoured by members of both the working and middle classes who disliked private enterprise and preferred profits to be distributed in the form of the dividend.

Section III
New Roles for Labour 1900–1914

No major economic changes took place in this short period, but by 1914 Britain's share of world trade was dropping, and her export trade was being re-directed to some extent from Europe and North America to Africa (where the European 'Scramble for Africa' had just taken place), to India, to South America, and to Australasia. Exports of coal and of machinery were increasing, and this at the expense of the export of goods, though the latter still accounted for three-quarters of all exports. As for imports, food had become more important than raw materials, and imports of manufactured goods increased rapidly. The truth was that Britain was no longer the Workshop of the World, for the world itself was becoming more industrialized. Yet the relative decline of the staple industries was masked by the boom which began about 1908, though the rise in prices led to a fall in real wages and to much industrial discontent. The pomp and glitter of the prosperous Edwardian period therefore rested upon insecure foundations.

Chapter XI
The Labour Party and the Unions before World War I

The Fortunes of the LRC

The setting up of the Labour Representation Committee in 1900 caused no great stir at the time, and there were few who regarded it as more than another pressure group aiming to strengthen the labour cause. Keir Hardie himself thought of it in this way, and as late as 1905 he hoped that in time it might become an 'influence second in importance only to that of the Irish National Party'. At the time when it was founded, the socialist journal the *Clarion* appears to have been rather more optimistic about its future, but even then its tone was cautious:

> At last there is a United Labour Party, or perhaps it would be safer to say, a little cloud, no bigger than a man's hand, which may grow into a United Labour Party.

This caution was justified, for the LRC certainly got off to a slow start. It had little time to make preparations for the 1900 General Election, and of its 15 candidates, only two were elected—Keir Hardie and Richard Bell, general secretary of the Railway Servants Union. It was almost impossible to create a new parliamentary party of only two members, especially as Bell was no socialist and was more of a Liberal than anything else. Indeed, he was too sympathetic for Hardie's liking to the group of eight Lib–Labs in the House. Further, the LRC was short of funds. Less than a dozen unions affiliated to it, representing only about 350 000 members out of a total trade union membership of two million or so.

In the early days it appeared that the LRC might well disappear altogether from the political scene. It was saved from this fate by a famous legal decision, and by a political bargain made with the Liberals. The legal decision resulted from a strike on the Taff Vale Railway in South Wales supported by the Amalgamated Society of Railway Servants. Although the strike was settled quite quickly in 1900, the railway company brought an action against the union itself for unlawful picketing, rather than against the individual pickets, something that had not been done before. The case went from the High

Court to the Court of Appeal, and finally to the House of Lords, who found in favour of the company. Since the union had now been declared responsible for the actions of its members, the railway company went on to sue the union for all its losses arising from the strike, and in December, 1902 was awarded £23 000 damages together with costs of the action—about £42 000 in all.

The Taff Vale Railway case caused great concern among the trade unions because it now appeared that whenever a trade union supported a strike, it might be made liable for all the losses incurred by the employer. Strange to say, some of the more conservative unions were not so opposed as one might have expected to the decision of the House of Lords. This is because they thought the more militant and hot-headed trade unionists would be restrained by the new legal situation. However, many unions were very alarmed by what had happened—the ASRS had been severely shaken financially by the case. Some historians have even seen the Taff Vale Case as the final blow in a sustained and calculated attack on the trade unions dating from the mid-1890s. There is really little evidence to support this view, but the fact remains that the Taff Vale Case was regarded by many unionists as a serious threat. The consequence was a very distinct increase in the support for the LRC as a means of getting an Act passed to reverse the Taff Vale judgement. By January 1903 affiliations had so increased that the membership affiliated to the LRC had gone up to 850 000. Thus, as the historian R. C. K. Ensor put it, a sudden wind filled the sails of the LRC and blew hard in its favour till the general election of 1906.

The other favourable influence assisting the LRC relates to that election. In 1903 Ramsay MacDonald entered into a secret electoral pact with Herbert Gladstone, acting on behalf of the Liberal Party. By this pact it was agreed that the LRC would support the next Liberal government on condition that LRC candidates were unopposed by the Liberal Party in some 30 constituencies. The advantages of this agreement for the Liberals were that they would save the cost of putting up a candidate in the constituencies concerned, and also avoid splitting the anti-Conservative vote. Jesse Herbert, secretary to Herbert Gladstone, saw the last point very clearly, and foresaw serious Liberal losses if the LRC advised their supporters to vote against Liberal candidates, especially as most of these voters had previously voted Liberal. In this event he predicted

> . . . the Liberal Party would suffer defeat not only in those constituencies where LRC candidates fought, but also in almost every borough, and in many of the divisions of Lancashire and Yorkshire. This would be the inevitable result of unfriendly action towards the LRC candidates. They would be defeated, but so also should we be defeated.

From the LRC point of view, the pact was obviously advantageous in giving them a good chance of winning most of the 30 seats. Secrecy was necessary, however, since conservative-minded Liberals would certainly object to any kind of deal with the LRC, while many LRC supporters were strongly opposed to any kind of a return to a Lib–Lab alliance.

By the time this pact was made in August 1903 the LRC had already picked up a further three seats in by-elections, so that the future was looking much more promising. Between August, 1903 and the end of 1905 the LRC, the Liberal Party, and the eight Lib–Labs all drew more closely together (Keir Hardie loyally keeping the pact secret, though he privately disliked it). In December, 1905 the Conservative government resigned. In the General Election which followed in January, 1906 there was little to choose between the election manifesto of the Liberal Party and that of the LRC. Both attacked strongly the idea of Protection, an idea which the Conservatives were accused of thinking of adopting. Part of the LRC manifesto reads:

> Protection, as experience shows, is no remedy for poverty and unemployment. It serves to keep you from dealing with the land, housing, old age, and other social problems! You have it in your power to see that Parliament carries out your wishes. The Labour Representation Executive appeals to you in the name of a million Trade Unionists to forget all the political opinions which have kept you apart in the past, and vote for—(the name of the LRC candidate).

The General Election brought a landslide victory for the Liberals who gained 377 seats in all, with a majority of 84 over all other parties. The LRC's share in the victory was 29 seats, with one further successful candidate joining the group after the election, making 30 in all. In addition, 24 Lib–Lab candidates were elected. The LRC now changed its name to the Labour Party, while its 30 representatives in the House of Commons set up their own organization with their own whips—the Parliamentary Labour Party. Keir Hardie was elected chairman, with Ramsay MacDonald as secretary and Arthur Henderson chief whip. At last the working classes had their own party in parliament, and no longer had to rely on the Liberal Party to represent them. Almost immediately the Labour Party scored a success in the passing of the Trade Disputes Act, 1906. The basis of this Act was a Bill introduced by the Labour Party to alter the law as laid down in the Taff Vale Case. The government accepted this measure in place of its own moderate trade union Bill, and as a result trade unions were given immunity against actions for damages for losses incurred during a strike. This effectively nullified the Taff Vale Case decision and constituted a very important legal advance for the unions. The law of picketing was also altered in a way which favoured peaceful picketing.

Thus the year 1906 was a year of triumph for the new Labour Party.

Their election successes, coupled with the passing of the Trade Disputes Act, appeared to mark the dawning of a new age. Some viewed the future with alarm and A. J. Balfour, the leader of the Conservative Party, seemed to think that the new Liberal government under its Prime Minister Campbell-Bannerman, would soon be swept away by the tide of socialist revolution. According to Balfour:

> CB is a mere cork dancing on a torrent which he cannot control, and what is going on here is a faint echo of the same movement which has produced massacres in St Petersburg, riots in Vienna, and Socialist processions in Berlin.

In fact, this opinion was quite absurd. Not only was Campbell-Bannerman with his overall majority of 84 perfectly able to cope with the Parliamentary Labour Party, but the new party was entirely peaceful and constitutional in outlook. Only 18 of the 30 Labour MPs were socialists, and none of them held revolutionary views.

Nevertheless, working-class voters might well have expected the Labour Party in parliament to make their presence felt as a lively pressure group. If so, they were to be disappointed. By the end of 1906 it was clear that the Labour MPs were exerting very little influence over the government, and in the next year a well-known socialist and member of the ILP, Victor Grayson, won the Colne Valley bye-election without official Labour support. In 1908 Ben Tillett complained in his pamphlet *Is the Parliamentary Labour Party a Failure?* that

> The House of Commons and the country, which respected and feared the Labour Party, are now fast approaching a condition of contempt towards its parliamentary representatives. The lion has no teeth or claws, and is losing his growl, too . . .

Some members of the ILP Council issued a so-called Green Manifesto entitled *Let us Reform the Labour Party*, and by 1911 discontent among some members of the ILP led them to join with the SDF (which had withdrawn from the LRC as early as 1901) to form a new party, the British Socialist Party. This was later to form the basis of the Communist Party of Great Britain after the war. Meanwhile, the electoral support of the Labour Party was not increasing. It is true that its number of seats increased to 45 by 1909, but this was because a number of miner MPs ceased to be Lib–Labs and transferred their allegiance to the Labour Party. By 1914, and after two general elections in 1910, this number was reduced to 36. No wonder Keir Hardie remarked, no doubt with some bitterness, in 1910: 'At the present time the Labour Party has almost ceased to count.'

Yet there are good reasons which explain and to some extent excuse the apparent inertia of the Labour Party in Parliament. The most obvious of these is that their choice was always limited to voting Liberal or Conservative, or abstaining; and they could hardly oppose the social reforms introduced by the Liberals, especially in and after 1908. Since the government had such a good overall majority there was no question of Labour threatening to outvote them—at least, not until after the general elections of 1910. But even though this then became theoretically possible, it was not a practical possibility, for general elections were very expensive for the Labour Party, and not worth risking unless a serious difference of opinion arose between the parties. Apart from this, the size of the Labour group depended very largely on the electoral pact, which was continued in the 1910 elections. For all these reasons, the situation was unfavourable to independent action by Labour, and—as Dr Pelling has put it—circumstances made the Labour Party the 'handmaiden of Liberalism'.

Nevertheless, some criticism may fairly be levelled against the Labour MPs themselves. They certainly did not make up for their inexperience by any show of militancy. Keir Hardie's habitual rebelliousness did not make him a good party leader, and there was a certain lack of unity due to mutual distrust between the trade unionists and socialist members. This lack of unity contributed to poor party discipline—debates were not well-attended, and members sometimes missed divisions. In fact, apart from Hardie, the Labour MPs were rather a dull lot, and Beatrice Webb had some harsh things to say about them in her diary in 1914:

> The cold truth is that the Labour members have utterly failed to impress the House of Commons and the constituencies as a live force, and have lost confidence in themselves and each other . . . there is little leadership but a great deal of anti-leadership.

The Osborne Judgement

It must be said, however, that in the same passage Mrs Webb did acknowledge that the trade unions were 'swelling in membership and funds', and it is clear that trade unionism made greater strides forward than the Labour Party between 1906 and 1914. At first the unions came up against an unexpected obstacle in the Osborne Judgement, 1909. The Osborne case was the result of a branch secretary of the Railway Servants Union bringing an action against his own union to stop it from imposing the compulsory political levy. Osborne objected to his union using part of members' subscriptions to finance a political party (i.e. the Labour Party), and the House of Lords ruled in his favour. The judgement dealt a severe blow at Labour Party finances, and in particular at the subsidies given by the unions to Labour MPs. No salaries were paid to MPs at this time, and several Labour MPs now found themselves in financial difficulties. It is sometimes supposed that Osborne was given secret support by employers in bringing his action, but it seems rather that he was a Lib–Lab who disliked being forced to support a party which included socialists, and he spoke for many liberal and conservative trade unionists. At all events, he was expelled from his union as a result, and his 18 years' contributions were confiscated and all benefits cancelled. As for the actions of the courts, it is not impossible that the judges were reacting against the privileges given to trade unions (as they saw it) by the 1906 Act.

For two years the Liberal government took no action in the matter, then in 1911 the situation was eased when in return for Labour support over the National Insurance Act, the government provided for payment of MPs (£400 a year). This still left trade unions fettered by the Osborne judgement, of course. Finally in 1913 the government passed another Trade Union Act whereby trade unions might once more use their funds to support a political party, but only under certain conditions. In the first place, each union had to hold a ballot of its members to decide whether a majority wished to establish a political fund. If they did, a political fund could be set up, separate from the general fund. Any member objecting to part of his subscription going into the political fund would be entitled to say so, thereby 'contracting-out'. In this case the whole of his membership fees would go into the general fund. The trade unions disliked the new 'contracting-out' procedure, for obvious reasons, but they did not wish to vote against it and bring down the government. As a leading TU official put it

> This act represents the most we could extract from them. They would have been glad if we had rejected it. So would the Tories have been glad also.

Industrial Strife and Syndicalism

Meanwhile the industrial scene had been relatively peaceful since the beginning of the century, due largely to the development of collective bargaining procedures in the well-organized trades. It was these procedures, worked out in a time of trade depression when the unions were not strong enough to risk going on strike, which seem to explain the industrial peace, rather than the threat of employers' legal actions following Taff Vale. From about 1908, however, things began to change, and by 1910 trade conditions had greatly improved. Employment prospects were much better, but prices were rising, real wages falling. The scene was therefore set for industrial strife.

There is the further point that new political beliefs in the form of syndicalism were now spreading among trade unionists. Syndicalism takes its name from the French word for trade union (*syndic*) and was gaining popularity at this time in both France and the United States. Its basic idea was that the workers should gain political power not by acting through parliament but by the unions in each industry taking over that industry and running it for the benefit of the workers, not the employers. Worker control of industry, of course, would lead ultimately to political control of the State. The means whereby these ends were to be achieved were, firstly, the creation of one big union for each industry, and secondly, the use of strikes, and particularly the General Strike. These ideas were set out clearly in a famous pamphlet, *The Miners' Next Step*, published in Tonypandy in 1912, syndicalism having gained considerable support by then in the South Wales mining valleys. Thus, this pamphlet advocated as an 'Ultimate Objective':

> One organization to cover the whole of the Coal, Ore, Slate, Stone, Clay, Salt, mining or quarrying industry of Great Britain, with one Central Executive.

As for its political programme, the pamphlet lays it down:

> That the organization shall engage in political action, both local and national, on the basis of complete independence of, and hostility to all capitalist parties, with an avowed policy of wresting whatever advantage it can for the working class.

Its general recommendations also include the following:

> Alliances to be formed, and trade organizations to be fostered, with a view to steps being taken to amalgamate all workers into one National and International union, to work for the taking over of all industries by the workmen themselves.

Views of this kind were spread enthusiastically by Tom Mann on his return from Australia in 1910. High employment, falling real wages, and syndicalism thus provide the background for severe industrial strife from 1911 onwards.

There can be no doubt of the serious nature of the strikes in 1911. There were dock strikes in London and Liverpool, the latter organized by Tom Mann. Troops were brought in, and two men killed in a riot. In August 1911 the first national railway strike began, and troops were again sent in. Two strikers were killed in Llanelli when trying to stop a train driven by blacklegs. Hardie thereupon published a pamphlet entitled *Killing No Murder: the Government and the Railway Strike.* Fortunately Lloyd George's skill as conciliator brought the strike to an end within a few days. Another mining strike in South Wales began in September, 1910 and lasted some 10 months. Rioting and looting took place in Tonypandy, and troops were sent into the area, though contrary to legend they were kept in the background to avoid provocation.

In 1912 the wave of strikes was intensified, the number of days lost through strikes being more than three times the figure for 1911. A national miners' strike over the minimum wage lasted from February to April, while in the following month the dockers went on strike in London. The National Transport Workers Federation, formed in 1910 by Mann in conformity with his syndicalist beliefs, called a national strike in support of the London dockers, but it proved a failure, and by August the London workers had to give in.

In 1913 the number of strikes reached a peak, but there was less bloodshed, and the most important strike occurred not in England but in Ireland. It was by the Dublin transport workers. Their union, the Irish Transport Workers Union, was led by Jim Larkin, a believer in syndicalism and the device of the General Strike. The English trade unions showed sympathy, and Keir Hardie attended the funeral of two men killed in the rioting, but no English union was prepared to come out in support. The strike ended in failure in January, 1914. However, syndicalist thinking appeared to be having some effect in the passing of a resolution at the Miners' Annual Conference in 1913:

That the Executive Committee of the Miners Federation be requested to approach the Executive Committees of other big Trade Unions with a view to cooperative action and the support of each others' demands.

Writing some time after the event, the President of the Miners Federation, Robert Smillie, pointed out that if there was a strike on the railways, the miners and other transport workers were always affected and often thrown out of work. Accordingly the three unions, the National Union of Railwaymen (formed 1913), the National Transport Workers Federation, and the Miners Federation held a conference in April 1914 and agreed in principle to a Triple Alliance whereby they would consult together in drawing up wage demands. As Smillie said:

The predominant idea of the alliance is that each of these great fighting organizations, before embarking on any big movement, either defensive or aggressive, should formulate its programme, submit it to the others, and that upon joint proposals joint action should be taken.

He also added significantly that although only the three unions named were to be included:

> it may well be found advisable to extend the scope of the alliance in the general interests of labour as a whole.

The Extent of Militancy

On the face of it, there certainly seemed a marked increase in militancy from 1910 onwards, with a rapid spread of syndicalism and much emphasis on solving industrial problems by direct action rather than by parliamentary pressure through the Labour Party. Indeed, some older historians have linked up the violence in industrial relations, the growth of syndicalism, and the apparent threat of a General Strike posed by the Triple Alliance with violence in other sectors of society—the violence of the suffragettes, the approach of civil war in Ireland, and even the international violence of the outbreak of the First World War in August 1914. They have gone on to suggest that something like a revolutionary situation existed in England in 1914, with an increasing stress on violent action and a loss of faith in parliamentary procedures.

Such an interpretation of events has a certain superficial attraction, but founders on the rock of hard historical facts. The influence of syndicalism was in fact very limited. Hardie said on one occasion that he rejoiced in the growth of syndicalism, but this did not make him a syndicalist. One of his ILP colleagues, Bruce Glasier, observed that:

> Syndicalism is now on the lips of all politicians—the majority of whom do not know what it means . . .

Ramsay MacDonald went rather further in calling it

> the impatient, frenzied, thoughtless child of poverty, disappointment, irresponsibility.

There is no evidence to show that the strikes which have been described owed anything to syndicalism at all, but rather were based on grievances of a traditional kind to do with pay and working conditions. The few amalgamations of unions were similarly not due to any syndicalist ideas, but to the need to gain further bargaining strength, and in no case resulted in one union for the whole industry. The National Union of Railwaymen, for example, failed to incorporate either the Associated Society of Locomotive Engineers and Firemen (ASLEF) or the Railway

179

Clerks Association. As for the Triple Alliance, recent research has made it clear that there was no intention in reality of bringing about a General Strike. Rather it was intended as a practical way of avoiding losses due to the unilateral action of any one of the unions concerned. As Smillie put it:

> When the miners struck in 1912 the cost to the railwaymen alone was about £94 000. Whenever any of these three great sections have struck the others have to stand by and suffer in silence.

There was the further point that the Alliance would increase bargaining power, and would probably intimidate the employers into acceptance of wage demands. All this is very different from planning a General Strike of the kind advocated by French syndicalists such as Georges Sorel.

If the influence of syndicalism is to be discounted, it may still be asked why there was so much labour unrest just before World War I. The answer remains that given earlier on—the high level of employment, which meant that labour was relatively scarce and trade unions strong, and the fall in real wages, which supplied the major grievance. Unionism now spread to an important degree among the unskilled, and this time on a permanent basis, unlike many of the new unions of the 1890s. What happened was that the rise in the cost of living drove many of the unskilled into strike action, and this in itself brought them into trade union membership. The Workers Union, for instance, established in 1898, had a membership of 4500 in 1910 which grew to 143 000 by 1914. So the membership of the whole trade union movement increased substantially. In 1910 it stood at 2 565 000, increasing by 1914 to 4 145 000—an extraordinary growth; in 1913 alone an additional 719 000 members were acquired. Part of this enormous increase was due to the National Insurance Act, 1911, which required all workers to become members of a friendly society as part of the scheme of health insurance, so that many joined the trade union for their trade if it also provided friendly society benefits. But the increase also owed much to the extension of unionism to the unskilled.

The Progress of the Labour Movement

Any survey of the development of the Labour Movement in the period 1900–1914 must inevitably concentrate on the fortunes of the Labour Party in the first instance, but it is the growth of unionism which is most striking. The sheer increase in membership is impressive, and by 1914 trade unionism incorporated skilled workers and unskilled workers in almost equal numbers. However, in spite of these great changes, trade unions remained traditional in outlook. They were still suspicious of the law (understandably, one might think) and rejected any proposals that trade unions should have a body of clearly defined laws applied to them, or even to strike procedures. They were wary of compulsory arbitration, though not of conciliation, and the number of conciliation boards increased from 162 in 1905 to 325 in 1913.

Administratively they remained very weak, mainly because full-time officials working behind desks were considered by the rank and file to have soft jobs. Their numbers were kept to a minimum, and their salaries fixed with regard to rates of pay of the average member. As a consequence most unions were at a disadvantage when engaged in negotiations with employers, who had much better administrative resources. As a national movement, trade unions also lacked unity, principally because of the divisions between leaders who saw a political future for the unions, and those who thought unions should confine themselves to industrial matters. Thus, in spite of their size and importance, trade unions present a curiously old-fashioned appearance in 1914. For the most part, they were content to accept the economic system as it was, concentrating on protecting their members' interests in the customary way, and anxious to maintain good relations with employers whenever possible.

A similar conciliatory spirit animated the Labour Party, though from time to time Keir Hardie might use violent language, for example, against the House of Lords, or the Royal Family. It would be wrong, however, to leave the impression that if the trade unions had made progress in the decade before the war, the Labour Party was at a complete standstill in 1914. This is not true because away from Westminster, local Labour organization was improving, even though individual membership still did not exist. The number of trades councils was increasing, and 85 had affiliated by 1915. Thus, the Labour Party was really stronger outside parliament than it was inside, and in Chapter XIV it will be seen how the coming of the First World War provided the opportunity for the Labour Party to move forward, and even to participate directly in government.

Chapter XII
The Liberal Welfare Reforms

The Origins of the Reforms

When the Liberals took office in December 1905 and then overwhelmingly defeated the Conservatives in the General Election held in January 1906, their victory was not the consequence of a declared policy of social reform. On the contrary, the major issues seem to have been tariff reform, the Education Act of 1902, and 'Chinese Slavery'. As to the first, it is clear that the Conservatives were divided over the need for tariff reform, while the Liberals, recently split over the Boer War, reunited under the banner of Free Trade. The Conservative Education Act also provided a unifying force for the Liberals, particularly their nonconformist supporters who strongly opposed financial aid to Anglican schools from the rates. 'Chinese Slavery' was the Liberal phrase for the government's action in allowing Chinese labourers to be imported into the recently conquered Transvaal, where they were treated almost as slave labour. The government's policy in this matter certainly antagonized many working-class voters. During the election campaign Liberal speaker after Liberal speaker dwelt on the evils of Chinese Labour. One remarked on how much better it would have been if the cost of the Boer War had been spent on land reform:

> . . . but out in South Africa there are 50 000 graves and 50 000 Chinamen working at 1s 0d per day instead.

Another speaker asked sarcastically:

> If the poorer Rand mines could not be worked without cheap foreign labour, why not bring in Chinese at 1s 0d or 1s 6d a day to work the poor S. Staffs mines?

No doubt this kind of argument helped to influence working-class voting, but even more powerful was the suggestion that tariff reform would mean taxes on imported food, and an increase in the cost of living. Thus, the Conservative defeat appears to have been due to their own policies (or the way they could be represented) rather than any positive programme put forward by the Liberals. The latter hammered away at the major issues, but there were only incidental references to the need for a new housing policy, or for old age pensions, or measures to combat unemployment. Yet by 1914 the Liberals had passed a number of extremely important social reforms which are landmarks in the social history of the working classes. Why was this so?

In the first place, it seems unlikely that working-class pressure was a primary cause. It is true that the Parliamentary Labour Party came into being in 1906, but as was seen in the last chapter it was not strong enough numerically to have much effect on the Liberal government, even after the 1910 elections had drastically reduced the government's massive majority. Trade union demands for social reform, on the other hand, may have helped to focus attention on the need for action, but it cannot be shown that it played a principal part in the passing of any one reform. As for the working classes as a whole, it has been argued that they were much more interested in improving wages and working conditions than in social legislation. It is a reasonable conclusion, therefore, that working-class pressure did not of itself produce the Liberal reforms.

A better explanation is that the reforms were the result partly of changing social attitudes of the time, and partly of political events. The influences which had led to the appointment of the Royal Commission on the Poor Law in 1905 continued to trouble the public conscience (or more accurately, perhaps, the middle-class conscience)—that is to say, the shocks administered by the surveys of Booth and Rowntree, the scandal of the poor quality Boer War recruits, concern about unemployment, and the growth of collectivist thinking. But in addition to these pressures, there were those who argued that if the British were to continue to compete successfully in world markets, then in the interests of national efficiency, something must be done about the third of the working classes below the poverty line. Others argued that the Empire itself could not be maintained without a healthy working class. Sidney Webb made this point, and Asquith agreed with him:

> What is the use of talking about Empire if here, at its very centre, there is always to be found a mass of people, stunted in education, a prey of intemperance, huddled and congested beyond the possibility of realizing in any true sense either social or domestic life?

Still others regarded it as essential that help should be given to the 'respectable' poor before they became corrupted by the lowest stratum of the working classes, the 'submerged tenth', for whom little could be done.

For all these reasons it seems likely that whichever party had won the 1906 Election, a number of social reforms would have been passed, and it is not surprising that up to 1908 the Liberals did pass several useful but minor reforms. From 1908 onwards, however, the pace quickened, and here the political circumstances of the time must be taken into account. In that year the Prime Minister, Campbell-Bannerman, was forced to retire by ill-health. He was replaced by Asquith, with Lloyd George moving to the Exchequer, and Winston Churchill to the Board of Trade. The government had recently lost several bye-elections and was finding its legislative programme increasingly obstructed by the Conservative majority in the House of Lords. Something had to be done to revive electoral support. As Lloyd George said to his brother:

> It is time we did something which appealed straight to the people—it will, I think, help to stop this electoral rot and that is most necessary.

The result was the introduction of a number of major reforms, starting with the Pensions Act 1908. This is not to say, of course, that the important reforms introduced from 1908 onwards were simply the result of cold-blooded, political calculation. On the contrary, both Lloyd George and Churchill were genuine reformers; Lloyd George in particular understood the feelings of ordinary men and women far better than the vast majority of MPs. Nevertheless, the political situation in 1908 provided the trigger for the second and major phase of Liberal reforms, though the form they took, as we shall see, owed much to the determination of Lloyd George and Churchill operating in a climate favourable to social reform. We may now examine the Liberal reforms in some detail.

The Reforms: the Young and the Old

School meals were not an entirely new departure in the early twentieth century, since in times of local distress in the previous century it was not unknown for school children to be provided with $\frac{1}{2}$d or 1d breakfasts or dinners by charitable bodies. After the revelations about the poor quality of some of the Boer War recruits, there was much concern at the state of health of the younger generation. As noted in Chapter VII, the Interdepartmental Committee on Physical Deterioration, 1904, recommended both the provision of school meals and medical inspection in schools. As regards the former, the Committee commented that:

> With scarcely an exception, there was a general consensus of opinion that the time has come when the State should realize the necessity of ensuring adequate nourishment to children in attendance at school; it was said to be the height of cruelty to subject half-starved children to the process of

education, besides being a short-sighted policy, in that the progress of such children is inadequate and disappointing . . .

In 1906 a Labour member introduced a bill for school meals which was supported by the government and passed into law as the Education (Provision of Meals) Act 1906. This act permitted local authorities to levy a halfpenny rate to pay the cost of meals for needy children. Such authorities were not compelled to provide meals, and at first many did not do so. However, it was a beginning, and the usual rule that the acceptance of any form of poor relief led to the loss of the vote was not applied in this case. In 1907 another advance was made with the introduction of school medical inspection. Sir Robert Morant, Permanent Secretary to the Board of Education, was aware that some Liberals were opposed to medical inspection of this kind, and therefore quietly included it, suitably obscured by other provisions, among the clauses of the Education (Administrative Provisions) Act, 1907. Then in 1908 the Children's Act was passed. This was a codifying act so wide in application that it has been termed the 'Children's Charter'. Not only did it bring up to date and generally revise the law relating to children but it also contained valuable new rules relating to child offenders, establishing juvenile courts and setting up the first Borstals as alternatives to prison for young persons. One part of the Act, for example, dealt with juvenile smoking, and laid it down that:

> If any person sells to a person apparently under the age of sixteen any cigarette or cigarette papers, whether for his own use or not, he shall be liable, on summary conviction, in the case of a first offence, to a fine not exceeding two pounds . . .

In the same year something was at last done about old age pensions. The idea was not new. They had been proposed as early as 1878 by Canon William Blackley, and again by Charles Booth whose investigations in London convinced him that much poverty was due to old age. Pensions were also advocated by Joseph Chamberlain, and public interest increased when New Zealand introduced pensions in 1898. In the next year the National Committee of Organized Labour on Old Age Pensions was established as a pressure group. Yet the cost of introducing pensions remained an obstacle. A non-contributory scheme of the kind envisaged by Booth would cost up to £16 m. A contributory scheme, on the other hand, would reduce the cost, but was strongly opposed by the friendly societies, who feared that they would lose contributions to their funds as a result.

There the matter rested in the early 1900s, but by 1906 opinions were changing. The friendly societies were beginning to realize that their funds were being increasingly depleted by sick payments to ageing members, and they were coming round to the view that a non-contributory scheme would take the strain off their funds. The Charity Organization Society was also beginning to accept the principle of old age pensions, though characteristically they favoured a contributory scheme. Finally in 1908 the government introduced and passed the Pensions Act. It brought in a non-contributory scheme for payment of 5s 0d a week to those of 70 years of age or over, with a reduction depending on any wages still being earned. The amount was kept deliberately small and was not intended to replace savings—Churchill referred to the pension as 'a lifebelt', intended to help the poorest. An important aspect of the new scheme was that pensions were to be provided out of national funds, and paid at the post office, so that they escaped the stigma of poor relief payments.

There is little doubt that old age pensions came as a great relief to many elderly people who were too proud to seek help from the poor law authorities. The numbers who applied for them showed, as Lloyd George said, that there was

> a mass of poverty and destitution in the country which is too proud to wear the badge of pauperism and which declines to pin that badge to its children. They would rather suffer from deprivation than do so . . .

The cost in the first full year, 1909–10, was more than eight million pounds. Lord Rosebery, the former Liberal leader, who had by now become much more conservative in outlook, thought the expense of the scheme would be ruinous:

> so prodigal of expenditure that it was likely to undermine the whole fabric of the Empire.

Churchill, however, put the cost in a different perspective in a speech at Nottingham in 1909:

> Nearly eight millions of money are being sent circulating through unusual channels, long frozen by poverty, circulating in the homes of the poor, flowing through the little shops that cater to their needs, cementing again family unions which harsh fate was tearing asunder, uniting the wife to the husband and the parent to the children.

Working Conditions and the Out of Work

Also in 1908 the Liberal government began to introduce legislation to improve working conditions. The first to benefit were the miners, and they secured the Eight-Hour Day which they had been demanding for years, and which was already in operation in at least one coalfield. This was the first time that the length of the working day had ever been fixed for men. In 1912 minimum wages were also to be fixed for the miners, though the government was reluctant to establish national wage scales, leaving wage rates to be negotiated district by district in conformity with local conditions. Meanwhile, shop assistants benefited from the Shops Act, 1911, which made the weekly half-day off compulsory. The trade union Acts should also be mentioned at this point—the Trade Disputes Act, 1906, and the Trade Union Act, 1913, both already described in Chapter XI. Another act, intended to bring relief to sweated workers, especially women workers, was the Trade Boards Act, introduced by Churchill in 1909. This Act tried to protect workers in notoriously sweated trades such as tailoring, paper box making, lace and chain making, by setting up trade boards to determine minimum wages and maximum hours.

There remained the problem of the unemployed, a problem which had been under discussion since the 1880s with little prospect of a solution being found. Chamberlain's Circular in 1886, and the Unemployed Workmen Act, 1905, (see Chapter IX) had attempted to find an answer through the provision of work by local authorities, but both had been unsuccessful. The first step taken by the Liberals to ease unemployment was the Labour Exchanges Act 1909, another Act piloted through Parliament by Churchill, but owing much to William Beveridge, the economist. Labour exchanges had already been tried experimentally under the 1905 Act, but Beveridge argued strongly for a national system of exchanges which would allow the man in casual employment to move quickly from one job to another in his own locality, and be spared the tramping from one factory to another in search of work. He would also be spared looking for work at a distance when there might still be a job going in his own area. According to Beveridge:

> The aim of such a system is not simply the fluidity, but the organized and intelligent fluidity of labour—the enabling of men to go at once where they are wanted, but at the same time the discouraging of movement to places where men are not wanted.

A national system began to operate from 1910, quite distinct from the Poor Law, and under the direction of William Beveridge. No workman or employer was obliged to use the system, but it soon proved of great use where jobs were available.

It could do nothing, of course, where no work was to be had, so that Churchill had next to consider how to help the man or woman faced not with a brief interval between jobs, but with a longer period of unemployment. Any scheme proposed would have to contain safeguards against the malingerer who was simply reluctant to work, and also be on a national basis, like the labour exchanges. Churchill's answer was incorporated into the great National Insurance Act, 1911, as Part II of the Act (Part I was concerned with Health Insurance, to be considered in the next section). The basic principle of the scheme was compulsory insurance against unemployment in trades where unemployment was known to be a common occurrence. If the risk was spread over large numbers, then the contribution by the person insured need be only small. In Churchill's words:

> By sacrifices which are inconceivably small, families can be secured against catastrophes which otherwise would smash them up for ever.

In fact, in order to make the scheme work, both employers and the state had to contribute as well. The contributions were $2\frac{1}{2}$d a week each from the employer and the workman, and approximately $1\frac{2}{3}$d from the government. About $2\frac{1}{4}$ million workers were compulsorily insured in industries which included building, mechanical engineering, and the production of iron. The benefits were kept deliberately small so as to discourage the work-shy, and to encourage saving for a rainy day— 7s 0d a week for a maximum of 15 weeks—not enough to feed, clothe, and pay the rent of a single man, let alone a man with a family. Like old age pensions, the benefits were simply intended to provide some help by (to use Beveridge's words) averaging a man's earnings between good and bad times, or as Churchill put it, pooling his luck with that of his fellow workers.

The administration of the scheme required weekly deductions from the workman's wages which, together with the employer's contribution, were used to purchase stamps to be fixed on a card by the employer. This method was copied from Germany, though not the scheme itself which was something quite new. Unlike Lloyd George's proposals for health insurance, Churchill's scheme went through relatively smoothly, the only point at issue being whether benefit should be paid to men who had been dismissed and had thereby (in the eyes of some) forfeited their right to assistance. Churchill was against this, relying on the mathematical calculations of the scheme to take care of this kind of thing, and remarking that he did not like 'mixing up moralities and mathematics'; but he had to give way on this point. In fact, the proposals proved actuarily sound, and as we shall see in Chapter XV, were expanded enormously between the wars in face of large-scale unemployment. Thus was provided a means of helping the unemployed outside the framework of the Poor Law.

Health Insurance

Part I of the National Insurance Act, 1911 was concerned with a very much wider scheme of insurance against ill-health, and its author was not Churchill, but David Lloyd George. The background to the insurance scheme has already been sketched in—the concern for the health of the nation in the early 1900s, the need for national efficiency which led to school meals and medical inspection, and the realization that much poverty was caused by sickness—and by now even the medical profession was becoming uneasy. Many doctors were already providing medical services on contract to friendly societies, but their terms of contract varied, and they were sometimes poorly paid. Then in 1905 the British Medical Association published a Report on Contract Practice which recommended the setting up of a public medical service for those classes not dependent on the Poor Law—the 'respectable' working classes. In 1908 Lloyd George visited Germany where he was 'tremendously impressed' (his own words) by what he had seen of the German scheme of insurance against sickness. Both Majority and Minority Reports of the Poor Law Commission advocated medical reform, the Minority Report going as far as to argue for the actual prevention of sickness rather than its treatment when it occurred. By 1911 Lloyd George was ready to introduce his Bill.

In accordance with basic Liberal principles he placed great emphasis on the insurance scheme which lay at the root of the reform. The working classes as a whole—that is, everyone earning up to £160 a year—were to be compulsorily insured against ill-health. The weekly contribution to be deducted from wages was to be 4d, while the employer was to pay 3d, and the state 2d ('9d for 4d' as Lloyd George put it, somewhat misleadingly). Provided an insured working man had paid his contributions, he would be entitled to 10s 0d a week when off sick, and free medical care from a doctor chosen from a panel or list of local practioners. The administration of the scheme was placed not in the hands of a government department, but was given to 'approved societies', a term covering friendly societies and insurance companies. In this way the measure conformed to fundamental beliefs among liberals that the individual must remain responsible as far as possible for his own welfare, and must not look to the state for support. At the same time he would be *entitled* to benefit, for he had paid his contributions. The scheme was thus clearly designed to attack national ill-health, and the povery resulting from ill-health, without implementing either the Majority or Minority Reports of the Poor Law Commission, and certainly without the kind of state intervention advocated by the Webbs.

Yet immediately when the Bill was brought in, Lloyd George ran into massive opposition. The trade unions objected to any deductions from wages, while the Webbs opposed the combination of insurance payments and government contribution. Socialists like Keir Hardie attacked the Bill for not getting down to the root causes of poverty, the capitalist system. According to Hardie, it was as if the Liberals were declaring

> We shall not uproot the cause of poverty but will give you a porous plaster to cover the disease which poverty causes.

The *Daily Mail* waged a campaign against the compulsory nature of the Act, and middle-class ladies protested at having to 'lick stamps' for their servants—for the same methods of collecting contributions were to be used as for unemployment insurance. The doctors protested at their scales of payment under the Act, and were as touchy as ever as to their professional independence; they had no wish to appear to be state employees. Perhaps the most serious obstacle was provided by the friendly societies and the great insurance companies, all of whom resented and feared interference with their business. These companies had something like 30 million life policies in operation, and employed 80 000 door to door collectors. Vested interests of this kind needed skilful handling, and Lloyd George had to struggle hard to gain their cooperation, being obliged to sacrifice his earlier proposals for widows' and orphans' benefits in order to avoid competition with the companies' death benefits. Lloyd George defended his Bill passionately, and in a striking speech claimed that he was driving an ambulance waggon to the rescue of the suffering working classes:

> This year, this Season, I have joined the Red Cross. I am in the ambulance corps. I am engaged to drive a waggon through the twistings and turnings of the Parliamentary road. There are men who tell me that I have overloaded that waggon. I have taken three years to pack it carefully. I cannot spare a single parcel, for the suffering is very great. There are those who say my waggon is half-empty. I say it is as much as I can carry. Now there are some who say I am in a great hurry. I *am* rather in a hurry, for I can hear the moanings of the wounded, and I want to carry relief to them in the alleys, the homes where they lie stricken . . .

In the end, Lloyd George's scheme was accepted, and the Bill was passed. According to Dr Jones, Secretary to the Cabinet and afterwards one of Lloyd George's biographers, it was the greatest Act of parliament ever to reach the statute book. Certainly the two insurance schemes were far-reaching in their effect. Lloyd George claimed that something like 15 m people would be insured:

> at any rate against the acute distress which now darkens the homes of the workmen whenever there is sickness and unemployment.

But even Lloyd George did not claim that the Act was a complete remedy, but only that it alleviated 'an immense mass of human suffering'. In fact, Keir Hardie was right in arguing that the health scheme merely treated the illness when it occurred, and failed to do anything positively to improve the health of the working classes. However, it is difficult to see how any larger plan would have stood any chance of acceptance, though Lloyd George hoped to extend the scheme in the course of time. Again, additional benefits were very limited under the Act, and were confined to minor items like a 30s maternity benefit. Only the person insured could claim benefit, not his wife or members of his family, for whom doctor's bills would still have to be paid. Yet it was a most important step forward, and the National Health Service of the present day owes much to it. So did the doctors, particularly those who were just starting to build up their practices, since by joining the Panel they gained an assured income from the capitation fees payable for each 'panel patient' they took on. Many doubled their incomes and gained a noticeable improvement in status.

The Reforms Assessed

There can be no doubt that taken as a whole the Liberal reforms constitute an impressive body of social legislation, the greatest ever passed by any one government up to that time. Nor do the reforms considered so far exhaust the list of Liberal social measures: there were a number of other minor reforms passed, such as the Workmen's Compensation Act, 1906 which improved an earlier Act, and allowed workmen to claim compensation from their employers not only for accidents sustained at work but also for illness or disease resulting from their industrial occupations. The Town and Country Planning Act, 1909 is another minor Act which increased the powers of local authorities to inspect and repair poor quality housing. Lloyd George's famous People's Budget of 1909 proposed to pay the cost of the new pensions scheme by taxes which seemed specially aimed at the rich, increasing income tax and death duties, and imposing a super tax on incomes over £3000. Worst of all from the viewpoint of the upper classes was his proposal to impose special land value duties, including a duty of 20 per cent on the profit made when land changed hands for development. Protests from the House of Lords, who ultimately rejected the Budget, provoked a withering counter-attack on their privileges from Lloyd George:

> Who is responsible for the scheme of things whereby one man is engaged through life in grinding labour, to win a bare and precarious subsistence for himself, and when at the end of his days he claims at the hands of the community he served a poor pension of eightpence a day, he can only get it through a revolution; and another man who does not toil receives every

hour of the day, every hour of the night, whilst he slumbers, more than his neighbour receives in a whole year of toil? Where did the table of that law come from?

This was to place a new emphasis on the ability and duty of the upper classes to pay for social reform. A number of Liberals also supported the idea of a 'national minimum' standard of living, including Churchill who in 1909 talked about wanting to 'spread a net over the abyss' so as to help the very poorest. Understandably, after 1911 the Liberal impetus in the direction of social reform somewhat slackened—the remaining years before the outbreak of war were increasingly occupied with the Irish problem and the suffragette agitation—yet even then there were extensive proposals for land reform, including a new Ministry of Lands and Forests, and a minimum wage for agricultural labourers. The Land Nationalization Society actually claimed the support of 98 members of the House of Commons.

Given this extraordinary concentration on social reform, the problem arises of how to put it into perspective and assess its general significance. What contribution did it make to the eventual setting up of the Welfare State? Did it in fact lay the foundations of the Welfare State, as some historians have asserted? At a first glance, there seems some justification for this point of view, since old age pensions and safeguards against ill-health and unemployment are familiar aspects of the present-day Welfare State. Nevertheless, strong arguments have been directed against this interpretation.

These arguments take two forms. The first is that the range of welfare services provided by the Liberals was far too narrow for any meaningful reference to a Welfare State to be possible. One historian, for example, has argued that the Welfare State of the post-World War II period was intended to assume responsibility for five types of social need—protection against interruption of earnings, health, education, housing, and full employment—and the Liberal reforms fell far short of this. Consequently, the argument runs, any reference to laying the foundations of the Welfare State is anachronistic. The other form of argument (it can also be thought of as an extension of the first form) is that the Liberal reforms in themselves were very limited. For example, old age pensions were quite inadequate in amount, health insurance covered only the insured, not his family, unemployment insurance was for only seven trades, and so on.

These arguments have some force, yet it is clear that both Lloyd George and Churchill thought that their reforms were only a beginning. For example, notes made by Lloyd George for one of his many speeches include the following points:

> Insurance necessarily temporary expedient. At no distant date hope state will acknowledge full responsibility in the matter of making provision for sickness, breakdown, and unemployment.

As early as 1908 Churchill had jotted down proposals for welfare services which included special state industries, a modernized Poor Law, railway amalgamation under state control, and compulsory education to the age of 17. In commenting on the Budget in 1909 he said that it was intended to fortify the homes of the people:

> We ought to be able to set up . . . an unbroken bridge or causeway, as it were, along which the whole body of the people may move with . . . security and safety against hazards and misfortunes.

He was well aware, however, of how much had to be done, and in his election address in 1908 looked forward hopefully to the future:

> Humanity will not be cast down. We are going on—swinging bravely forward along the grand high road—and already behind the distant mountains is the promise of the sun.

It seems therefore that these two Liberals, at least, thought that their reforms were not final solutions to the problem of working-class poverty and insecurity. No historian would argue, of course, that the Liberals *created* the Welfare State before 1914—manifestly they did not—but whether they laid the foundations is still, it is suggested, a matter for debate. One thing which is undeniable is that they did begin a system of pensions and of insurance against sickness and unemployment, however limited the scale might have been; and social services of this kind are fundamental to the Welfare State of the present day.

Another interesting aspect of the liberal reforms is the question of how far they really went in collectivism or state interference on behalf of the masses. For the socialist, with his belief in the public ownership of the means of production, distribution, and exchange, state action was both inevitable and desirable. It is quite clear that the Liberals utterly rejected state intervention of this kind, and considered Liberalism to be completely different in character. As Churchill put it in the speech in 1908 already mentioned:

> Socialism wants to pull down wealth, Liberalism seeks to raise up poverty. . . . Socialism assails the maximum pre-eminence of the individual—Liberalism seeks to build up the minimum standard of the masses.

Yet in practice the Liberal reforms certainly involved much more vigorous action by the state than before. For example, old age pensions were non-contributory, and paid out of a national fund; insurance against sickness was compulsory for all workers, and so was unemployment insurance for 2¼ million; miners' hours were fixed by the state, which also made provision for fixing miners' wages, and the wages in the sweated trades. How could the Liberals claim to be still supporting the cause of individual freedom in the face of all this?

The answer seems to be that they considered they were merely protecting the weakest who were unable to protect themselves. The Liberal measures were intended to give them the freedom which the capitalist system did not allow. Churchill's remarks about spreading a net over the abyss, and about the old age pensions being a lifebelt, are important in this connection. Moreover, the Liberals' belief in self-help can be seen in the importance attached to the insurance principle which was a way of allowing self-help to operate, just as it had always done, through the friendly societies. Further, benefits were kept low in order to encourage savings. A comparison may perhaps be made here with the Benthamites with their acceptance of a cetain degree of state interference in order to allow individualism to function to the greatest extent.

Nevertheless, Liberal thinking of this kind seemed markedly different from Liberalism of the mid-nineteenth century, and it was often termed New Liberalism because of its greater emphasis on collectivism. Historians have disagreed over the nature of New Liberalism. Some see it as a distinctly new development in Liberal thinking, stressing the increasing support for positive state interference from 1909 on. One historian has argued that the Liberal Party was increasingly appealing for support to the working classes throughout the period, offering them what was termed at the time 'progressivism'—social justice, state intervention, and an alliance with the Labour Party. Other historians, however, have taken the opposite point of view, preferring to stress their belief that the Liberal reforms owed much to the two great outsiders, Lloyd George and Winston Churchill, rather than to the Party as a whole. For these historians, the reforms contained little that was new in principle, and radical Liberalism was not a different kind of Liberalism, but only the old Liberalism adapting itself to meet the challenge of the 'condition of England' problem. To do this it had to provide a way forward which was an alternative to socialism, and at the same time recognizable as Liberalism, so that both the middle-class and working-class vote would be retained.

From the point of view of the working classes at the time, the theoretical basis of New Liberalism was of little consequence. Inside Parliament, of course, the Labour Party had no alternative but to accept the reforms in principle, though they objected to some of the details; and the price of their agreement to the contributory nature of the 1911 Act was the introduction of salaries for MPs in the same year. Outside parliament, however, it is hard to gauge the reaction of the average man and woman to all the legislation. Old age pensions were undoubtedly welcomed, but many workpeople disliked the compulsory deductions from wages under the Insurance Act, while free school meals were to be obtained in some places only after a good deal of bureaucratic questioning and prying into the means of the family. It has even been argued that the working classes on the whole were suspicious of all the welfare reforms since they associated such legislation with middle-class interference into their lives. Whether this is true or not, the fact remains that a radical new plan of campaign had been developed to meet the most urgent social needs of the working classes, and to do this outside the Poor Law system. In this way the stigma attached to seeking Poor Law relief was avoided, and the way ahead was to be along the lines laid down by the pre-war Liberal governments, and not by any reorganization of the nineteenth-century Poor Law system.

Chapter XIII
Class, Family and the Quality of Life

The Notion of Class

In this chapter an attempt will be made to discuss three aspects of the development of working class life in the nineteenth century, with particular reference to the pre-war scene. The first is the idea of class. Some observers believe that it was only in Victorian times that working people became aware that they constituted a large social group or class with their own distinctive characteristics, quite different from the middle class. The phrase 'working classes' itself was new in the early nineteenth century, gradually replacing older expressions such as 'the lower orders'. Marx and Engels, of course, were in no doubt as to the existence of the working class, a class engaged in a constant struggle with the capitalist employing class. In the *Communist Manifesto*, written in 1848, this working class was described as the Proletarians or the Proletariat, Engels adding an explanatory note in the 1888 edition that by this was meant

> . . . the class of modern wage-labourers who, having no means of production of their own, are reduced to selling their labour power in order to live.

Thus the idea of a single homogeneous class, brought into existence by industrial capitalism, and lacking all property save their own labour power, is central to the idea of Marxism, together with the concept of class struggle.

Modern Marxist historians have refined and amplified this concept. E. P. Thompson, for example, has sought to show how the working class was created or 'made' in England early in the nineteenth century, while other Marxist historians have tried to demonstrate the existence of class consciousness in typically nineteenth-century towns such as Oldham. Other non-Marxist historians have also attempted to trace the evolution of a working class in the early days of industrialization. Professor Harold Perkin, for example, has claimed that 'it was between 1815 and 1820 that the working class was born'—thus pinpointing its origin with truly remarkable precision. This came about because the landed aristocracy had 'abdicated their responsibility' towards the lower orders—that is, they had abandoned their traditional paternalism towards the working classes. This abdication would have taken effect earlier, but for the fact that patriotism during the Napoleonic Wars delayed the birth of the working class (and indeed, of the middle class also) until after the end of the wars in 1815. As was noted in Chapter V, sectarian religion was a powerful aid here, since according to Professor Perkin, it helped to give the working class a sense of separate identity.

However attractive these theories may appear to be at first sight, it is not easy to see how they work out in practice. There are really three points at issue. The first is, how far did a single working class come into existence before 1850, uniform in mode of life, united in outlook and values? Secondly, did class consciousness increase among working men and women in this period? Thirdly, was there more class conflict between the workers and the other classes at this time?

In answer to the first question, it is hard to see how a single working class can be held to exist when there was such a variety of working-class occupations at the mid-century, and when there was such a wide gap between the skilled and the unskilled. This point was emphasized in Chapter I, and was made again with reference to working-class housing in Chapter II. Even within the same industry there were social divisions between different grades of workers—for example, in the flint glass industry between the head of the chair (the gaffer) and the footmakers, and certainly between gaffers and the labourers who worked on the furnaces at week-ends. In the iron industry, the hierarchy was even more pronounced—first the foremen, then the master rollers, then the puddlers, then the under-rollers and assistant puddlers, and so on down to the general labourers and the boys. W. O. Foster, MP, the owner of large iron works, was reported in 1866 as saying that these gradations (or 'cliques' as he called them) made it difficult to organize working men's clubs because:

> Some receive considerable wages, some little. The high grade of iron workers associate with second and third class tradesmen and do not want to meet in a club the faces they have seen all day.

Not all industries were organized like the iron industry—miners seem to have had much less of a hierarchy—but sub-divisions among the working classes were certainly common. Thus, according to a working-class author writing in 1873:

> Between the artisan and the unskilled labourer a gulf is fixed. While the former resents the spirit in which he believes the followers of genteel occupations look down upon him, he in turn looks down upon the labourer. The artisan creed with regard to the labourer is, that they are an inferior class, and that they should be made to know, and kept in their place.

Another working-class writer observed in 1879 that labourers were grateful to be spoken to 'like as if we was the same flesh and blood as other people', and that

> There is no place in which class distinctions are more sharply defined or, if need be, violently maintained, than in the workshop. Evil would certainly befall any labourer who *acted upon* even a tacit assumption that he was the social equal of the artisan . . .

As for the second question, it is extremely difficult to determine how far class consciousness actually increased in the first half of the century. It seems reasonable to assume that working people in the previous century were aware of their own lowly social position, and that this awareness was intensified among factory workers and others affected by the industrialization of the nineteenth century. Whether this awareness became the kind of self-awareness mixed with hostility towards the middle class which Marxists would identify as class experience or (a wider term) class consciousness, is a debatable matter. Certainly working-class leaders on occasion used aggressive language, particularly during the most militant phase of Chartism, though this was not necessarily a reliable guide to what the masses were thinking. Again, a man suffering from unemployment and near-starvation may speak violently against the employer class, but this is no proof that he is converted to the Marxist brand of class consciousness. In the simplest terms, it may well be that some sections of the working classes had a better understanding of their economic and social role in society by say, 1850 than in 1815, because of their experiences during industrialization; but as it was still only a minority whose lives had been transformed by powered machinery, it would be dangerous to assert that the working classes as a whole had gained a new, class-conscious identity.

The third question, that of the existence of class conflict, is bound up with the question of class consciousness. This is because if class consciousness involves a hostile relationship to another social group (in this case, the middle classes), then actual conflict is likely to result. It may at least be somewhat easier to detect actual happenings which will demonstrate the existence of class conflict than to prove the existence or non-existence of such an elusive concept as class consciousness in some other way.

Yet even here, though a certain amount may be done with the eye of faith, it is difficult to pinpoint sufficient instances of class conflict to show clearly and irrefutably the existence of a class struggle or a class war. It is true that earlier on there seems an increasing middle-class fear of the 'mob'—a word used more and more after the French Revolution instead of the customary 'lower ranks' or 'lower orders'. Again, between 1839 and 1841 the Chartist movement rejected middle-class support and was for a time militantly working class in outlook. But thereafter what might be termed class cooperation was resumed, and by 1849 O'Connor was stressing the common interests of the middle and working classes against the aristocracy—a union of 'mental labour on the one hand and manual labour on the other'.

Further, by the mid-century the middle classes were making a clear distinction between the 'well-disposed' or 'well-affected' section of the working classes, and the so-called *residuum*, or very poor. The former group included the aristocracy of labour and the semi-skilled who shared many of the beliefs of the middle classes—in particular, their faith in individualism, self-help, saving, and so on. Far from showing hostility to this section of the working classes, the middle classes were prepared to accept them as supporters of the new industrial society, and to incorporate them politically by the grant of the vote. The *residuum*, on the other hand, were not considered sufficiently responsible or reliable as yet to be given that privilege, though in time they might be found worthy of it. Middle-class attitudes of this kind, patronizing though they might seem by the standards of today, scarcely denote a state of class conflict.

Nor is class conflict readily to be seen in industrial relationships. Whether the landed aristocracy abandoned paternalism or not, *some* employers, at least, continued to feel some responsibility for their workers up to the mid-century and beyond. This showed not only in their involvement in charitable work in times of depression, as noted in Chapter VI, but also in direct relationships with their workpeople. Apart from such instances as the provision of reading rooms for adult workers or schools for workers' children, works outings were common, and so were dinners given by the employer to celebrate some event in the family such as the coming of age or marriage of an eldest son. Of course, it is possible to explain this kind of thing as a calculated attempt by the employer to keep his workers quiet, but it seems more likely to be the expression of a traditional form of paternalism. Its extent would obviously vary from one district to another, but it was probably strongest in Birmingham and the Black Country. In this region labour relations were generally good and examples are plentiful of cooperation between employer and workmen, principally because of the opportunities for advancement up to the mid-century in what was still in many parts of the region a small-master economy. When in a small firm the employer worked at the same bench as his workmen, and when indeed the workman still had some hope of becoming an employer himself one day, there was rather less scope for the growth of class antagonisms.

All this is not to say, of course, that industrial disputes never occurred—naturally they did, as was seen in Chapter III, and strikes and lock-outs might arouse bitter feelings on both sides. But this is a different matter from class warfare, and it was perfectly possible for the model unions of the mid-century to advocate conciliatory attitudes to employers yet at the same time go on strike when a principle was at stake. What is significant is that such strikes rarely resulted in vindictive or retaliatory action by the employers when the strike was over; it was not unknown for a dinner to be held to restore goodwill. No doubt traditional attitudes of deference on the part of the workmen helped to bring this about. Mid-Victorian society was certainly a deferential society—working-class deference was the counterpart of middle-class paternalism. Together they made it difficult for class conflict to develop as a disruptive force in society.

The tenor of the argument so far then has been that although the working classes (or rather, working-class leaders and important numbers of the working classes) become increasingly aware of their role in an industrial society, this did not lead to anything recognizable as class struggle or class conflict by the mid-century. Some historians, however, find the simple division of society into three classes (upper, middle, and working) far too simple, and basically unhelpful in describing the realities of the situation. In particular, the older classification leaves no room for the important group of clerks, semi-professional men, and aristocrats of labour who, it is argued, really have a place in the social hierarchy between the middle class and the mass of the working classes. Again, is it right to put all members of the working classes into one large category?

Considerations such as these have led one historian to suggest a five-class model of society rather than a three-class model. The first class would then be an upper class, aristocratic, landholding, and exclusive. The second class would be a middle class consisting of industrial and commercial property owners, senior military and professional men. Next would come a middling class, central to the whole social structure, and consisting of young professional men, aristocrats of labour, and other literate people. The fourth and fifth classes would both be working classes—the first being composed of factory workers and domestic industry workers, on the whole non-deferential, prepared to stand up for themselves, and demanding government intervention to secure satisfactory working conditions. The other working class would include agricultural labourers, domestic servants, urban labourers and so on, much more deferential and non-demanding than the other group of workers.

This model is most interesting and raises a number of questions as to how best to categorize working people; here they are spread over three classes—the middling class, and the two separate working classes. Although the middling class is a useful category, for the life-style of a skilled worker might be very similar to that of a lower middle-class clerk, the dividing of the rest of the working classes into two groups of contrasting outlook is more open to question. It would be unprofitable, perhaps, to take this kind of theorizing much further, though enough has been said to indicate the difficulties of describing working people in the first half of the nineteenth century in terms of either a single class or several classes.

So far the discussion has concentrated upon the first half of the century; what of the second half? There seems no reason to suppose that working and living conditions in the period 1850–1914 produced further radical changes in the nature and attitude of the working classes. If it is difficult to detect a naked class struggle produced by industrialization before 1850, it is equally difficult to trace it after 1850, when the strains of industrialization were reduced, and social reform became an accepted obligation for every government. However, some important qualifications must be made to this statement. The first is that as domestic industry declined, industrial workers became more and more used to working in a relatively large work place in an urban environment. Further, as the lot of the unskilled improved, the gap between them and the aristocrats of labour lessened. One labour historian goes as far as to argue that the aristocracy of labour of the mid-century kind had almost disappeared by 1900, that is, there was no longer a group clearly identifiable as being much better off than the semi-skilled and unskilled workers. Whether this is so or not, the gap had certainly narrowed. To these qualifications there must be added the facts that the acquisition of the vote, the spread of education, and the development of new unionism all helped to produce an enhanced class consciousness among the working classes.

Thus it appears that by 1914 there was much more uniformity among the working classes than in the mid-nineteenth century. They were shaped by the same compulsory educational system and read the same popular press, while the overwhelming majority lived the same kind of life in the large industrial towns. From 1900 onwards they had their own political party in parliament. It is little wonder, therefore, that the average working man was more aware of the nature of his class in 1914 than in the previous century. Yet this does not of itself mean that he saw himself drawn into inevitable class conflict with his employer, or the middle class as a whole. On the contrary, to the despair of Keir Hardie, the enemy he enlisted against in 1914 was the working classes of Germany, and not, as Marx would have preferred it, the enemy within the gates—the middle class of his own country.

The Working-Class Family

Older historians used to assume that the nature of the working-class family was drastically altered by the development of modern industrial society. Before industrialization the most common type of family was thought to have been the 'extended family'—that is, a large family group of grandparents, parents, and children, sometimes also including aunts and uncles and even cousins, all living in one household. Somehow, under the impact of industrialization, this large family unit was replaced (or so it was believed) by the modern 'nuclear family' consisting of man and wife, with or without children.

Modern research has revealed no trace of the process by which this transformation took place. Indeed, it now appears that in this country the pre-industrial extended family is something of a myth. Investigations have shown that as far back as numerical records go, the ordinary family in England has usually been a nuclear family. The leading expert in this field has pointed out that the mean household size has remained remarkably constant in England at 4·75 persons per household at all times from the late sixteenth century to the early twentieth century; and such a figure clearly leaves little room for the widespread existence of the large extended family. We may start our enquiry into the working-class family in the nineteenth century, therefore, by assuming that the majority of families (though naturally not all) were nuclear families. Investigations have shown, for example, that the percentage of extended families in Preston in 1851 was only 23 per cent, and in York 21·6 per cent.

If then the typical family unit was that of man and wife and offspring, this did not mean that relatives were not close at hand. Often they were, but clearly this would depend on whether the parents had recently moved into the community, perhaps leaving the grandparents behind in an agricultural village, or whether they themselves had been born in the community. In many areas of domestic industry children would grow up and get married in the area in which they were born. Often the son would follow his father's trade, and would live close to the family house, sometimes even in the same street. The result was that in places where industry was well-established before the nineteenth century it is usual to find a network of related families. For example, a daughter of a nailer would marry a nailer, and move into the house near or next door to her father and mother. In this way working-class families had strong ties with each other from one generation to the next, whole streets being inhabited by a mass of people closely related to each other. In the course of time this could happen even in new industrial towns as newcomers had their families who grew up, married, and settled in the area. This resulted in patterns of family life in the same street which persisted in some working-class areas—for example, in the East End of London—right into the post-World War II era. It also helped to strengthen the sense of working-class unity, and suspicion of strangers (even if they were working-class) from other parts.

The family was also prominent at work. This is obvious enough in agriculture, and in domestic industry where the family was in fact the work unit. For at least the first half of the nineteenth century the father was all-powerful in leading this work team. He was the strongest and most skilled worker until his sons were grown up. The wife and children had to adjust themselves to a routine of his devising, and everything depended on his skill and energy. If he was lazy or a drunkard, the burden of work fell overpoweringly on them. They had to work or they would starve. The mother had a particularly hard life, having to look after the children, cook meals, and clean the house in addition to working in the family workshop. The children also had a hard life, though the boys could look forward to the day when they were old enough to marry, leave home, and become head of a family themselves.

From the twentieth-century standpoint it requires some effort to visualize just how lowly the status of the mother and the children in the family work unit really was. Methods of birth control were rarely used until the end of the nineteenth century, and even then they were usually limited to the middle classes. The working-class wife therefore had no safeguards against repeated pregnancies. Even if she was carrying a child she still had to work at the bench, and once the newly-born baby was weaned it would be looked after by a girl of six or seven (often a sister) so that the mother could get back to work. Such 'nurses' were common enough—today they would be called baby-sitters. In theory, the working-class wife should have had her hours of work restricted by the Workshops Act 1867, but as was noted in Chapter VII, it was not customary to prosecute a man for overworking his wife. A wife had no legal means of extracting housekeeping money from her husband, and sometimes not much of his wages would survive the husband's visit to the pub on his way home on pay day.

Further, the whole of a wife's possessions passed by law to her husband on marriage, and although this was usually of consequence only to the middle-class woman, the law emphasized the subordinate position of all women in a male-dominated society. Not until the Women's Property Act, 1882 could women retain their own property after marriage. It should be added, too, that every husband had the right of reasonable chastisement of his wife, a right which was often exercised. In the middle years of the century, wife sales still continued, though increasingly frowned upon. Thus a newspaper of 1840 contained the following item–

Disgusting Exhibition
On Saturday week, a fellow named Gibbon sold his wife to a country fellow for 2s od. The latter was proud of his purchase, while the woman cried with joy at getting release from her master.

Feminine degradation could scarcely go much further than to be bought and sold like a slave.

The children in domestic industry had a similarly low status. It was sometimes alleged that nailers, for example, always had large families so as to provide plenty of labour for use in the family workshop. There seems little real proof as yet of this assertion, but undoubtedly nailers' children had to work hard. They had no protection from the law in the first half of the century, and were subjected to long hours of work and sometimes to physical ill-treatment. In a sense, they were trapped by their environment; they grew up in a household dominated by the workshop, and knew no other way of life. They suffered from having a mother who of necessity could have little time for them. This is so even when the children had to go to school in the second half of the century. As a woman Inspector of Factories remarked in 1892:

> It is impossible to have a clean house and cooked food without someone to clean and cook, and it is only when the wife is half-time, or has a grown-up daughter, that a decent home can be looked for.

Were family conditions any better when members of the family worked away from home in a factory, or ironworks or down the pit? It seems fair to assume that such families were free at least from the strains inseparable from domestic industry, though even here it was common enough for sons to work in the same work-teams as their fathers. Moreover, in the early cotton factories, as noted in Chapter I, the whole family might work on one mule until the invention of bigger mules broke up the family work unit because of the need for more children on a single mule than any one family could usually supply. Work away from home for the younger members of the family might result in a wider circle of acquaintances, and bring some relief from parental control. As for home circumstances, presumably much would depend on whether the mother stayed at home or went out to work. This aspect has not been investigated on a wide scale as yet, but research suggests, perhaps surprisingly, that only a minority of mothers went out to work. In the Lancashire cotton mills, for example, most women workers appeared to have stayed in the home after marriage. In Preston in 1851 it is estimated that 26 per cent of wives worked, but only 15 per cent of wives with children had a job away from home. The figure seems to have been higher in Oldham and in Northampton, where over one-third of mothers with children aged 11 or under went out to work.

By the end of the nineteenth century, many of the characteristics of the working-class family had undergone a radical change. As compared with the mid-century, domestic industry was no longer the norm, and the family work unit was an increasing rarity. The result was that women who had formerly worked long hours in the family workshop were now released from industrial work. If they did have a job in industry, it would generally be in a factory or workshop where the hours were limited by factory legislation, and where they might even be members of a union. Children were also liberated from industrial work at an early age by the factory and workshop Acts, and had to attend school. Their well-being was increasingly the concern of local welfare services, and as we saw in the last chapter, children's clinics were established, school meals were provided, and medical inspection in schools began, all in the last few years before the coming of World War I. Children of agricultural families also benefited from changes of this kind.

The one person in the working-class family to lose as a result of all this was, of course, the father of the family. Earlier in the century he had indeed played a dominant role, particularly in the family work unit, but also in the industrial family working away from home, and in the agricultural family. Now his authority was considerably diminished, not only over his wife but also over his children. As a parent he had formerly had great authority; but compulsory education and the growth of welfare services compelled him in effect to surrender part of his authority to school teachers, attendance officers, medical officers, and other welfare workers. Further, boys no longer automatically took up their fathers' trades, partly because improved local transport made a wider choice of jobs available, partly because new jobs such as those of tramdriver, electrician, or motor mechanic came into existence. Thus it was the father whose role in the family changed markedly. Though he might still have great influence over the family by reason of his personality, he was no longer the all-powerful figure of former times. His wife and family, on the other hand, certainly lived less restricted and narrow lives by 1914.

The Quality of Life

Was working-class life superior in quality at the beginning of the twentieth century to what it had been say, 50 years previously? The changes in the family just discussed seem to show an improvement for the women and children, at least—but what of the working classes as a whole? This is not such an easy question as it appears at first sight. It is proposed to try to answer it first by reference to the standard of living, and then to consider other, more qualitative aspects of change over the period.

In Chapter VI the standard of living problem was examined for the first half of the nineteenth century, and it was there suggested that the debate for that period remains open. When we come to the second half of the century, there is much less controversy to record. It is generally agreed that real wages improved in the 1850s and 1860s, especially those of the skilled worker. This period is always regarded as the period of the great Victorian boom, and even though efforts have been made recently to suggest the extent of the boom has been exaggerated, it remains true that the period was one of striking prosperity compared with the depression of the early 1840s. This prosperity continued into the early 1870s, but from about 1873 onwards prices began to fall and continued to decline, with recoveries from time to time, until the mid-1890s. This fall in prices so alarmed contemporaries that the period 1873–96 was described as the 'Great Depression', even though production was maintained, and there was only a limited increase in unemployment. What was depressed, in fact, was the high level of prices and profits which had characterized the earlier period. Money wages nationally did not fall as fast as prices, so that real wages actually rose, and rose quite steeply, too, between 1882 and 1890. Thus, a man who kept his job during the Great Depression was better off at the end of the Depression than at the beginning. After 1900 real wages at last began to fall, but without serious loss of the previous gains. About 1905 the fall was checked for a while until another minor fall occurred from about 1908. The figures seem to show a substantial improvement in real wages in the period 1860–1900 of 60 per cent or more for the average urban worker, even allowing for unemployment.

These facts and figures appear to be generally accepted by historians, so that few would dispute the statement that the standard of living rose for the working classes as a whole in the second half of the nineteenth century. However, generalizations about what happened to the working classes nationally over a considerable period of time must always be treated with reserve. The surveys of Booth and Rowntree make it clear that there was still a vast amount of poverty in London and York by 1900, and as was seen in the last chapter, unemployment, sickness and old age remained major social problems which the Liberals sought to tackle. There is the further point that industrial conditions during the Great Depression varied from region to region. In the Black Country, for example, where the iron industry and the mining industry were both in decline, due largely to the exhaustion of mineral resources, the Great Depression was very real, and by no means a 'myth', as one historian has called it. Unemployment was widespread, and there was a great deal of suffering among the working classes, especially the unskilled, who were always the first to be dismissed when trade was bad. In 1880 the headmaster of a board school wrote to the local newspaper about the mounting arrears of school pence. Because of the depression in trade in the Black Country, many parents were unable to pay, and the children were suffering hardships at home:

> . . . the tattered clothes and the attenuated faces of many of the children showing that at their homes there had been a protracted struggle for mere existence . . .

Later in the same year a nailer wrote to the paper asking why the children must suffer so, and claiming that unless something was done for the nailers their condition would be worse than that of the Irish:

> We are half-starved, over head over heels in debt, and with no means of getting out of it.

Even in a prosperous area, the movement of real wages did not necessarily conform to the national pattern; in Sheffield real wages rose to much lower levels than national earnings between 1851 and 1914.

However, these qualifications apart, all the quantitative evidence seems to point to a general rise in the standard of living, and so does the qualitative evidence of improvement in the environment. This was discussed in Chapter VII, and it can hardly be disputed that both living and working conditions had improved substantially by 1914. Educational opportunities were certainly wider, and improvements in transport made social life more varied and enjoyable. Social problems like drunkenness still remained, of course, and diseases like tuberculosis still remained a scourge, but the fall in mortality rates (especially in infant mortality rates) points unmistakably to an overall improvement in material conditions.

Does this mean that the quality of life had actually improved? It is a fair assumption that it had, for the majority, at least. Industrialization and urbanization had produced grave social problems before 1850, but thereafter two influences were at work—on the one hand, the rise in real wages, on the other, the improvement in the working and living environment. Coupled with the latter is the rise in educational standards, and of cultural levels in general. Working-class manners were less brutish, women and children treated with more consideration, cruelty less tolerated, juvenile crime greatly abated since 1850. Working-class life for many had become more civilized in a number of different aspects.

Yet there was still a spectre at the feast—the plight of the poorest in the great cities at the turn of the century who constituted the gravest social problem of the time. It is hard to say precisely just how numerous they were, but if the skilled workers were about 31 per cent of the total occupational structure, and the semi-skilled were 39 per cent, then the unskilled were about 10 per cent—the 'submerged tenth' of the popular press. The standard of living of the typical unskilled labourer was undoubtedly still very low, and may not have improved at all since the 1850s. His diet had always been poor, and much of the cheapest food by 1914 was of a worse quality than before. Factory-made jam, for example, had little fruit in it, and tinned condensed milk was low in fat content. In consequence, malnutrition was rife among the poorest, who could not afford meat, fresh milk, butter and eggs. The standard of living of the very poor in the city slums was therefore as bad as it had ever been, and this remained the greatest social failure of what was otherwise an age of improvement for the working classes.

Section IV

Labour in Peace and War 1914–1945

The First World War provided further opportunities for trade rivals such as the USA and Japan to take over British overseas markets, and after a brief post-war boom, economic gloom settled on the staple industries. The cotton industry suffered from severe foreign competition, the coal industry was now antiquated in its methods of production and also had to compete with oil as a new fuel, the steel industry was similarly technically inefficient, shipbuilding was at a standstill due to war-time over-production and the decline in world trade. The result was heavy unemployment in the staple industries, made worse by world depression following the Wall Street Crash of 1929. In 1932 the government was forced to abandon Free Trade to protect home industry. Meanwhile newer industries such as motor manufacture and the electrical industry supplied mostly the home market and were prospering. Building actually boomed in London and the South-East in the 1930s. Prices fell faster than money wages, so that real wages rose. This strange mixture of expansion and decay, higher real wages and widespread unemployment in the old centres of industry, dissolved away with the outbreak of the Second World War and as the economy was geared increasingly to war production. By the end of the war Britain had made great sacrifices and was almost ruined financially, but was determined to rebuild a fairer economic system without unemployment, and with social security for all.

Chapter XIV
The First World War

Military Service

The greatest impact on the working classes of what was called at the time the Great War was that of service in the armed forces, and in particular, in the Army. There was a good deal of popular support for the war; the announcement at the Foreign Office of the British declaration of hostilities provoked round after round of cheers, and there was a rush to the recruiting offices. A famous poster issued on 7 August 1914 showed Lord Kitchener, Secretary of State for War, pointing his finger straight at the onlooker, with the caption, 'Your King and Country Need You'. Men of all classes responded in their many thousands. In one week alone in September, 1914 about 175 000 volunteered and 750 000 by the end of the month. In all, two and a half million men volunteered for service before conscription was adopted in March 1916. With the coming of conscription, war service was extended beyond the ranks of the volunteers to a large proportion of the entire male population. Those who refused military service on grounds of conscience—the COs, or conscientious objectors—numbered only 16 000, many of whom were middle-class rather than working-class, and by the end of the war about one in three of adult males had undergone military service.

Once in the army, whether as volunteer or conscript, there was every chance that after a brief period of training the working man would find himself in France, and in the trenches. The horrors of life (and death) in the trenches are too well-known to need extended description here. In winter, the trenches were often flooded and this together with the deep mud made movement very difficult. Wounds often turned gangrenous because of the mud and wet. One soldier described the mud as:

> very viscous, very tenacious. It stuck to you, not only your puttees—they were solid mud—but it also stuck to you all over, slowed you down, got into the bottom of your trousers. It wasn't liquid, it wasn't porridge, it was a curious sucking kind of mud because when you got off the track with your load it drew at you, not like a quicksand, but like a real monster which sucked at you.

In summer with the better weather massive attacks or 'big pushes' were mounted, when horror piled on horror. The battle of the Somme in 1916 will serve as a good example of this. Before the battle began, a non-stop barrage of artillery fire was directed on the enemy lines for seven days, using 52 000 tons of ammunition on a front of 25 000 yards. Meanwhile, troops moved up into position. Their morale was high, and one officer described his men on the way to the front:

> They got going without delay; no fuss, no shouting, no running, everything solid and thorough—just like the men themselves. Here and there a boy would wave his hand to me as I shouted good luck to them through my megaphone. And all had a cheery face . . .

On 1 July the British attacked at 7 am, long lines advancing with fixed bayonets, wave after wave, and at walking pace, as if on parade at Aldershot. They were torn to pieces by the German guns. A German officer noted that after a while the British began to advance at the double, but still the slaughter went on.

> The noise of battle became indescribable. The shouting of orders and the shrill British cheers as they charged forward could be heard above the violent and intense fusilade of machine guns and rifles and the bursting bombs, and above the deep thunderings of the artillery and the shell explosions. With all this were mingled the moans and groans of the wounded, the cries for help, and the last screams of death . . .

At the end of the day, the British casualties numbered 57 470 of whom 19 240 had been killed. It was the greatest loss ever suffered by the British army in a single day, before or since. When the battle came to an end in November with very little gain in territory, the total British casualties amounted to 419 654.

The battle of the Somme was only one of the large-scale battles on the Western Front in the First World War. An equally massive attack was launched by the British in 1917—the third Ypres campaign or the battle of Passchendaele—which cost another quarter of a million casualties. Its peculiar horror was that it was fought over territory which rain had made virtually a swamp, even in September. The chances of drowning were therefore added to the customary hazards of mutilation or death resulting from rifles and machine guns, mortar bombs, shells, and (from April 1915 onwards) poison gas. Even between the major battles there was a good deal of minor activity, so that the threat of death was ever present in the trenches, as was the dirt and discomfort, the cramped shelter of the dug-outs, and the grim No Man's Land between the two front lines (defended by barbed wire at times as thick as a man's finger) and strewn with military debris with here and there the rotting corpses of the slain. When the fighting at last came to an end in November 1918 on the Western Front and on the other minor fronts elsewhere, just on three-quarters of a million men from Britain (9 per cent of all men under 45) had been killed, and 1·6 million had been wounded. Of these, the majority were working men, though the casualty rate among middle-class junior officers was also extremely high.

The frightful conditions which the fighting men had to endure in France were kept out of the newspapers so as to avoid a loss of morale, though the daily casualty lists printed in the papers told their own story. So did the hospital trains arriving regularly at Victoria and Charing Cross stations with their loads of gravely wounded men. Emergency hospitals had to be set up in schools and other places. The Great Hall of Birmingham University was so employed, and there is still an inscription in the Entrance Hall of the building which reads–

FROM AUGUST 1914 TO APRIL 1919 THESE BUILDINGS
WERE USED BY THE MILITARY AUTHORITIES AS THE
1st SOUTHERN HOSPITAL. WITHIN THESE
WALLS MEN DIED FOR THEIR COUNTRY.
LET THOSE WHO COME AFTER LIVE IN THE SAME
SERVICE.

Yet incredibly, although morale became low at times on the Western Front, it never broke. There were no mutinies of any consequence in the British armies. The typical Tommy Atkins grumbled, swore, ate his bully beef, drank his tea, and slogged on. It was as if a separate macabre world of suffering and death existed in France, entirely apart from the old civilian life in England. In such circumstances a camaraderie developed, a spirit of brotherhood in the trenches which helped to make tolerable what otherwise could not have been endured. The average soldier hoped that if he got hit, it would not be too severe a wound, but that it would be just enough to get him sent back to England—a 'Blighty one'. As for being killed, it was often said that if a bullet had your name on it, there was nothing you could do about it. So men learned to endure, to suffer, and if need be, to die. They had to help them the music hall songs of the day. 'Tipperary' was written before the war but was revived in 1914 and became a great favourite. Many songs took the form of sentimental ballads such as 'Roses are blooming in Picardy', or 'There's a long, long trail awinding . . .'. Others were adopted as marching songs such as 'Pack up your troubles in your old kitbag', or

Take me back to dear old Blighty
Put me on the train to London Town . . .

In previous wars the bulk of the fighting had always been done by relatively small professional armies, enlarged to some extent by volunteers. In the First World War very large numbers of volunteers and later conscripts increased the size of the British Army to an unprecented degree, and a larger proportion of working men than ever before found themselves in uniform. Consequently the memories of service in the Great War remained strong in working-class families for many years afterwards. Few families escaped death or injury to father or son, uncle or cousin. Disabled men, often short of a leg or an arm, were common enough sights in the streets after the war—sometimes selling matches in the gutter, wearing their campaign medals; while the names of those who had failed to return were recorded on the war memorials erected up and down the country. They remain today as monuments to the sacrifices made in France and elsewhere by the British working man.

The Home Front

At home the economy was increasingly geared to the needs of the armies, so that employment prospects improved for the many different kinds of workers contributing to the war effort. Both the railways and the mines were brought under government control, and the number of munitions factories was greatly increased. By March 1918 the government actually owned 250 mines or quarries, and exercised direct control over about 20 000 workplaces. As volunteers joined the army, the government found themselves faced with a labour shortage. For example, about a fifth of those working in the coal-mining industry joined up in the first year of the war. It therefore became vital to exercise some control over the national work force, and by 1915 recruiting officers were being advised not to accept volunteers in certain occupations, and some skilled men were even brought back from the trenches. Throughout the war unemployment remained at a low figure, and an official Report issued towards the end of the war stated:

> According to the Trade Union percentage of unemployment at the end of June, 1914 it was 2·4 per cent; at the end of July, 1914, 2·8 per cent; in 1918 it has been at the end of June, 0·7 per cent; at the end of July, 0·6 per cent; at the end of August, 0·5 per cent.

The same Report also drew attention to the 'remarkable decline in pauperism':

> Alike in the Metropolis and in the other great urban areas, it had fallen by July 1918 to two-thirds of what it was in July 1914.

The government had somehow to persuade the trade unions to suspend traditional restrictions on production, and in particular to permit the use of unskilled or semi-skilled labour (especially women) to do skilled work. This could often be made possible when the job was broken down into a number of less skilled operations of a mechanical kind. Naturally there was much opposition on the part of the trade unions to this, but by early March, 1915 an agreement had been reached in the engineering industry (the Shells and Fuses Agreement) on this point. Shortly after, a conference at the Treasury produced another agreement (the Treasury Agreement) to the effect that trade unions engaged in war work would voluntarily forgo the right to strike, disputes being referred to arbitration. Growing alarm at the shortage of shells led to the creation of a Ministry of Munitions, and to the passing of the Munitions of War Act in July 1915 which put into statutory form the two agreements just described: strikes and lock-outs in war industries were prohibited, arbitration became compulsory, profits were to be limited, trade union restrictions on production were suspended, and no worker was to leave a job in munitions without a certificate of consent from his employer.

This Act gave the government substantial control over working practices in munitions factories, though the government still lacked information as to the exact numbers remaining in the major occupations. It therefore compiled a National Register of all males and females between the ages of 15 and 65, based on a special census held in August 1915. Clearly this looked very much like clearing the ground for military conscription, which was bitterly opposed by the unions. However, after the failure of the Derby Scheme for voluntary enlistment during the remaining months of 1915 (by the end of the year only 1 150 000 single men of military age out of the 2 179 231 on the National Register had signified willingness to serve) conscription became inevitable. It became law in March 1916 between the ages of 18 and 41, with exemptions for men with special economic or personal responsibilities, conscientious objectors, and men in certain reserved occupations. There was so much friction with the unions over this last category that by December the government permitted the issue of trade cards by the unions themselves which decided who was to have exemption—an extraordinary accession of power by the unions.

Although as we have seen strikes were forbidden by law from 1915 onwards, they took place from time to time—for example, on Clydeside in March 1916, and in Coventry in November 1917. Sometimes the strikes were sufficiently serious for the government to intervene in the interests of maintaining production, as in July 1915 when the miners' demands in South Wales were met after only five days; the government really had no alternative but to get the miners back to work as soon as possible. By 1917 industrial unrest became very marked, due to a number of issues, such as the attempt to introduce dilution (the use of unskilled labour on skilled work) into firms not engaged directly on war work. By now the government was desperate for more recruits and was 'combing out' as many fit men from industry as possible. The trade card scheme was abolished, and a new schedule of protected occupations was issued. By far the greatest cause of unrest, however, was the high cost of food, and a series of Commissions of Enquiries into Industrial Unrest in June 1917 made this quite clear. The Report on conditions in the North East stated that:

> The high prices of staple commodities have undoubtedly laid a severe strain on the majority of the working classes, and in some instances have resulted in hardship and actual starvation. It is no doubt true that in some instances wages have risen to such an extent as to largely compensate for the increased cost of living, but there are workers whose wages have been raised very slightly, if at all, and some whose earnings have actually diminished.

Later on that year the proposals to extend dilution were dropped and the leaving certificates (always detested by working people) were abolished. Nevertheless, the drive to find yet more men for the army went on, with fewer and fewer exemptions from military service being allowed during 1918.

The extent to which the high cost of living affected the standard of living of the working classes during the war would depend on variations in wages and prices from place to place and from year to year. However, on balance it seems that the rise in wages kept up with prices over the war period as a whole, so that the working classes were no worse off in 1918 than they had been in 1914. In the words of the 1918 Report quoted from earlier in this section:

> We have found on the evidence of the budgets of working-class expenditure that in June 1918 the working classes as a whole were in a position to purchase food of substantially the same nutritive value as in June 1914. Indeed, our figures indicate that families of unskilled workmen were slightly better fed at the later date, in spite of the rise in the cost of food.

This improvement also showed itself in the fact that the number of meals provided free by local educational authorities during the war fell by about a half, and the health of school children improved.

> From London it is officially reported after the inspection of all the children entering school, that 'the percentage of children found in a poorly nourished condition is considerably half of the pecentage of 1913'. A similar improvement is shown by the figures furnished by Birmingham, Bolton, Bradford, Bristol, Glasgow, and Nottingham.

Further, wages continued to rise immediately after the war, while prices fell after 1920, so that those in work were better off by some 25 per cent compared with their pre-war situation. It must also be remembered that in spite of long hours worked in war-time factories, the unskilled had far greater opportunities for work in war-time than ever before, and this was particularly true for women workers. Indeed, there was no lack of middle-class complaints about women war workers being able to afford fur coats, and spending money wildly.

Though the working classes were able to benefit in these ways, working-class education and housing suffered set-backs during the war. The shortage of labour was so great that children were tempted to leave school early to go to work, so much so that in the first three years of war some 600 000 children left school before reaching the official school-leaving age. While at school they were taught by elderly teachers, all the younger men having gone to the war. Of curse, some children left early in order to bring money into the home, the principal wage-earner being in the army. As regards housing, the shortage of accommodation at the outbreak of war grew steadily worse, since building was at a standstill. Poor housing conditions were among the grievances revealed by the Enquiries of 1917, though rents were fixed at 1914 levels by the Increase of Rent and Mortgage Interest (War Restrictions) Act, 1916. By 1918 the pre-war shortage of 120 000 houses had increased to 600 000.

Working Women

So far in this chapter great emphasis has been laid on the demands made by the war on manpower, and these demands had a marked effect on the social position of women of both the middle and working classes. Many middle-class women benefited greatly from the shortage of labour, replacing men as clerks in offices of all kinds. The number of women in banks increased greatly, and the total employed in commerce rose during the war from 505 000 to 934 000. In national and local government, including education, the increase was from 262 000 to 460 000. Middle-class women also went into nursing, or joined the newly established women's service organizations such as the Women's Auxiliary Army Corps (WAACs) or the Women's Land Army. For many, these activities meant employment away from home or even living away from home, so that middle-class women began to acquire a new social freedom, and a new independence which made chaperones a thing of the past.

This new freedom had beneficial results for working-class women as well, though paid employment was no novelty for them, of course. What was new for them was the far wider job opportunities which now opened up for them. Employers of sweated labour found it hard to keep workers as women flooded into better-paid occupations. The most striking of these was employment in munitions factories, where the number of women more than quadrupled to nearly a million by 1918. The work was arduous and meant working shifts of 12 hours or more. A Report on the Health of Munition Workers commented that:

> A day begun at 4 or even 3.30 am for work at 6 am, followed by 14 hours in the factory, and another two or two and a half on the journey back may end at 10 or 10.30 pm in a home or lodging where the prevailing degree of overcrowding precludes all possibility of comfortable rest.

Working with high explosive could also result in TNT poisoning which turned the skin yellow. Yet it could mean a starting wage of 30s a week, and by the end of the war £2 a week was common, and an assistant forewoman might earn £3 a week or more. These figures should be compared with a woman's average wage before the war of 11s 7d a week. Other occupations taken over by women included those of bus conductor and railway porter—in fact, transport experienced the biggest relative increase of women workers, from 18 000 in 1914 to 117 000 in 1918. An official report in 1918 commented that:

> The occupations are multifarious, ranging from carrying on a solicitor's business to the work of a bricklayer's labourer . . . the barriers which excluded women in the past, traditional or social as they were, have largely vanished . . .

The one occupation to lose numbers of female workers was that of domestic servant, the number employed declining by about a quarter by 1918, though there were still about 1¼ m in domestic service by then.

Both middle- and working-class women therefore made a massive contribution to the war effort, and it was to have a marked effect on their social standing. Economic independence brought a much greater social independence than ever before. Women smoked in public, visited public houses more openly, went out alone more often. There was even more sexual freedom, and some tolerance shown to the war-time babies fathered by single soldiers departing for the front; but this did not do much to remove the age-old stigma attached to illegitimacy. The illegitimate rate was about 30 per cent higher at the end of the war than at the beginning.

In many ways then the extreme shortage of manpower allowed women to assert a new independence during the war. Naturally it was not entirely new. The middle-class educated woman was beginning to claim more freedom before the war, and was prominent in the suffragette movement. Even the working-class women might be a member of a trade union before 1914. Nevertheless, the war saw striking advances for women of all classes, and an increasing self-confidence which was often commented on. In this connection, Professor Marwick has drawn attention to a notable passage in the *New Statesman* for 23 June 1917 which says of working women:

> They appear more alert, more critical of the conditions under which they work, more ready to make a stand against injustice than their pre-war selves or their prototypes. They have a keener appetite for experience and pleasure and a tendency quite new to their class to protest against wrongs even before they become 'intolerable'.

In these circumstances it became clear that women deserved some recognition for their war services just as much as the men who had fought in the trenches. The male prejudice which had been a great barrier to the grant of the vote before the war was now greatly lessened; and the ending of suffragette agitation with the coming of war also made it easier for the vote to be given without seeming to be yielding to female militancy. No doubt the cause was assisted by the need to do something about extending the male franchise. Although in theory all male householders had the vote before 1914, in practice the law was complicated and subject to a number of qualifications, so that about a third of men were still without the vote. Then again, men serving overseas had lost their residential right to a vote, thus making it even more urgent to review the whole matter. In October 1916 a Speaker's Conference was convened to consider franchise reform, and it reported in January 1917 in favour of 'some measure of woman suffrage'. The problem then presented itself of the age at which women should have the vote. Since women were in the majority in the population, it seemed too great a step to enfranchise all women of 21 and above, as they would then out-number the male voters. Eventually it was decided to give the vote to all men of 21 and over, based on a simple residence qualification, and to all women of 30 and over, provided they or their husbands possessed the minor local government property qualification necessary to vote in local government elections. The Bill incorporating these terms was passed in February 1918 as the Representation of the People Act, 1918.

An important consequence of this Act was the passing of a further Bill to make it illegal for women to be excluded from public posts because of their sex—the Sex Disqualification (Removal) Act, 1919. This Act provided that:

> no person shall be disqualified by sex or marriage from the exercise of any public function or from being appointed to any civil or judicial office or post.

As a result women might now serve on juries or become magistrates, and members of most professions, though they were still unable to become ministers of the Church of England or members of the Stock Exchange. In 1919 the first woman MP—Lady Astor—took her seat in the Commons. The 1919 Act was of much greater importance to middle-class women than to working women, but it was not without indirect importance in demonstrating the increasing freedom of women generally. Thus the First World War brought great gains in improved confidence and status for women of the working classes, though it must not be forgotten that with the return of the men from the trenches and the closing down of the munitions factories, many women found themselves deprived of their jobs.

The Labour Movement

From what was said earlier in the chapter, it is obvious that full employment during the war would be to the benefit of the trade unions. Generally speaking, trade union membership tends to go up when jobs are plentiful, and to decline when there is unemployment, simply because a man is better able to pay his dues when he is working than when he is not. This is born out by the figures:

	TU Member- ship	Percentage Increase
1912	3·416 m	8·8
1913	4·135 m	21·0
1914	4·145 m	—
1915	4·359 m	5·0
1916	4·644 m	6·5
1917	5·499 m	18·3
1918	6·533 m	18·5
1919	7·926 m	21·4
1920	8·347 m	5·3

It has been argued that the rate of increase during the war was no greater than the rise before the war, but it must be remembered that there was an exceptional and non-repeatable rise in 1913, due to the need for working men and women to become members of a friendly society under the Health Insurance Scheme of 1911. The figures above show large increases towards the end of the war and an even larger increase in the first year or so of the peace.

Important as this expansion of membership was—a virtual doubling of numbers between 1914 and 1920—this is not the only indication of the increased importance of the trade union movement. Because of the need for maximum production, the government had to handle the trade unions very carefully, and examples of this have already been given in the form of the Treasury Agreement, the issue of trade cards by the unions, and the abolition of leaving certificates. In 1915 Arthur Henderson, the Secretary of the Labour Party, joined the coalition government as President of the Board of Education, and unofficial adviser on labour matters. In addition, minor positions in the government were given to two other Labour MPs—William Bruce, a miner, who gained an under-secretaryship, and G. H. Roberts, a printer, who became a government whip. When the coalition government was re-constructed by Lloyd George in December 1916, Henderson was promoted to the inner war cabinet, while John Hodge of the steel workers became Minister of Labour, and George Barnes of the engineers became Minister of Pensions. Roberts, Bruce, and another labour MP, James Parker, were also offered minor posts.

For trade unionists to serve in high office in this way was unprecedented, and it must be remembered that the Parliamentary Labour Party was still very small, and before the war their chances of gaining experience of office in the near future appeared remote. It should be stressed that the government had no great need of support from the Labour Party as such. It was trade union cooperation that they needed, and one way of gaining it was to invite Labour MPs to join the government.

This cooperation between the unions and the government had the unexpected result of fostering the development of the shop steward movement. Shop stewards had existed before the war, of course, but their activities had been confined to administrative matters such as the collection of union dues, and negotiations over piece rates. After 1914 trade union leaders worked hand in glove with the government at the highest levels and remote from the shop floor, deciding on nation-wide pay settlements. By the end of the war national pay agreements existed for the railways, coal mining, most sections of the transport industry and certain other industries. Moreover, following recommendations of the Whitley Committee in 1917, joint councils representing both employers and unions were set up in a large number of industries—73 Whitley Councils in all by 1921. In these circumstances, the shop steward on the spot became the obvious person to turn to when disputes arose on the shop floor, for example, over dilution. The importance of the shop steward, aided by a works committee, therefore increased. In some places shop stewards from a number of works formed a Workers Committee, and these committees for a time provided the basis of a national movement which actually held four national conferences. The outlook of the Workers Committees was strongly political and indeed, in theory, revolutionary. Many of the leading shop stewards had been syndicalists, and one interpretation of the movement has it that it was a protest against an increasing regimentation of the workers which was being imposed by the government, employers, and trade unions all working together. It is true that the movement was strongest in the engineering industry, where there was much resentment against the loss of privileges by the skilled worker as dilution was extended. Whatever the correct explanation of the origins of the shop steward movement, it declined as a force after the end of the war, though the shop steward remains in himself an important trade union official today.

To turn to the development of the Labour Party during the war: from what had been said already, it is clear that the war brought an unexpected opportunity for expansion to the Labour Party. Yet at first the Party was divided by the outbreak of war. An important minority strongly disapproved of the diplomatic moves which had led to the coming of war, and were aghast at the prospect of working men of one country killing the working men of another. Among such protesters were Ramsay MacDonald and Philip Snowden. MacDonald resigned from the leadership of the Party, and together with members of the ILP formed the Union of Democratic Control. The UDC depended largely on support from middle-class intellectuals, and advocated that the war should be ended by negotiation, followed by open diplomacy afterwards—an implied rejection of the secret diplomatic commitments which had allegedly caused the war. MacDonald was replaced as Chairman by Arthur Henderson, but the split in the Party was never allowed to grow very wide, and MacDonald did not seek to limit the war effort in any way. As he put it:

> We condemn the policy which has produced the war, we do not obstruct the war effort, but our duty is to secure peace at the earliest possible moment.

MacDonald even kept his seat on the Executive of the Labour Party in his capacity as representative of the ILP, but the word 'pacifist' was used of him (and was used for other supporters of the UDC) and this helped to lose him his parliamentary seat in the 1918 General Election.

In 1917 the March Revolution occurred in Russia, causing a great stir among left-wing political movements throughout the world. The new coalition Prime Minister, Lloyd George, sent Henderson (now a member of the Inner Cabinet, of course) to Russia to strengthen relations with the new Russian government, and on his return Henderson supported the sending of Labour Party representatives to an international socialist congress in Stockholm. This congress was intended to discuss peace terms, and it was anticipated that there would be delegates representing German socialists. Although a special Labour Party conference backed Henderson, the War Cabinet could not; and having been kept waiting outside the room for some time (the 'doormat incident') Henderson was at last invited in, only to be reprimanded by Lloyd George. Henderson thereupon resigned, though his place was taken by George Barnes, and the Labour Party remained part of the coalition government.

This did not end the Labour Party's concern for a just peace settlement, and the Party took the initiative in drawing up a Statement of War Aims which anticipated President Wilson's Fourteen Points, and was made public in January 1918. Labour's War Aims included many of the general principles which were subsequently observed (in theory, at least) in drawing up the peace treaties, with particular support for democratic forms of government:

> Whatever may have been the causes for which the war was begun, the fundamental purpose of the British Labour Movement in supporting the continuance of the struggle is that the world may henceforth be made safe for democracy.

A further development was the drawing up in 1918 of a new constitution for the Labour Party by Henderson, helped by MacDonald and Webb. This constitution provided for a more efficient organization of local Labour Party branches, and encouraged individual membership as well as the corporate membership of the affiliated unions. In addition, this constitution for the first time referred to the socialist objectives of the Party in the famous Clause Four, albeit in somewhat vague terms:

> To secure for the producers by hand or by brain the full fruits of their industry, and the most equitable distribution thereof that may be possible, upon the basis of the common ownership of the means of production and the best obtainable system of popular administration and control of each industry or service.

Finally, in June 1918, the Party produced a new programme of reform, drawn up by Sidney Webb, and entitled *Labour and the New Social Order*. This programme included such reforms as the establishing of a 'national minimum' of living standards for working people, democratic control of industry, and the proper use of surplus wealth for the community.

All this might seem to indicate a strong movement to the left and indeed towards socialism by the Labour Party, but recent research suggests that this is not necessarily so. Once more it must be emphasized that it was the trade unions who were really the senior partners in the Labour Movement, and not the Labour Party. The growth of the unions during the war intensified the growth of class loyalty, and this is by no means the same as belief in socialism. This growth of class consciousness or class loyalty, it has been argued, became a substitute for socialist ideology, so that in spite of Clause Four (put in by Webb to appeal to socialist middle-class supporters) the Labour Party, the political wing of the trade unions, remained very much a 'labour' and not a 'socialist' party. According to this interpretation, therefore, it would be wrong to suppose that the left wing of the Labour Movement was stronger in 1918 than in 1914. If anything, the Labour Movement had turned to the right by 1918, and certainly away from socialism. The unions as a whole might have been collectivist—and state control of the economy during the war encouraged this attitude—but they were not socialist.

This view is certainly supported by the nature of the two Labour governments between the wars, as we shall see in the next chapter. Once the war had ended in November 1918 the Labour Party withdrew from the coalition and stood on its own platform in the December election. No doubt it profited from the Representation of the People Act passed earlier in the year, which greatly extended the working-class vote. Many of the newly enfranchised working men and women could have seen little reason to vote Liberal, since that party continued to be split between the supporters of Lloyd George who remained within the coalition, and the supporters of Asquith, who stayed out. Although the coalition under Lloyd George won a great victory in the election (usually called the 'Coupon Election', from the letter of support sent by Lloyd George and Bonar Law, the Conservative leader, to all coalition candidates), the Labour Party won 57 seats and secured two million votes, as compared with less than half a million votes in the last general election in December 1910. The outlook appeared promising for the Labour Party, particularly as the South Wales miners now abandoned their former Lib–Labism for good, and provided firm support for the Labour Party. Twenty-five of the 57 new Labour MPs were members of the Miners Federation of Great Britain.

Daily Life on the Home Front

In addition to the broad changes at work and in the home which have been discussed, there remain certain effects of the war on the working classes which have still to be considered. Many of these affected the nation as a whole. One consequence of the war, for example, was a tremendous increase in government regulations under the Defence of the Realm Acts of 1914, 1915 and 1917. These acts applied to all classes and covered a multitude of subjects from military court martial of civilians to lighting regulations. Black-out precautions became necessary with the onset of Zeppelin raids, but it was not until the end of 1916 that the black-out was widely enforced. Beatrice Webb recorded in her diary the reactions of herself and her husband to the raid on London on 8 October 1915 in which 38 people were killed and 87 injured:

In another few minutes a long sinuous airship appeared high up in the blue-black sky, lit up faintly by the searchlights. It seemed to come from over the houses just behind us—we thought along Victoria Street—but it was actually passing along the Strand. It moved slowly, seemingly across the river, the shells bursting far below it—then there were two bursts which seemed nearly to hit it and it disappeared—I imagined it bounded upwards. The show was over. It was a gruesome reflection afterwards that while we were being pleasantly excited, men, women and children were being killed and maimed.

Towards the end of the war, Londoners began to take shelter in Underground stations as they were to do again in World War II. Altogether there were 51 raids by Zeppelins, and 57 raids by aeroplanes, killing and injuring 4820. There were additional casualties resulting from coastal attacks by German warships in December 1914 on Hartlepool, Whitby and Scarborough, while Dover suffered cross-channel shelling throughout the war. Altogether civilian casualties amounted to 5611, including 1570 deaths, all but 157 of these being in air raids.

Another danger threatening the home population from 1917 onwards, with the intensification of the German U-boat menace, was the shortage of food. During 1917 shortages of basic foodstuffs became more and more apparent in spite of the voluntary rationing system adopted in February 1917. Towards the end of the year the government produced its own standard quality bread, margarine and tea, and then in April 1918 meat was rationed together with certain other foods. An official publication in July 1917 explained that:

The foods rationed at present are meat, including bacon; fat, including butter, margarine and lard; and sugar. Definite quantities of these are allowed to each person.

In fact, each person was issued with a certain number of coupons (four a week for meat) which had to be handed in when food was purchased. Although for a time the threat to food supplies was acute, the German submarine campaign had been beaten by the end of 1917, and rationing never became severe before the war ended.

As daily life became more regimented and drab, workers naturally looked forward to their leisure hours. The cinema was already becoming the working man's theatre by 1914—there were some 3000 cinemas in existence when war began—and this form of entertainment became much more popular during the war, especially as professional cricket and football were abandoned in 1915. The public house continued to be the working man's club, but by early 1915 fears were being expressed that heavy drinking was impeding war production. Men were spending their time in the pub instead of at the bench. It must be remembered, of course, that in 1914 licencing hours were extraordinarily long—in London from 5.30 am to past midnight, and in other towns from 6 am to 11 pm. Only on Sunday were hours restricted to two hours or so at midday, and four or five in the evening. Lloyd George drew attention in February 1915 to the major cause (as he saw it) of absenteeism:

> It is mostly the lure of the drink. They refuse to work full-time, and when they return, their strength and efficiency are impaired by the way in which they have spent their leisure. Drink is doing us more damage in the War than all the German submarines put together.

Strong measures were taken to combat the drink menace. Beer was weakened, and spirits heavily taxed. King George V took the pledge for the duration. A Central Control Board was set up to regulate licencing hours, district by district, and by 1915 there was a general restriction of hours to two and a half at midday, and three hours in the evening. The closing of London's pubs by 10 pm brought a remarkable decrease in the drunken commotion which had been usual about midnight in the capital. By the end of the war the limiting of drinking hours, always thought to be so uncivilized by continental standards, seems to have done much to reduce drunkenness. The number of convictions for drunken behaviour certainly dropped very markedly: in 1914 the average weekly convictions in England and Wales numbered 3338. By the end of 1918 this figure had been reduced to 449. Thus the needs of war-time production had a considerable and unexpected result for the drinking habits of the working classes.

The Aftermath

It is hard to sum up in a few lines the consequences of the war for the working classes. Perhaps a start can be made by emphasizing again the effect of military service. If a man found himself in uniform, service in France or at sea or in one of the minor theatres of war such as the Middle East would provide a stark and unforgettable experience. The sacrifices of the working classes in the armed forces were unprecedented, and it is worth repeating that the vast majority of names in the casualty lists were those of working men. This is not to gainsay the sacrifices of men of other classes, but the fact remains that the First World War made enormous demands on manpower, and those demands could only be met by the working classes.

For those who stayed at home the situation was different. The long-term effects of the war were to maintain or even improve the working-class standard of living, to give new opportunities to working-class women, to improve the lot of the unskilled and worst-off, and—above all else, perhaps—to strengthen the trade unions in such a way as to brighten the political prospects of the Labour Party. Socially, however, there were no striking changes. The class system remained in all its puzzling complexity, and although there had been comradeship in battle, there was still a social gap between the officer and gentleman and the working man in the ranks. Social reform had been brought to a standstill by the war, and in 1918 it remained to be seen whether Lloyd George's promise of 'Homes Fit for Heroes' would be fulfilled. The working classes could only hope that their sufferings had been worth while. In the meanwhile they mourned their dead, of whom Wilfred Owen (killed in action in 1918) wrote so movingly in his 'Anthem for Doomed Youth':

> What passing bells for those who die as cattle?
> Only the monstrous anger of the guns,
> Only the stuttering rifles' rapid rattle
> Can patter out their hasty orisons.
> No mockeries for them from prayers or bells,
> Nor any voice of mourning save the choirs—
> The shrill, demented choirs of wailing shells;
> And bugles calling for them from sad shires.

Chapter XV
Between the Wars

Economic Change between the Wars

The period between the two World Wars is well-known as one of heavy unemployment, and this has led to misleading ideas about the 20 years as a whole. It may therefore be helpful at the outset to say something about economic change in this period in order that what happened to the working classes may be seen in due perspective.

The major point to be made by way of a start is that the period was one of considerable economic growth and was by no means character-ized by stagnation throughout. Immediately after the war there was a short boom which collapsed by the end of 1920, but though there was little growth in the next few years, by the mid-20s growth was resumed and continued steadily till 1929. During the whole of the 1920s the rates of growth of income, production, and consumer expenditure were very similar to those of the period 1870–1914 (though export growth was very slow) while productivity increased dramatically by over 3 per cent per annum. Between 1929 and 1932 a severe economic depression set in, but income and expenditure rates kept up surprisingly well, and recovery was swift. Growth rates in the 1930s were very similar to those of the 1920s, but exports were still contracting, and productivity increased at a somewhat lower rate. If the 20s and 30s are now taken together, it can be said that their growth rates were very similar to those before the war, save for the two features already noted—that is, the fall in exports, and the increase in productivity. Exports actually contracted by 1·2 per cent between the wars, compared with a 2·7 per cent expansion between 1870 and 1913. Productivity, on the other hand, showed a 2·8 per cent increase from 1920 to 1938, compared with a 0·6 per cent increase from 1870 to 1913, and 0·2 per cent in the 1900s.

Nor can it be shown that Britain was noticeably behind all the other European countries in industrial development during this time. It is true that Britain lagged in output up to 1929, though productivity was about average, but in the 1930s Britain did well when compared with other countries. Between 1929 and 1932 most countries suffered worse from depression than Britain, while only Germany, Norway, and Sweden grew faster than Britain over the period 1929–38. In the shorter period 1929–37 Britain's growth rate of 3·4 per cent (far better than in the 1920s) was surpassed by only Sweden and Denmark. All in all, from 1913 to 1937 Britain's industrial performance was at least average when compared with her European rivals, and industrial production between the wars grew by about 62 per cent.

All this may seem somewhat paradoxical in view of the admitted growth of unemployment which reached unparalleled heights in the early 1930s. How could industrial growth be taking place when at the same time so many were out of work? The answer lies in the structural changes which were occurring within industry. In the simplest possible terms, the old staple industries—textiles, coal mining, iron and steel, mechanical engineering, and shipbuilding—were now in decline as overseas markets were lost to competitors. By 1929 these five industries were responsible for nearly half the insured unemployed; between the wars employment in these industries was reduced by over a million. The situation was made worse, of course, by the rise in productivity referred to earlier. This meant that output per man grew each year at an average rate of 1·2 per cent, thereby reducing the demand for labour. It is no wonder that with the staple industries so depressed, our export trade was so drastically affected. The new industries, on the other hand, were not so dependent on exports. The proportion of exports to total production in these industries rarely exceeded 25 per cent; their growth was based very largely on the home market. Such industries included motor manufacturing, rayon, electrical supply and manufacturing, chemicals, aircraft, aluminium, rubber, food processing, and films. Building must also be grouped with these industries because it too was expanding, even though it was an old and not a new industry. Thus, industry between the wars was undergoing considerable readjustment, with the great industries of the nineteenth century suffering severe problems, while the new industries were forging ahead.

This then is the basic explanation of the strange situation which developed between the wars, and it had momentous consequences for the working classes. Whether they prospered or decayed depended to a large degree upon their trade or occupation. If they worked in the staple industries the likelihood of unemployment and of long spells on the dole was strong; if in one of the newer industries or in building, the chances of keeping a job were far better. Moreover, as we shall see in the next section, prices fell for most of the inter-war period, while money wages stayed reasonably stable. The man who remained in continuous employment therefore found his real wages rising. The result of all this was that industrial workers could be divided very roughly into two groups—those suffering intense economic depression in the staple industries on the North East coast, in Lancashire and Yorkshire, and in South Wales; and those enjoying a moderate prosperity in the Midlands, in London and in the South East—anywhere, in fact, where the newer industries had developed. Since they depended on electrical power rather than coal, they had no need to establish themselves on coalfields. So far as industry was concerned, there were two Englands between the wars—one the England of the depression and of the dole, and one the England of prosperity and regular employment. The two existed side by side, yet geographically apart, and in some ways almost unknown to each other. The social history of the working classes between the wars is necessarily based on this strange and even tragic state of affairs.

The Standard of Living

It will be recalled that in Chapter VI the standard of living of the working classes in the first half of the nineteenth century was discussed, and it was remarked there that it seemed self-evident at first that the standard of living must have declined. Similarly it might appear from the amount of unemployment between the wars that living standards must have fallen. But to take this for granted would be to ignore the improved position of those who stayed in work and profited from the fall in prices, quite apart from improvements in working conditions and in the home environment. When an overall survey is made of living standards, it is possible to argue that a substantial increase in the standard of living of wage earners did in fact take place.

To take money wages first: it has already been mentioned in the previous chapter that in the post-war boom wages continued to rise, and they reached two and a half to three times their pre-war level. They fell back after 1921, remained stable till the early 1930s, declined mildly to 1934, then rose slowly up to 1938, when they were still about double their pre-war figure. Money wages were on the whole lower in the staple industries, due either to short-time working, or, in the case of textiles, the predominance of women workers. Prices by comparison fell from 1920 to 1934, when they then rose slightly.

The results of these movements combined was to produce a marked improvement in real wages throughout the period. In detail, real wages fell slightly after the peak of 1920/1, remained stable until the late 20s, then rose to 1935, thereafter declining very marginally. By 1938, real wages were 30 per cent up on 1913, and real income per head had risen by about 31 per cent. In addition to this, the pre-war Eight-Hours Movement made great gains immediately after the war bringing the average week down from the 53–54 hours pre-war to 48 hours. There was little further reduction in the working day after 1921, but by 1938 most workers were working an hour less a day compared with pre-war, that is, there had been a reduction of about 11 per cent. There is the further point that although holidays with pay were still somewhat exceptional in the 1920s—not more than 3 m workers benefited by them before 1929—in 1938 the Holidays with Pay Act was passed, extending the entitlement to about 11 m workers by June, 1939. This covered about half the manual workers in the country.

Studies of family expenditure have attempted to show how the increase in real income was spent. Perhaps 25 per cent went on more nutritious food (the consumption of potatoes per head declined) while up to 45 per cent was spent on clothing, rent, fuel and light, household equipment, newspapers, tobacco and transport. The 30 per cent remaining went on semi-luxury items such as entertainment and holidays, and on consumer durables such as electrical appliances and radios. Taking account of the rise in prices, consumer expenditure per head rose from £75·38 in 1910–14 to £92·76 in 1933–8—an increase of 23 per cent.

There seems little doubt that there was a significant rise in the standard of living of the wage-earner—and it must be stressed again that all the figures quoted refer to the man or woman continuously in work, and not to the long-term unemployed. The key reason, of course, was the rise in real wages and the decrease in hours, though other factors also played a part. As we shall see later, the health of the nation also improved between the wars. It was very noticeable that recruits in the Second World War were in much better physical condition than their predecessors in 1914–18:

Men examined for Military Service 1917–18 and 1939–46

| Grade | Percentage in each grade | |
	1917–18	1939–46
I	36·0	70
II	22·5	14
III	31·5	7
IV	10·0	9

Thus, the working classes *as a whole* appear to have been better fed, better clothed, and better housed than was the case a generation earlier. The exception must be the army of the unemployed, to whose plight we must now turn.

The Unemployed

How extensive was unemployment between the wars? There is no lack of figures to provide an answer. Generally speaking, unemployment never dropped below the million mark after 1920, and it reached a peak of nearly three million in 1932. This figure represented 23 per cent or nearly a quarter of the population insured against unemployment. To it must be added the out of work who were not covered by the National Insurance Acts, these including agricultural workers, domestic servants, and the self-employed. When these groups are taken into account, the true total of unemployed in September 1932 has been estimated at 3 750 000. After this peak the figures began to fall, but remained at over 20 per cent of the insured population for the following two years. By way of comparison, in times of virtually full employment in the early 1960s the figure for unemployment dropped to about a quarter of a million, some of whom were basically unemployable, others merely short-time unemployed changing from one job to another.

As for the industries and areas concerned, figures again make it very plain that it was the declining staple industries in the great nineteenth-century industrial areas which were hardest hit. Thus, unemployment percentages in these industries are as follows:

	1932	1937
Coal mining	33·9	14·7
Woollen and worsted	20·7	10·2
Cotton	28·5	11·5
Shipbuilding	62·2	23·8
Pig-iron making	43·5	9·8

Some of the worst areas were in South Wales, on Tyneside, and in Durham. Many of these had unemployment rates of over 50 per cent, and some over 70 per cent. In the Bishop Auckland district in South-West Durham, 80 per cent of men in Tow Law were unemployed, and almost 100 per cent in Shildon. These figures may be compared with the average national unemployment rate among the insured of 14·4 per cent for the period 1921–38. In London, where the sight-seeing visitor to the capital would see no obvious signs of unemployment among the population, the percentage unemployed was only 9·8 in 1930 (in the North-East it was 24·5, and in Wales 31·2).

The composition of the host of the unemployed naturally varied from one point in time to another, but certain generalizations may be made. The first is that, as might be expected, the unskilled worker was much more liable to be unemployed than the skilled worker. A survey in 1931 showed that 30·5 per cent of unskilled labourers were out of work, compared with 14·4 per cent of skilled and semi-skilled industrial workers, and only 5–8 per cent of white-collar workers. Secondly, certain groups may be distinguished—the older men, who had little hope of ever getting another job once they were out of work; the highly skilled, who refused to take unskilled work; and the young, who either had never had a job, or had lost their jobs once they were old enough to claim adult wages. Thirdly, there was a group of special significance—the long-term unemployed, that is, those who had been unemployed for more than a year.

This last category provided one of the most melancholy aspects of unemployment between the wars. It was one thing to be unemployed for a matter of weeks or even months, but quite another to suffer unemployment for year after year. Yet in the 1930s the proportion of the unemployed who had been out of work for over a year grew from 16·4 per cent in August 1932 to 25·0 per cent in August 1939. In July 1933 the number of long-term unemployed was as high as 480 000. In West Auckland in 1935 only 100 men out of a 1000 had had work in the preceding seven years. In Crook in 1938, 71 per cent of the men had been unemployed for over five years. In the Rhondda in South Wales, 45 per cent had also been unemployed for more than five years. The contrast between the Rhondda and a relatively prosperous place like Deptford in London was remarkable. In the words of a 1938 Report:

> Only 6 per cent of the Deptford unemployed were long-unemployed, but 63 per cent in the Rhondda. . . . Among every 1000 workers, 4 in Deptford, but 280 in Rhondda have failed to get a job for at least a year . . . The difference between a prosperous and a depressed area is thus not in the neighbourhood of 1 : 7, but 1 : 70. In a depressed community, there are 70 long-unemployed men whereas in a prosperous community there is one.

Faced with an unemployment problem of this size, what could the government do? Nothing on this scale was expected when the war ended, though it was anticipated that there would be some temporary unemployment as soldiers were demobilized and war workers were discharged. To cover this, special 'out-of-work' donations were made available in early 1919 on a non-contributory basis to both ex-service men and former war workers, to tide them over until they had settled in jobs. Thereafter it was hoped that the insurance scheme of 1911 would take care of unemployment, especially after the Unemployment Insurance Act, 1920, had extended the scheme to all workers earning less than £250 p.a. Nevertheless, it soon became clear that the scheme could not cope financially with such large numbers out of work. It had been designed to meet the cost of occasional unemployment of limited numbers out of the contributions paid, and could therefore accommodate cyclical unemployment, but not deep-seated and sustained unemployment. Since it was unthinkable that the unemployed should be sent to the workhouse for relief as soon as they had used up their contributions, they were allowed to continue drawing benefits from contributions they would make in the future. This 'uncovenanted benefit' was defined as being confined to persons who are normally employed in insurable employment and who may be expected by the payment of such contributions in respect of such employment in future to assist in extinguishing the deficit.

This was something of a polite fiction. The plain fact was that the government did not wish to abandon the idea of insurance, but were being forced to improvise to meet exceptional circumstances.

However, 'uncovenanted benefit' was available from 1921 onwards to help insured· workers when their entitlement under the insurance scheme ran out. Those who had no claim at all to insurance payments would still have to seek relief from the Poor Law. The first Labour Government of 1924 failed to offer any solution to the problem of how to finance the unemployed, though it did increase the weekly benefit from 15s to 18s. After 1924 uncovenanted benefit became known as extended benefit. In 1925 the Blanesburgh Committee was appointed to investigate the whole business of the insurance scheme, and in its report in 1927 recommended that standard benefit and extended benefit should be merged, and should be given to anyone with 30 weeks' contributions. Other workers without this number of contributions could draw for the time being so-called 'transitional benefit'. These recommendations came into effect in 1928 as a result of the Unemployment Act, 1927.

In practice, this meant that those drawing transitional benefit were really being given disguised Poor Law relief, though it was paid at the labour exchange as was ordinary benefit. It is not surprising that by 1928 the Insurance Fund was £28 m in debt. Meanwhile, the Poor Relief system proper was also under great strain, for many unemployed who for one reason or another could not claim either form of benefit (or whose rates of benefit were too low) were forced to seek outdoor relief. Whereas there were only 281 000 on outdoor relief at the end of 1918, by June 1922 the figure was 1·24 m, rising to over a million and a half during the coal strike in the second half of 1926. The financial problems of the Poor Law Unions (some actually went bankrupt) led to reform in 1929, when the Boards of Guardians were abolished, and their powers transferred to the County Councils, to be administered through their newly-created Public Assistance Committees. In this way the Majority Report of the Royal Commission of 1909 was implemented, and the old Poor Law Administration came to an end. However, this change in administration made little difference from the point of view of the unemployed, although in 1930 the second Labour Government abolished the requirement that applicants for benefit should be 'genuinely seeking work', which made it easier to obtain transitional benefit. Within two months the numbers receiving this form of benefit sailed up from 140 000 to 300 000.

By 1931 the problem of how to support the mass of unemployed who had exhausted their insurance benefits was still unsolved, and the Unemployment Fund was still seriously in deficit. In the autumn of 1931 the Labour government faced a severe financial crisis (to be discussed at greater length later in this chapter). Although the cabinet was able to agree on major cuts in government expenditure, it split hopelessly on a proposal to cut the dole by 10 per cent. The Labour government therefore resigned, to be replaced by a National coalition government which reduced the dole from 17s (fixed in 1928) to 15s 3d, reduced ordinary benefit to a period of 26 weeks only, and put the administration of transitional benefit into the hands of the Public Assistance Committees, making it subject to a Means Test.

Thus, from late 1931 to 1934, the worst years of the inter-war Depression, the working-class unemployed who were out of work for more than 26 weeks found themselves in the hands of the new Poor Law authorities, and subjected to a searching enquiry into their family income before any further benefit could be paid. Savings, pensions, and income of all members of the family, young and old, were taken into account before the calculation of benefit. Such enquiries were bitterly resented by the many working men who were out of work through no fault of their own. Fathers were humiliated by being made to rely on the earnings of their children, who would sometimes leave home rather than be forced to support their parents. The Means Test remains today the most bitter memory of the 1930s for many of the surviving working classes, and as an enquiry into family income it was not completely abandoned till 1941.

At last in 1934 after 15 years of improvisation, the government passed an Unemployment Act which tried to reorganize the relief of the unemployed on an efficient and financially sound basis. Part I of the Act dealt with the Insurance Scheme, restoring the cuts of 1931 but paying benefit for only 26 weeks as before. Groups of workers not previously covered by the scheme were brought into it, so that with the agricultural workers covered by a separate provision about 14·5 m workers were insured by 1937. The new scheme was to be run by an independent statutory committee, and like the original scheme, it was intended to help workers normally in work. Part II was concerned basically with long-term unemployment, and provided for all who needed help whether because they had exhausted their entitlement to insurance benefit or for any other reason. An Unemployment Assistance Board was set up to operate on a national scale (previously the assistance given by PACs varied from one authority to another), taking over from the PACs some 800 000 on transitional payments, and later on 200 000 receiving poor relief. Its funds were to come directly from the Treasury. The Means Test was retained, but in a less rigorous form. When the UAB began operations in 1935 there was some preliminary confusion as its rates of benefit were discovered to be lower in many cases than the rates previously paid by the PACs. For a time applicants could claim either rate of benefit, whichever was the higher, but by

1937 the new Act was working satisfactorily.

The significance of the 1934 Act is that the government had at last faced directly the need to put the insurance scheme on a viable basis, and to provide separately for serious unemployment. In fact, the new insurance scheme worked well, and accumulated a surplus. The setting up of the UAB had important consequences for the Poor Law, for the relief of the able-bodied unemployed was removed almost entirely from the PACs. There was now little left of the old 1834 Poor Law system. In 1936 only 13 per cent of those relieved were on indoor relief (children, the sick, and the aged), all other classes being given outdoor relief. The workhouse test and even the term 'pauper' had been abolished in 1930. The old idea that the Poor Law should deal with all classes of people needing assistance, but on the basis of deterring the able-bodied from applying, was clearly dead.

However, if the government had at last devised a more efficient way of relieving the unemployed, little was done to solve the problem of unemployment itself. While in other countries it was often the practice to establish public works schemes in order to provide work, comparatively little was done here. This was in spite of the fact that such schemes were advocated by the Liberals, and also by the leading economist of the day, John Maynard Keynes. Both the Labour government and the National government which followed it preferred to adopt highly conservative policies of cutting government expenditure and refraining from any efforts to create employment. This was in accordance with the orthodox Treasury doctrine, described by Winston Churchill in 1929 as the belief that:

> very little additional employment and no permanent additional employment can in fact, and as a general rule, be created by State borrowing and State expenditure.

What little was done was in the 1920s rather than the 1930s. In the period December 1920 to January 1932, the Unemployment Grants Committee spent £69·5 m in helping local authorities with public works, but not more than 60 000 men were employed on such schemes in 1931, when the total unemployed was more than 2·5 m. Thereafter this kind of assistance was suspended. In 1934 four areas were officially designated distressed areas (later re-named 'special areas'), one in Scotland, one in South Wales, and the others in West Cumberland and Tyneside. Some financial aid was given to firms settling in these areas, but again it was on a modest scale. On the whole, therefore, the working classes could not expect very much help from direct government aid to industry between the wars. They, like the government, could only sit out the economic blizzard and hope for better times to come.

234

Life on the Dole

What life was like on the dole necessarily varied from one family to another, depending on the courage and optimism of the head of the family, the provident housekeeping of the mother, and the attitude of the children. The absence of alternative employment in shipbuilding towns or in mining villages scarcely improved the spirits of those who had to live in them. J. B. Priestley visited the North-East in 1933 and described what he saw in Jarrow:

> One out of two shops appeared to be permanently closed. Wherever we went there were men hanging about, not scores of them but hundreds and thousands of them. The whole town looked as if it had entered a perpetual penniless bleak Sabbath. The men wore the drawn masks of prisoners of war.

Jarrow was the town which afterwards became famous for the march of 200 of its unemployed to London in October 1936 to petition the government for work to be provided in the area. Priestley went on to visit other towns, such as Stockton where there were

> . . . grassgrown shipyards and workshops with grimy broken windows, and middle-aged men who look like old men, sucking their empty pipes and staring at nothing, and grey-faced women remembering new clothes and good meals and holidays and fun as if they had once lived in another and better world.

Faced with an environment of this kind, hope could soon give way to despair. Some, of course, moved out of the area altogether, but this was less easy for the family man who had lived in the district all his life and whose skills had been learned in local employment. Most men therefore stayed where they were, and in the meantime passed the time as best they could. In summer, they could go for walks or cycle rides, or work on their allotments, or simply hang about the streets. In winter, there was the problem of keeping warm and saving fuel. Lying in bed late in the morning was a help in this direction, while the warmth in public libraries was free. Cinemas were also warm, when they could be afforded, and so were pubs. The more serious-minded would spend much time reading in the public library, or might attend day or evening classes. Those without the taste for reading would pass the time in other ways, chatting, or listening to the radio, or doing the football pools or putting a few pence on a horse. Life became so dreary that small sums were often spent on entertainment of this kind, particularly on cinema-going, which provided a welcome release from the monotony of having no work to do.

235

In many places clubs were set up for the unemployed, often by local voluntary bodies, though national bodies such as the YMCA and the Salvation Army also played a part. In the course of time a national movement developed under the leadership of the National Council of Social Services. By 1935 there were about 400 clubs in existence, with a membership of a quarter of a million. One such club was visited by Priestley in Blackburn in 1933. It was housed in a building which had previously been a school, but had been condemned. Classes were held in woodwork, and the men could repair their boots and shoes, and knock up cupboards or bookcases for their homes. There were socials and singsongs and table tennis. Some of the younger men did not take the woodwork very seriously at first, but after a time gained some satisfaction from doing at least something with their hands. Some clubs or towns were adopted by towns or counties in more prosperous parts of the country—for example, Jarrow was adopted by Surrey, and Redruth by Bath.

In the end, the impact of unemployment is best seen in its impact on individuals. The young suffered least, perhaps, since many went straight from school onto the dole, and scarcely knew what it was like to be in regular employment. They simply adjusted to a new and dull form of existence, unless they were prepared to leave the district and take the chance of finding work elsewhere. It was different for the older man, especially if he was married with a family. In some cases he might actually be better off on the dole than in a poorly-paid job because the benefits scale took dependents into account; but this was not so generally, and the Means Test was intended to make sure that only the minimum allowance was payable. For most men, unemployment meant an apathetic form of existence, a feeling of uselessness, a loss of personal dignity. Many felt a sense of resentment that through no fault of their own they were deprived of the right to work, and were denied the opportunity of using the skills which gave them their self-respect. It is surprising that so few turned to political remedies for their grievances; only a very small minority gave any support to Moseley's British Union of Fascists (formed 1932), probably rather more being attracted to the Communist Party or to the Communist-led National Unemployed Workers Movement, which organized hunger marches.

It was probably the housewife who suffered most of all. She had to go on cleaning the house, and clothing and feeding the family, whatever happened. Her work went on, and often had to be done on a smaller housekeeping allowance than ever before. Food was given priority, but there was little left over once it had been purchased and the rent paid. Certainly new clothes or household equipment could rarely be bought. Clothes had to be patched, and household breakages had to await replacement indefinitely. Usually the children continued to eat reasonably well, the mother preferring to go without if necessary. The dole certainly prevented anyone from actually starving, but it did not go very far beyond that. The greatest damage inflicted by the dole therefore was not physical, but psychological. The housewife was scarcely responsible for the failure of the economic system to work properly, yet she was condemned to an endless scrimping and saving in an attempt to make both ends meet. Similarly her husband, however willing to do an honest job, simply could not find work. Such deprivation was bound to leave psychological scars.

Social Reform

One of the most important reforms between the wars has already been dealt with—the extended schemes of help to the unemployed, however improvised and inefficient they were until well on into the 1930s. The pre-war health insurance scheme remained basically unchanged between 1918 and 1939, and was run by the approved insurance companies throughout. Although these societies provided a reasonably efficient service, they varied greatly in size and there was some unavoidable duplication of administrative effort. A Royal Commission on National Health Insurance in 1926 recommended some reform of the system, and the Minority Report even advocated that approved societies should no longer be used to administer the scheme; but no government action was taken. The greatest weakness of the scheme from the working man's point of view was that it still provided only a low sickness benefit, and it still excluded all dependents. Further, hospital treatment was not free unless it was given in Poor Law infirmaries. The Local Government Act, 1929, permitted local authorities to take over such infirmaries and run them as municipal hospitals, but few took advantage of this provision. By 1939 just under half of all public hospital services were still provided by Poor Law infirmaries and dispensaries.

In the last chapter it was pointed out that by the end of the First World War the housing problem had grown considerably worse. In spite of the depression of the inter-war years, important progress was made by 1929 in tackling this problem. Soon after the war had ended, Addison's Housing and Town Planning Act, 1919, placed the responsibility for remedying housing shortages firmly on the local authorities, and government housing subsidies were made available to both local councils and to private builders. This Act proved very expensive to the government, who paid £800 for houses costing only £300 a year later, but 213 000 houses were built under this Act. The Conservative government of 1923 passed a further Act, giving a subsidy in aid of private building which resulted in the building of another 438 000 houses. Under the first Labour Government, 1924, Wheatley's Act gave subsidies of £9 per year for 40 years for houses to be let at controlled rents subsidized out of the rates; this Act gave a further boost to council house building—another 520 000 houses were built.

These Acts of the 1920s, together with the boom in private house building of the 1930s, really ended the physical shortage of houses. Large council estates now became a familiar sight. Between the wars local authorities built 1·1 m houses. Private builders built 400 000 houses with public subsidies, and 2·5 m houses without subsidies. All in all, about four million houses were built. Although this might be said to have solved the acute shortage of houses, it did not of itself solve the problem of slum accommodation. The Housing Act, 1930, gave subsidies to local authorities for slum clearance, while the National government in 1933 planned to replace more than a quarter of a million houses, rehousing more than a million people. Much still remained to be done even then, and the Overcrowding Survey of 1936 (undertaken as a result of the Housing Act, 1935) showed severe overcrowding in some industrial areas. In Jarrow, for example, 17·5 per cent of families were overcrowded, and the Infant Mortality figure was high at 114, while by way of contrast in Oxford the comparable figures were 1 per cent and 31. There was also a marked difference between overcrowding in Scotland, where 22·6 per cent of working-class houses were over-crowded, and in England, where the figure was only 3·8 per cent.

Some improvements were also made in the Old Age Pension scheme. In 1919 the weekly payment was raised from 5s to 10s per week. In 1925 an important further act was passed—the Widows, Orphans, and Old Age Contributory Pensions Act. By its provisions the previous old age pensions scheme was merged with the health insurance scheme, so that a pension (to which contibutions were to be made) now became available between the ages of 65 and 70 to all insured workers. There was also a widow and children's benefit built into the scheme. At the age of 70 the previous non-contributory scheme would then operate as before. An important feature of the new arrangement was that there was to be no means test for those contributing under the Act, either between 65 and 70, or after 70. Yet even now, the pension was intended only to supplement savings. Chamberlain, the originator of the new scheme, remarked that:

> It is not the function of any system of state insurance to supersede every other kind of thrift. We rather regard the function of a state scheme as being to provide a basis so substantial that it will encourage people to try and add to it and thus achieve complete independence for themselves . . .

Something must also be said of educational reform. Fisher's Education Act, 1918, proposed important reforms which were intended to widen educational opportunities for the working classes. The school leaving age was fixed at 14 without exception, and the system of part-timers was to end in July 1922. Local authorities were required to organize advanced instruction for older pupils, and day continuation schools were to be set up for school leavers at 14 up to the age of 16, and later to 18. Unfortunately the depression which developed from 1921 onwards and the Geddes economy cuts of 1922 destroyed most of this programme, though the school leaving provisions remained unaffected.

Nevertheless, during the 1920s there was an increasing demand for secondary education for the working classes as a whole, and not merely for the clever minority who were able to gain free places in the secondary schools established under the 1902 Act. Such an idea was very different from the conventional view that all that working-class children needed was a basic, elementary education. The newer view was expressed very forcibly in a Labour Party publication in 1922 entitled *Secondary Education for All*, which attacked the belief that secondary education was needed only by the privileged middle and upper classes:

> The very assumption on which it is based, that all that the child of the worker needs is 'elementary education'—as though the mass of the people, like anthropoid apes, had fewer convolutions in their brains than the rich—is in itself a piece of insolence.

It then went on to demand free secondary education for all, and a raising of the school leaving age first to 15, and then to 16.

When the Hadow Committee issued its Report in 1926, it showed clearly enough the influence of the new attitudes. It recommended that the term 'elementary education' be abandoned, and replaced by 'primary education' for the stage up to 11, and 'secondary education' for the stage from 11 onwards. This second stage should take place either in the county secondary schools (to be renamed grammar schools) or in other secondary schools, to be known as modern schools. The latter type of school might be set up as a separate school, or be formed from the upper forms of existing elementary schools; their curriculum would be less academic than that of the county grammar schools, but would still include a modern language and some science. Such schools were intended to be different from the grammar schools, but equal to them in status:

> It is not an inferior species, and it ought not to be hampered by conditions of accommodation and equipment inferior to those of the schools now described as 'secondary'.

In practice, progress was slow in implementing the Hadow Committee's Report. All depended on the willingness of local authorities to provide new buildings or divide up existing schools, and some authorities proved more energetic and progressive than others. Although the Report suggested that the school leaving age should be raised to 15, this was not done, and few children stayed at school after 14. Further, shortage of money acted as a brake throughout, especially when the financial crisis led to severe cut-backs in government grants for buildings, and also to cuts in teachers' salaries, and to a means test being imposed on parents whose children won places in grammar schools—these places had previously been completely free. Even when the Education Act, 1936, did raise the school leaving age to 15, it was not to take effect till 1 September 1939 and there were many exemptions proposed (the outbreak of war prevented the Act being carried out). Yet in spite of all these set-backs, some real progress was made. Thus, in 1920 only 33 per cent of pupils in the county secondary schools occupied free places; by 1931 the figure had risen to 47 per cent. In that year about 25 per cent of older children were in separate secondary schools or departments, the figure rising to about 64 per cent by the end of 1938. The numbers of secondary schools and of the children in them showed a noteworthy increase:

Year	No. of Sec. Schools	No. of Pupils in Sec. Schools
1913	1027	187 647
1921	1249	362 025
1937	1397	484 676

Though progress was slow, and the new secondary (or senior) schools never gained the respect accorded the older secondary grammar schools, it remains true that a valuable step forward had been taken in providing some form of secondary education for working-class children. It should also be noted that the increase in the number of free places, though no longer entirely free after 1931 except for the poorest families, meant increasing chances for the able working-class boy or girl to attend grammar school and university. Their numbers were very small, but undoubtedly progress was being made, and the scene was set for the major advances in secondary education which were to come after World War II.

It is difficult to assess the effect of social reform between the wars taken as a whole, but government expenditure on social services certainly increased from £101 m in 1913 to £596 m in 1938. When allowance is made for the increase in prices, this means that expenditure had risen by about three times. As was noted earlier, the health of the nation noticeably improved. The death rate which averaged 13·9 in the years 1911–14, dropped to 11·9 for the years 1935–8. Infant mortality rates also declined from 105 in 1910 to 56 in 1940, and deaths among children from tuberculosis, measles, diarrhoea and bronchitis were fewer. Regional variations are once more important here: in 1935 in the South-East the infant mortality rate was only 47, but in Wales it was 63, in Northumberland and Durham 76, and in Scotland 77.

The Extent of Poverty

So far in this chapter it has been suggested that overall the condition of the working classes improved markedly between the wars when judged by the criteria of real wages, working conditions, housing and standards of health. It has also been pointed out that there was a good deal of variation in living standards from one region to another, and especially between the prosperous and the depressed areas. How much real poverty was there as compared with pre-war?

In 1936 Rowntree carried out another survey of poverty in York, and the results provide an interesting comparison with his figures for the same city in his survey of 1899, published in 1901. In the earlier survey, discussed in Chapter IX, he calculated that 27·84 per cent of the total population of York were below the poverty line. In 1936 the comparable figure was 17·7 per cent. As regards primary poverty, or abject poverty, where income was insufficient to meet basic needs, the figures were as follows:

Primary Poverty in York

	Percentage Total Population	Percentage Working Classes
1899	9·91	15·8
1936	3·9	6·8

Clearly there had been a striking improvement. As Rowntree put it:

> In other words, the proportion of the working-class population living in abject poverty has been reduced by more than one half. . . . I suggest that we should probably not be very far wong if we put the standard of living available to the workers in 1936 at about 30 per cent higher than it was in 1899.

Of those who were below the poverty line, three-quarters of the poverty was due to three major causes: low wages, even though in regular work (32·8 per cent); unemployment (28·6 per cent); and old age (14·7 per cent).

Although Rowntree believed that great progress had been made since 1899, the fact remained that 17·7 per cent of the total population, or 31·1 per cent of the working classes, were still suffering from either primary or secondary poverty. There could be no satisfaction, he thought, in the fact that these workers

. . . have incomes so small that it is beyond their means to live even at the stringently economical level adopted as a minimum in this survey, nor in the fact that almost half the children of working-class parents spend their first five years of their lives in poverty and that almost a third of them live below the poverty line for ten years or more.

Other surveys were also carried out between the wars, but it is difficult to make direct comparisons because of the different poverty lines adopted. In Bristol, for example, only 10·7 per cent of the working classes in 1937 were in poverty, and 9·1 per cent in London in 1928. In a survey of Merseyside 1928–32, the figure was 16 per cent, but if adjusted to Rowntree's standard of minimum needs, it would have been 30 per cent. In all the surveys, unemployment was an important cause of poverty, accounting for about a third of all poverty, with inadequate wages as an equally important cause. One way of assessing poverty, of course, was to calculate the nutritional needs of a family, and then see whether the family income was enough to buy sufficient food. Sir John Boyd Orr did this in 1936 and claimed that a half or more of the entire population was under-nourished. His figures were heavily criticized at the time since they made no allowance for regional variations, and were based on a very small sample. His standard of need was also found unacceptable by some authorities. He himself admitted that the annual consumption of food per head had increased in every respect save for flour between 1909–13 and 1934. In a subsequent work he reduced his figure of a half to a third. Another estimate for undernourishment in 1937 was a fifth of the population rather than a third.

With so much disagreement over what constituted an acceptable minimum income, and over nutritional needs, it is hard to draw definite conclusions as to the extent of poverty by 1939. Probably Rowntree's conclusions as to the reduction of the extent of abject poverty, but the continuance of poverty of a general nature for 17·7 per cent of the total population (31·3 per cent of the working classes) will serve as a general guide, with higher figures for the depressed areas, and lower figures for prosperous areas. Thus, there was less grinding poverty than before the First World War, and poverty of all kinds had been considerably reduced, but poverty in itself still remained a serious social problem; and unemployment and low wages were together responsible for more than half of it.

The Labour Movement

Once the war was over, the government was obliged to review the war-time legislation by which the unions had given up some of their basic rights, such as the right to strike. Compulsory arbitration of disputes was accordingly abolished, and by the Restoration of Pre-War

Practices Act, 1919, the various trade practices suspended by the Munitions of War Acts were restored. The Industrial Courts Act established an industrial court for arbitration in industrial disputes, though resort to it was to be voluntary. Thus, the trade unions regained the rights and privileges they had had before the war, and their membership continued to increase in the post-war boom which lasted till mid-1920.

However, post-war prosperity did not bring industrial peace. On the contrary, men coming back from the war expected a better way of life than they had had before, and were not slow in going on strike. Even before the war had ended, there were strikes in the police in London in August, 1918 and again in 1919, while the strike in Liverpool led to violence and the calling in of troops. In September 1919 there was a national railway strike lasting a week. Earlier in the same year the Miners Federation demanded a 30 per cent pay rise, a six-hour day, and nationalization of the mines. The government, which still had overall control of the coal mines, refused these demands, whereupon the Federation decided on a national strike. Lloyd George acted swiftly, appointing a Coal Industry Commission to enquire into wages, hours, and nationalization. On this Commission Labour was well-represented with three members to speak for the mining unions, two economists favourable to Labour, and the socialist historian, R. H. Tawney. One of the interim reports of the Commission declared roundly:

> . . . the present system of ownership and working in the coal industry stands condemned, and some other system must be substituted for it, either nationalization, or a method of unification by national purchase and/or joint control.

Four final reports were issued in June, 1919, one of which was a separate report by the chairman, Sir John Sankey, which recommended nationalization, as did a second report signed by the six miners' supporters; but the remaining two reports opposed it.

Although there was no single majority report supporting nationalization, seven out of the 13 members of the Commission were in favour. Nevertheless Lloyd George took no further action, other than to accept in principle the nationalization of royalties; his largely Conservative coalition government would never have accepted state ownership of the whole industry. All the miners got out of the Sankey Commission was the Coal Act, 1919, which introduced the seven-hour day. It is little wonder that they were left very resentful, the Welsh miners' leader, Vernon Hartshorn MP, declaring that the Commission had been nothing but a bluff, and that the miners had been 'deceived, betrayed, duped'.

The year 1920 saw further industrial strife, including the famous political incident in May when London dockers refused to load a ship, the *Jolly George*, which was intended to convey munitions to Poland to assist that country in her war against the newly-formed Soviet Union. Later in the year the Triple Alliance was revived, and the miners went on strike on 16 October with the backing of the railway men and the transport workers. Once more the government was forced into action, granting the miners a wage increase to last six months. The miners therefore called off their strike after a fortnight. The one notable peaceful settlement of the year was the result of the dockers' unions and their employers taking a wages claim to the Industrial Court. The unions won their case, largely owing to the arguments skilfully presented by the representative of the Transport Workers Federation, Ernest Bevin, thereafter known as 'the dockers' KC'.

In 1921 the coal mines were handed back to their owners by the government, whereupon the owners immediately announced severe wage cuts, which the miners rejected. Once more the Triple Alliance was brought into action, but just before the sympathetic stikes of the transport workers and the railway men were due to take effect the railway men (and later the transport workers) refused to call their men out. Their excuse for this was that in their view the miners had not exhausted the possibilities of negotiation with the owners. The day of their withdrawal, Friday 15 April, became known as Black Friday. The miners felt betrayed, and went on strike alone, but were compelled to accept the wage cuts after a two months' strike. The Triple alliance had failed, and became known derisively as the 'Cripple Alliance'.

By this time the post-war peak of trade union membership of 8·3 m in 1920 had begun to decline—the figure for 1921 slipped down to 6·6 m. Days lost in striking reached new heights in 1921 at 85·87 m days, but this figure also declined thereafter to only 19·85 m days in 1922. The years 1921–2 therefore show an ending of the post-war expansion of the unions, and also of industrial militancy. The depressed state of trade undoubtedly played a part here. However, the trade union movement became better organized with a number of amalgamations among unions, the most important of these being the formation of the Amalgamated Engineering Union in 1920, the Transport and General Workers Union in 1921, Secretary Ernest Bevin, and the Union of General and Municipal Workers in 1924. Another notable advance was the replacement in 1921 of the old Parliamentary Committee of the TUC by a much more powerful General Council which could co-ordinate industrial action as required.

Meanwhile the Labour Party had been quietly making progress, winning 14 bye-elections between 1918 and 1922. In the General Election which followed the resignation of the Lloyd George coalition government in 1922, Labour won 142 seats compared with the Liberals 116, and so became the official Opposition in the House of Commons. The Parliamentary Party could claim to be much more of a national party by now, not only because of the number and geographical spread of the seats, but also because only half of its seats were held by trade union MPs. The Conservatives returned to power under Bonar Law, who was replaced when he retired due to ill-health in 1923 by Stanley Baldwin. After only six months in office Baldwin startled the country (and no doubt his own party) by an unexpected declaration in favour of Protection of the home market as a means of solving unemployment. Another General Election was held, this time in December, 1923. Both the Labour Party and the Liberals were strongly in favour of Free Trade, while the Conservatives were scarcely united over the issue. They lost 88 seats, while the Labour seats increased to 191 and the Liberal seats to 158. Undoubtedly the electorate had voted against Protection and for Free Trade, so that although the Conservatives were still the biggest party in the Commons with 258 seats, they could be outvoted by the two Free Trade Parties. They therefore resigned, and since Labour was the bigger of the two opposition parties, the Liberal leader Asquith offered to support the Labour Party if it should form a government. In this unexpected way, Ramsay MaDonald, who had returned to parliament in 1922 and become leader of the Parliamentary Labour Party, was given the chance to form a Labour government only 24 years after the party had been founded. It was a remarkable opportunity, and one that he could hardly fail to grasp. As he himself said:

> If we shirk our responsibilities now we should inflict upon ourselves the defeat our enemies could not inflict upon us.

So MacDonald formed the first Labour (minority) government in January, 1924. There is a well-known entry in King George V's diary which reads:

> Today 23 years ago dear Grandmama died. I wonder what she would have thought of a Labour Government!

Space does not permit a detailed account of the history of the first Labour government, which in any case would be more appropriate in a political history. Nevertheless, this government was of immense significance for the working classes. For the first time in the history of this country, a party led by working men had gained political power and were able to show their ability to shoulder the responsibilities of government. It is true that the government's record in home affairs proved to be undistinguished—Wheatley's Housing Act was its most important reform—but it could not afford to be adventurous without offending its Liberal supporters. In fact, it was a very moderate government in outlook, with MacDonald being both Prime Minister and Foreign Secretary, and Philip Snowden following highly orthodox financial policies as Chancellor of the Exchequer. In its relations with the trade unions, MacDonald was determined to put the national interests first and when a dock strike took place in January, he was prepared to use troops to move supplies. Ernie Bevin is reputed to have remarked at this:

> I only wish it had been a Tory government in office. We would not have been frightened by *their* threats.

Shortly after, a London tram strike looked as if it might spread to the London Underground, whereupon MacDonald considered using emergency powers to cope with the situation. Luckily for him, the strike was settled without the powers having to be used. It is worth noting in passing that in 1931 MacDonald was to be faced again with a choice between supporting his party interests and acting in the interests of the country as a whole, but with a very different outcome.

In foreign affairs MacDonald had rather more success, chairing the London Conference which accepted the new scheme for German reparations, the Dawes Plan. Yet it was in this sphere that opposition began to mount. MacDonald proposed treaties with Soviet Russia which included a proposal of a loan to Russia. This was unpopular with both Conservative and Liberal parties, and they combined to defeat the government over a relatively trivial matter, the 'Campbell Case'. This case concerned the prosecution of a communist, J. R. Campbell, for sedition, but the prosecution was discontinued for lack of evidence. The Opposition suspected favouritism shown to the accused, and brought the government down over a vote of confidence.

In the election which followed, Labour actually increased their popular vote, but lost a number of seats, ending up with 151 seats in all. The Liberals fared much worse, dropping from 158 seats to 42. The Conservatives romped home with 419 seats, and Baldwin became Prime Minister again. It may be that Labour would have done better if the best-known of all pre-election scares had not occurred—the Zinoviev Letter. This purported to be a secret letter from the President of the Third Communist International in Moscow to the British Communist Party (formed in 1920 from the British Socialist Party and other smaller socialist bodies) which fell into the hands of the Foreign Office and the British Press. It contained lurid instructions on how to spread communism in Britain. For example, one passage ran:

> Armed warfare must be preceded by a struggle against the inclinations to compromise which are embedded among the majority of British workmen, against the idea of evolution and peaceful extermination of capitalism.

The letter goes on to suggest that if communist cells were set up in the army and in the factories, then in the event of war breaking out

> it is possible to paralyse all the military preparations of the bourgeoisie and make a start in turning an imperialist war into a class war.

Whether this letter was genuine, or a forgery designed to frighten off potential Labour voters, is still disputed to the present day. On the whole, it seems unlikely to have done more than lose some votes for Labour, and it is difficult to believe that but for the Zinoviev Letter the Labour Party would have won the election. It did provide some consolation for their defeat, but their record in office could not have made a great impression on the electorate. Nevertheless, the Party had shown that it was fully capable of governing Britain, and the election result more than ever confirmed that Labour and not the Liberals were now the second great political party in the state. The first Labour Government also showed that even if they had a majority in office, the Labour Party was not likely to try to introduce sweeping socialist measures, so that the electorate had little to fear in this respect.

By the middle of the next year trouble loomed again in the mining industry. The return to gold in 1925 at the pre-war parity made coal exports relatively dearer, and the Dawes Plan had allowed German reparations to be paid in coal. Our exports of coal were therefore adversely affected, and the coalmine owners proposed their usual remedy when trade was bad—a cut in wages. The new General Council of the TUC responded very vigorously, calling a meeting on 25 July 1925 of the railway, transport and sailors unions who agreed to stop all movements of coal when the miners went on strike. Thus, the Triple Alliance was suddenly revived, and the government was faced with a real possibility of something like a General Strike. Alarmed at this, Baldwin appointed a commission of enquiry under Sir Herbert Samuel, and granted a temporary subsidy to the employers. The trade unions had scored a considerable victory, and the day on which Baldwin's decisions were announced was henceforth referred to as 'Red Friday'. However, the government immediately began to make extensive preparations in case a General Strike did occur. A private organization, the so-called Organization for the Maintenance of Supplies, was given Government approval. England and Wales were divided into ten regions with a Cabinet minister in charge of each, local committees were appointed, and volunteers were recruited. In contrast to all this, the TUC did nothing, though the Secretary of the Miners Federation, A. J. Cook, rather comically declared that his mother-in-law had been buying an extra tin of salmon when she went shopping for some little time past. More seriously he declared:

> I am going to get a fund, if I can, that will buy grub so that when the

struggle comes we shall have that grub distributed in the homes of our people. I don't care a hang for any government, or army or navy. They can come along with their bayonets. Bayonets don't cut coal.

In March 1926 the Samuel Commission reported, recommending that the subsidy be withdrawn, the coal industry reorganized, and wages reduced, though on a national and not district basis. The working day they considered should remain the same. The Report pleased neither side. The owners wanted district agreements on wages, and a return to the eight-hour day. The miners refused to accept either wage cuts or longer hours—in the words of Cook's slogan, 'Not a penny off the pay, not a minute on the day'. The owners proved equally stubborn, Lord Birkenhead recording his opinion subsequently that:

> it would be possible to say without exaggeration that the miners' leaders were the stupidest men in England if we had not had frequent occasion to meet the owners.

Negotiations continued between the government, the owners, the Industrial Committee of the General Council of the TUC, and the miners. From the miners' point of view, the proposed cuts were very serious—in Durham a reduction of 18s 4d per week, and in South Wales from 78s 0d to 45s 10d—a massive cut of 32s 2d on average. On 30 April the owners issued lock-out notices, so that the pits were closed, and the government declared a state of emergency. The negotiations intensified over the next two days, the General Council taking overall charge of the union side. On 2 May agreement seemed near, when on the evening of that day Baldwin suddenly broke off negotiations with the representatives of the General Council. His grounds for doing this were that notices had already been sent out by the unions for a General Strike, and that certain 'overt acts' had already taken place, including (as he put it) 'gross interference with the freedom of the press'. He thanked the trade unionists for their efforts, but concluded, 'Goodbye. This is the end'.

It was indeed the end. The TU leaders were astonished at his words. The interference with the press was a reference to a refusal by the printers of the *Daily Mail* to set up a leading article rejecting the idea of a general strike as being revolutionary in nature. The General Council repudiated the action of the printers, and went back to 10 Downing Street to resume discussions. But Baldwin had gone to bed, and it became clear that he regarded the talks as having ended. The General Strike began the following day, 3 May 1926.

The General Strike remains perhaps the greatest single incident in the history of the Trade Union movement up to the present day. What were its causes? In one sense it can be argued that Baldwin himself caused it, as it was Baldwin who had broken off the negotiations, mainly over the not very important *Daily Mail* incident. Baldwin, it is claimed, was exhausted by the protracted negotiations, and simply gave way to the demands of the more militant members of the Cabinet such as Churchill and Birkenhead, who were spoiling for a fight. On the other hand, it has been suggested that even if Baldwin had resumed the talks, it would only have postponed the final breach, since the miners were completely against making any concession whatsoever. At a deeper level, a major cause was clearly the inefficiency of the coal industry and the owners' refusal to see any remedy other than wage cuts. The General Council were equally determined to support the miners. This leads on to a further consideration: the TUC saw the whole situation as essentially an industrial dispute in which trade union loyalty had to be shown. In their eyes it was never a political matter, and they tried to use the term 'National Strike' rather than 'General Strike', since the latter term was used by syndicalists to describe the action necessary to bring worker control of the state and overthrow capitalism. Unfortunately for the unions, in spite of their protests to the contrary, the government considered that the strike was a direct challenge to their authority, designed to coerce them into forcing the owners to give in. Baldwin declared that the strike was 'a gross travesty of every democratic principle', and that 'the Cabinet found itself challenged with an alternative Government'. Thus, the General Council were trapped into calling a strike which their opponents could very plausibly represent as an attack on the constitution.

The General Strike lasted nine days, during which time the government's carefully prepared plans worked very well. Considering the complete lack of preparation before the strike by the unions, their local committees or councils of action proved very effective. Not all unions were called out, but only unions in key industries, including workers in transport, iron and steel, electricity and gas, building, printing, and the press. On the whole, the strike was peaceful, though clashes did take place between middle-class volunteers and pickets, and between strikers and the police. There resulted 3 149 prosecutions for incitement to sedition and for breaches of the peace in England and Wales. Nevertheless, Baldwin tried hard to avoid provoking violence, and succeeded in keeping Winston Churchill, the most aggressive member of the Cabinet, out of harm's way by putting him in charge of the government's official newsheet, the *British Gazette*. At the same time Baldwin refused to re-open negotiations until the strike was called off, and maintained throughout that the strike was 'a challenge to Parliament, and the road to anarchy and ruin'. To this the unions could only reply that the strike was purely industrial in nature, and not political at all. The logic of the situation, however, was somewhat against them.

Meanwhile Sir Herbert Samuel had returned from abroad and in his private capacity began talks with the TUC leaders. By 11 May a Memorandum was drawn up containing possible terms for settlement of the dispute. Because the General Council could see that the government had no intention of giving in, they grasped eagerly at the chance of ending the strike, even though the government was not committed to the Samuel Memorandum in any way. The General Council therefore formally accepted the Memorandum, in spite of protests from the miners, and on the following day, 12 May, called off the strike. Arthur Pugh, of the Iron and Steel Trades Federation, headed a deputation of the General Council to the Prime Minister, explaining that:

> we are here today, sir, to say that this general strike is to be terminated forthwith in order that negotiations may proceed . . .

It was in fact a defeat for the unions, though the strike was still solid, and most of the strikers astonished that it had been called off so soon.

The immediate consequence of the General Strike was that when the strikers returned to work on 13 May, many were dismissed on the spot, and it seemed momentarily that the strike might break out all over again. Baldwin was forced to warn employers against victimization. However, the miners still stayed out and Baldwin's proposals for a new wages agreement were rejected by both sides. In June the government passed Bills suspending the 7-hour day, and encouraging amalgamations of mining companies. By the end of the year the miners had to give in; their families had suffered greatly during the strike. The owners were triumphant. In most cases they were able to pay reduced wages based on district agreements, and to impose the 8-hour day. Some of the miners' leaders were victimized, and were barred from employment anywhere in the industry. In 1927 the government passed the Trade Disputes and Trade Union Act, banning sympathetic strikes, substituting 'contracting-in' for the 'contracting-out' of the 1913 Act (the Labour Party's income from the political levy was thereby reduced by over a quarter), forbidding civil servants to join trade unions or associations connected with the TUC and redefining the law so as to make legal picketing more difficult. The Act was regarded by the Labour Movement as a mean-spirited act of revenge, and insulting to moderate trade union leadership. It was repealed by the post-war Labour Government in 1946.

The General Strike therefore proved to be a disastrous episode in the history of the trade unions, and for the rest of the inter-war period the trade union movement made only limited progress. Membership was already dropping before 1926, and dropped again in 1927 when it was 4·9 m compared with 5·2 m in 1926; but during the depressed years of the early 30s it dropped further to only 4·4 m in 1933. Thereafter the figures improved, reaching 6·3 m in 1939. However, the movement gained from the moderate leadership in this period of the secretary of the TUC, Walter Citrine, and of Ernest Bevin, the Secretary of the largest union, the Transport and General Workers Union. One noteworthy aspect of trade union history after 1926 was the reduction in the number of days lost in striking. This is sometimes thought to be the consequence of an increased reluctance to go on strike, although another explanation is that there were fewer national (as opposed to merely local) stoppages after 1926 than before, and none at all after 1932. Whatever the reason, during the period 1927–39 the average annual loss of working days was only just over 3 m as compared with 28 m days as an annual average for 1919–25.

It is sometimes said that the Labour Party actually profited from the General Strike in that the trade unions now realized that political action rather than industrial action was the key to the future. Certainly the Labour Party appears not to have suffered any immediate loss of prestige as a result of the strike, and leaders of the Party were careful to leave the management of the strike to the General Council. Ramsay MacDonald actually disapproved of general strikes, and wrote afterwards that:

> The General Strike is a weapon that cannot be wielded for industrial purposes. It is clumsy and ineffectual . . .

In 1929 the Labour Party was given another opportunity of achieving political success in contrast to the industrial failure of the TUs in 1926. The General Election of 1929 left Labour as the largest party of all with 288 seats, the Conservatives winning 260, and the Liberals 59. Ramsay MacDonald thereupon formed the second Labour Government, again with the voting support in the Commons of the Liberals.

Unfortunately for the Labour Party, this second period of office (which again will not be described in detail) ended in catastrophe—the utter collapse of the government. Although there were some minor successes in foreign affairs, little was achieved at home, social reforms being limited to a Coal Mines Act, which reduced the shift to seven and a half hours, and to another housing act in the same year. Much worse than this was the government's failure to reduce unemployment, which grew worse as world depression followed the Wall Street crash in America in 1929. By December 1930 it had reached 2·5 million. Jimmy Thomas, who as Lord Privy Seal had been put in charge of the problem of unemployment, could provide no solution. The one member of the government whose plans for economic reform might have proved effective, Oswald Moseley, resigned when his suggestions were rejected. In August 1931 a government financial crisis developed when the May Committee report estimated that by April 1932 there would be a deficit of £120 m. It recommended increased taxation and cuts in government spending. A run on gold began. The Cabinet met repeatedly to try to decide on the necessary taxes and economies, at the same time seeking loans from abroad. Finally it became clear that the

New York bankers would provide loans only if the government made substantial economies, including a cut of 10 per cent in the dole. On this issue the Cabinet could reach no agreement, 11 supporting the cut in the dole, and nine opposing it. Ramsay MacDonald had no alternative but to submit the resignation of his cabinet to the King. MacDonald wrote bitterly in his diary of his last meeting with his cabinet:

> Consternation when I reported, but in the meantime news of terrible run on Bank. It was plain that I should be left almost alone with Snowden, Thomas, Sankey. 'Finis' is being written. They chose the easy path of irresponsibility & leave the burden to others. Henderson I knew, but as regards some others, I have once more experienced weak human nature.

In this way, the second Labour government came to an ignoble end.

Worse was to follow. The King, supported by Baldwin and Samuel, prevailed upon MacDonald to form a new National coalition government to see the country through the emergency. Only three of his former colleagues were prepared to join the new government—the three whom he thought would stand by him, Snowden, Thomas, and Sankey. Baldwin became a member of the new government on behalf of the Conservatives, and Samuel for the Liberals. The Labour Party as a whole refused to give their support. The National Government introduced the cuts (including the 10 per cent cut in the dole) and on 21 September abandoned the gold standard. Gradually the crisis eased, and in October a general election was held in which the National Government offered itself for re-election, asking for 'a doctor's mandate' to cure the country's financial ills. It was supported by a tiny group still loyal to MacDonald, by the Conservatives, and by the Liberals with the exception of the Lloyd George family group. The Labour Party alone opposed it. The National Government swept the board, winning 556 seats. The total Labour seats dropped dramatically from 288 to 46. It was a devastating defeat.

Thus, not only did the second Labour Government collapse, but its leader had apparently deserted his party, and Labour had suffered a shameful defeat. It is understandable that the Labour Party should have expelled Ramsay MacDonald, who remained Prime Minister without a party till his retirement in 1935. From their point of view, he was a traitor—Attlee subsequently termed his action 'the greatest political betrayal in our annals'. Not only had he supported the cut in the dole, but he had clung to office, and after 1932 when the Liberals withdrew from the government he was Prime Minister of what was virtually a Conservative administration. It was freely alleged that he had actually plotted the downfall of the government, or, if he had not gone quite as far as that, he had been only too glad to take advantage of the crisis to leave his Labour colleagues. Thus Sidney Webb wrote in a private letter in mid-September:

> But we have reason to believe that J.R.M. has had the idea of a 'National Govt' in his mind for some months at least. Underlying everything, there is the fact that he has come to dislike almost every section of the Labour Party, for one or other reason.

In fact, research has shown that MacDonald acted genuinely and sincerely in putting the needs of the country (as he thought) before his party. Without the economy cuts he was convinced that the foreign loans would not be forthcoming, and the country would be ruined, bringing disaster to employed and unemployed alike. The unemployed therefore had to accept the 10 per cent cut until the emergency passed. Once it was over, MacDonald expected to go back to the Labour Party as Henderson had done in 1918, and he did not anticipate the holding of a general election, and a further spell in office. However, his failure to consult the Party and explain his views told against him, and for the rest of his lifetime (he died in 1937) and for many years afterwards his name was hated in the Labour Party, in spite of his great services to the Party earlier on.

In the General Election of 1935 the National Government, now led by Baldwin, won a comfortable victory, but the Labour seats improved to 154, and this was the position when war came in 1939. The second Labour Government had indeed been a great disappointment for the Labour Party, but when the whole inter-war period is brought under review, then it can be said that great progress had been made. By 1939 the Labour Party had certainly replaced the Liberals as one of the two great political parties, something that could hardly have been predicted with any confidence in 1918. It is true that it had failed to produce any sweeping measures of socialist reform, but that in itself was perhaps one cause of its greatly increased electoral support. It had shown itself to be an essentially democratic, non-revolutionary party of moderate reform and as such gained supporters from the middle-class sectors of the electorate as well as the working classes. Ironically enough, the man who probably did more than any other leader to achieve this result was MacDonald, who in seeking to put the interests of the country before those of party, found himself regarded as a traitor to the working classes.

Leisure Interests

In spite of the shadows cast by persistent unemployment, the inter-war years saw a notable increase in leisure-time activities. Not only was there more leisure-time available after working hours and on Saturdays, but the increase in the standard of living allowed a greater variety of interests to develop. Pre-war patterns of leisure continued, of course. The pub was still an important social centre for the working man, and still the meeting place for societies such as the Foresters and the Odd Fellows. It was also the venue for domino players, while darts became more popular. The war-time restrictions on opening hours continued into peace-time, however, and drunkenness became much less of a problem than it had been pre-war. In the 1930s the consumption of beer actually fell. The other great interest of the working classes, professional sport, grew further in importance. In 1923 King George V presented the Cup at Wembley, and leading footballers like Alex James and Dixie Dean became known nationally, though their wages were much less than the earnings of football stars of the present day, and much nearer those of the skilled workman. Cycling continued to be very popular, though touring cyclists had to put up with an increasing volume of motor traffic.

To these familiar forms of working-class leisure activity there were added three new kinds of entertainment and pleasure, all of them based on technological advance. Wireless communication had been used during the war, and in 1922 the British Broadcasting Company was established. In 1926 a royal charter was granted to a new organization, the British Broadcasting Corporation. The early wirelesses, or radios as they began to be called by the 1930s, were often built from kits by enthusiasts, at first with headphones, later with separate speakers, and finally with speakers built into the set. Aerials were elaborate affairs in the early 20s. The *Radio Times* gave advice in its first issue of 28 September, 1923 as to the best kind of aerial the listener could erect:

> The deciding factor in this case is height, and we will take as a standard a single wire aerial 40 ft high and 60 ft long with the lead in the ground floor.

The programmes were often very dull from the working-class point of view, but news programmes had a universal appeal, and in the 30s there was late night dance music from London hotels, Saturday night variety programmes, and comedy shows such as ITMA with Tommy Handley (It's That Man Again) which began a 10-year run in July 1939. By 1939 nine million radio licences had been issued, and radios were to be found in nine out of 10 homes. In this way a revolution in home entertainment occurred to be eclipsed only after World War II by television, which had commenced transmission in 1936, but existed on only a tiny scale when war began.

The second major technological advance was the advent of the talking picture in 1927. Motion pictures were not new of course in 1918, and the cinema became increasingly popular in the early twenties, the films being given a piano accompaniment, or even a small orchestra in the London cinemas. With Al Jolson in *The Jazz Singer* in 1927, a new era began. By the 1930s cinema-going had become a habit with vast numbers of the working classes. This was the period in which chains of Gaumont and Odeon cinemas were built, and three hours' entertainment in warm and relatively luxurious surroundings could be purchased for less than a shilling in the cheapest seats. The attendance figures are quite staggering: by 1937 some 20 m visited the cinema weekly, of whom a quarter went at least twice a week. The fare provided was very different from that of the present day, and included musicals, westerns, epic dramas, comedies, gangster and prison films, and Walt Disney cartoons. It was the classic age of the Hollywood dream factory, portraying ways of life utterly remote from that of the British working man and woman, yet a source of cheap enjoyment for millions. The influence of the films was held to be very wide. According to the *New Survey of London Life and Labour* in 1934:

> Girls copy the fashions of their favourite film star. At the time of writing, girls in all classes of society wear 'Garbo' coats and wave their hair *à la* Norma Shearer, or Lilian Harvey. It is impossible to measure the effect that films must have on the outlook and habits of the people. . . . Certainly today the cinema is *par excellence* the people's amusement.

This passage may actually exaggerate the influence of the cinema on feminine fashion and on the 'outlook and habits of the people'—fears that American accents would spread proved quite unfounded—but nevertheless the cinema in the 1930s was the supreme example of working-class mass entertainment.

The third technological advance was the development of the cheap motor car. Before the war the motor car was only for the well-to-do, and something of a rich man's toy. After the war mass production increased the number of cars registered from fewer than 200 000 in 1920 to nearly 2 million in 1939. New models included the famous Baby Austin, the snub-nosed Morris Cowley, and the original Ford Popular selling at about £100. However, car ownership was still too expensive for the vast majority of the working classes, though many working-class men owned motor bikes, and sometimes motor cycle combinations. Motor transport also improved greatly, not only in speedier and more comfortable motor buses but also in the form of the open coaches known as charabancs. Both buses and charabancs became familiar means of transport to the working classes, the charabancs and later the more modern enclosed motor coach were much used for excursions.

Other leisure activities outside the home still included going to church or chapel, but attendance continued to decline between the wars. Weekday entertainments were extended by the beginning of greyhound racing on modern tracks in 1926, and by dirt-track racing, a new sport made possible by the development of the motor cycle. An increased emphasis on outdoor pursuits and the enjoyment of the countryside made walking in the country more popular for town dwellers—'hiking' was the new name for it. There was even a popular song about it:

I'm happy when I'm hiking
Pack upon my back
I'm happy when I'm hiking
Off the beaten track . . .

Those with less of a taste for fresh air thronged the dance hall, or palais de danse, which was also very popular as a means of meeting the opposite sex. Day excursions by rail to the seaside still attracted many, and holidays away from home increased. The Youth Hostels Association was founded in 1930, while the first Butlin's holiday camp was opened at Skegness in 1937.

At home, more and more newspapers were read, the Labour *Daily Herald* reaching a circulation of two million. The *Daily Mirror* became a tabloid in 1934, but its headlines and language were modest by the standards of today. The greatest innovation in the home, as we have seen, was undoubtedly the radio, but by the 1930s a new form of betting came into the home in the form of football pools. They had 10 m clients by 1938. Cigarette smoking increased and pipe smoking declined. Life in the trenches seemed to have spread the smoking of cigarettes, and between the wars some eight out of 10 men smoked cigarettes, and four out of 10 women.

This sketch of leisure activities between the wars is by no means exhaustive. Nevertheless, enough has been said to show that leisure assumed a new dimension in these two decades, and this in spite of the poverty-stricken enforced leisure of life on the dole. A genuine break with Victorian attitudes had been achieved, and as the opportunities for relaxation increased, so simple pleasure-seeking by the masses became more and more acceptable to public opinion. The week-end of recreation at home or out of doors became more of a reality for the working classes as well as for the middle classes. The Victorian work ethic, that fierce imperative which decreed that the working man should work long hours and earn his bread in the sweat of his brow, no longer reigned supreme. Times were changing fast when war came again in September 1939.

Chapter XVI
The Second World War

Military Service

With the coming of the Second World War in September 1939 the working classes once more found themselves quite literally in the front line. Conscription had already been in force since June, so that there was no need for the campaigns for voluntary recruitment which were a feature of the earlier years of the First World War. Age groups were called up steadily by the Ministry of Labour and National Service up to the age of 41, with exemptions from service for those in certain reserved occupations. Single women were also conscripted, but on a much more modest scale than for men: only those in the age group 19–24 were called up, and they were given a choice between the women's services, Civil Defence, and certain civilian jobs essential to the war effort. By the end of the war there were still fewer than half a million women in the ATS, WRNS, and the WAAF, many of these being volunteers, as compared with five million men in the armed forces. Conscientious objection to war service was again permitted, and 58 000 men and 2000 women sought exemption on religious or other grounds. Of these, 2900 were given complete exemption, and 40 000 conditional exemption, usually in the form of non-combatant duties. There was less ill-feeling about conscientious objectors than in the first war, and in any case COs serving in Bomb Disposal Units could scarcely be accused of cowardice. By the summer of 1940, only 0·5 per cent of all conscripts registering for service were COs. Overwhelmingly, the working classes responded to conscription in the conviction that the war had to be fought and won, and their contribution to victory was no less massive than in 1914–18.

A major difference between service in the second war and service in the first was the number of overseas theatres of war in which the working-class soldier served, and the nature of warfare. It is true that in 1939 as in 1914 a British Expeditionary Force was sent to France, but when the war suddenly came alight in May, 1940 with the German invasion of Belgium and Holland, the result was not trench warfare but a war of movement leading to the evacuation from Dunkirk, and a period of four years before British troops were again in France in any force. During that time British troops were to fight in the desert wars of

North Africa, in Italy, and in the jungles of Burma, before returning to France on D-day in 1944. Meanwhile, heavy fighting had taken place at sea to keep the sea lines open (the Battle of the Atlantic), and in the air, both in the Battle of Britain and in the prolonged bomber offensive over Germany. If the horrors of trench warfare were avoided in the second war, the realities of active service were still grim enough, though efforts were made to avoid the appalling casualties which characterized the large-scale offensives of the first war. Moreover, throughout the six years the belief remained strong that the war was being fought in a just cause and that Nazism had to be exterminated, at whatever cost to the nation. Thus the disillusionment of the later years of the 1914–18 war, the sense of needless sacrifice, were absent in the war against Hitler, and so equally was the old-fashioned and boastful patriotism. People grumbled, as always, but got on with it. John Pudney's poem on a bomber pilot killed in action catches this spirit very well:

> Do not despair
> For Johnny head-in-air
> He sleeps as sound
> As Johnny underground
> Fetch out no shroud
> For Johnny in the cloud
> And keep your tears
> For after years
> Better by far
> For Johnny the bright star
> To keep your head
> And see his children fed

In fact, casualties were far fewer than in the previous war, though heavy enough. Some 300 000 were killed in the armed forces, together with 35 000 in the merchant navy. This time there was far less of a gulf fixed between the forces and the civilians because of the air raids which brought the civilian population into the war as never before. Indeed, in the first three years of war there were more women and children killed than there were soldiers. Casualty rates in the armed forces were probably highest in Bomber Command, and at times approached the casualty rate in the trenches in France in the first war. Fortunately, the chances of recovering from serious injury in the second war were considerably improved by the development and use of penicillin and the sulphonamide drugs, while servicemen in the East grew accustomed to mepacrine as a precaution against malaria.

Life and Death in the Blitz

For the working classes who remained in civilian occupations, first the threat of air raids and then the actuality of bombing brought experiences of an unparalleled kind. In September 1939 there took place a mass official evacuation from danger areas of primary school children and also of mothers with children under five. About a million and a half were moved into safer areas, and a further two million evacuated themselves as well. Since air raids did not begin till the following year, by January a million or so had returned home, only to leave the cities again when bombing started in the autumn. Many working-class children from the cities had their first sight of fields and cows as a result of evacuation, and they took some time to adjust to a new world. The condition of the poorest children caused great concern; some were verminous, wet their beds, and appeared completely uncivilized. For the first time middle- and upper-class households were confronted with the realities of poverty, and were accordingly shocked. One owner of a large country house wrote:

> I had little dreamt that English children could be so completely ignorant of the simplest rules of hygiene, and that they would regard the floors and carpets as suitable places upon which to relieve themselves.

However, the majority of working-class children went to working-class families, the theory being that they would settle in better than with middle-class families. For some evacuees, separation from their parents and their homes was extremely painful, but most benefited in the long run from a healthier environment. Children who were left behind found their schools closed until November, while free milk and school dinners came to a halt. Even in the spring of 1940, half of London's school children were still not receiving full-time teaching.

Later in 1940 and as the Battle of Britain came to an end, large-scale bombing of London began—the London blitz—with raids every night from 7 September to 2 November. During this period and up to 13 November, an average of 160 bombers dropped every night about 200 tons of high explosive and 182 canisters of incendiaries (a canister commonly contained about 72 separate bombs). The raids were usually worse at full moon—for example, on 15 October there were 410 bombers which dropped 538 tons of bombs, killing 400 and starting 900 fires. In November the attacks were directed more to provincial industrial centres. On 14 November Coventry was bombed for 10 hours, at a cost of 554 deaths and 865 seriously injured. Finally the Germans extended their attacks to the ports such as Bristol, Merseyside, Southampton, Portsmouth, and Plymouth. On Sunday 29 December, another great attack was launched on London, destroying much of the City in the Cripplegate area, and starting 1500 fires. The all-clear sounded about midnight, and in the outer suburbs 12 miles or so away a great red glow in the sky could be seen, showing where London was burning. Fortunately the death toll was comparatively small—163 were killed. During January bad weather limited the German attacks, and there were no major raids in February, but the following months of March, April and early May saw a further intense onslaught. On 10 May London suffered the worst attack of the war, with 1 436 killed and 1 792 seriously injured. In June 1941 Hitler attacked Russia, and the blitz virtually came to an end, though there were to be more air attacks later in the war.

Many more bombs fell on the working-class East End of London than on the West End, so that the London working-class areas suffered disproportionately from air attack. Besides this, East End housing was much flimsier and more easily destroyed than property in the West End, where the owners could in any case afford to remove themselves to a safe distance. In Stepney by 11 November four out of 10 houses were damaged or destroyed, the East Enders' ordeal having begun on 7 September with a mass daylight raid on the London docks which continued into the night, killing 430 civilians. By June 1941 more than two million houses throughout the country had been hit, 60 per cent of them being in London. By the end of the war the figure had increased to an estimated 3¾ million, while in the central areas of London, only one out of 10 houses escaped damage of one kind or another. As for casualties, about 43 000 were killed by bombs in 1940 and 1941, and in the remaining years of the war this figure increased to a final total of 60 000. Of these deaths, nearly half were in London. About 86 000 were seriously injured, and 151 000 suffered minor injuries.

Thus the urban working classes were faced with unprecedented dangers, and they rose magnificently to the challenge. Air raid wardens, rescue squads, bomb disposal units, firemen, policemen, and the ambulance service all cooperated in rescuing victims and saving life whenever humanly possible. They were helped by an army of voluntary workers; most of the men and women in Civil Defence were part-time volunteers, and the same applies to the Salvation Army helpers and the Women's Voluntary Service. There was very little panic (though nerves were stretched dangerously close to breaking point by May, 1940) and there were few cases of mental disorders caused by bombing. In fact, the suicide rate fell, and the figures for drunkenness were more than halved between 1939 and 1942. Some looting took place, though not on a serious scale. In London, six out of 10 people went on sleeping at home during the raids, either in the house on the ground floor, often under the stairs, or in the outdoor Anderson shelter in the garden. However, many London houses lacked gardens, and it was not until mid-1941 that an indoor shelter (the Morrison shelter) became available. London Underground stations became a favourite place for shelter, and 79 stations were used for this purpose. By the end of September, 1940 there were 177 000 people sleeping in them. Some stations were deeper and safer than others. In October, 1940 four stations were hit in three nights, while in January, 1941 the Bank station suffered a direct hit, 111 being killed.

Three aspects of the London blitz are often recalled by those who experienced it. The first is the sheer noise of a raid—the racket of anti-aircraft fire, the drone of enemy aircraft, the whine and explosion of HE bombs, and the clanging of fire brigade and ambulance bells. The second is the aftermath of a raid, when the initial feeling of relief at having survived the night was tempered by the depressing sight of smashed buildings, by long detours on the way to work so as to avoid streets closed by unexploded bombs, by the acrid smell of burning, and by sheer fatigue due to lack of sleep. A third aspect is the comradeship resulting from danger shared by all classes of people in shelters or in rescue work. Class differences fell away, and the habitual reserve of the man in the street, whatever his class, could hardly be maintained in an air raid. As Lord Marley is supposed to have said, somewhat quaintly, in 1941:

It is quite common now to see Englishmen speaking to each other in public, although they have never been formally introduced.

Bombing of the cities did not cease entirely when Germany invaded Russia in June, 1941. It revived again in January 1944 and continued till mid-April. London was again heavily hit, and so were Hull, Bristol, and South Wales. After D-Day on 6 June, it seemed unlikely that the Germans could spare any bombers for raids on Britain, but on 13 June the first flying bombs (VIs) reached England, nicknamed 'doodle-bugs' by the public. By the end of August, nearly a million and a half people had left London. The boroughs in South and East London suffered worst, and Croydon worst of all. A total of 142 flying bombs fell on this borough, destroying over 1000 houses, and damaging many more. By mid-July, the bombs were being combatted in a variety of ways—AA guns were moved to the coast, the bombs were attacked in the air by new and faster aircraft, while London was protected by an intensified ballon barrage. By August, 80 per cent were being destroyed, and on 7 September Duncan Sandys, who was in charge of defence counter-measures, declared that: 'The Battle of London is over, except possibly for a last few shots'. In this he was largely correct, though another 79 reached London during the next seven months.

Unfortunately for Duncan Sandys, on the day after his pronounce-ment the first V2, a rocket 45 feet long and weighing 14 tons, fell on London. By November an average of six a day were landing on London, 518 in all. They were enormously destructive, four rockets landing in Croydon damaging 2000 houses altogether. Casualties amounted to 2724 deaths and more than 6000 badly injured. There was no defence against the rockets, because they travelled too fast to be intercepted in any way. Yet there was no panic, partly because there was little comment by the Press or the government, although Churchill told the Commons that the new weapon was not a serious threat; and partly because the rockets moved faster than the speed of sound, and therefore gave no warning of their approach. Thus the Londoner would simply hear a tremendous explosion, followed by the sound of the rocket's descent, and only then would know that he or she had survived another V2 attack. Only the overrunning of the rocket sites by the allies brought the attacks to an end, the last V2 falling on Orpington on 27 March 1945.

German air attacks on London and the provincial cities thus lasted for a period of well over four years, though with varying degrees of intensity. The blitz proved that London could take it, as the saying went at the time, and the same applied to other cities as well, though London alone took the last onslaught of V1s and V2s. At no time did morale collapse, and at no time in the war was there greater national unity. As A. J. P. Taylor has said, the raids were a powerful solvent of class antagonism. As much as anything then, the blitz stressed the need for joint effort, and a unity of purpose which made the war truly a People's War in which all classes worked together.

Life at Work

In many ways life at work during the Second World War resembled life at work in 1914–18. Once more working hours became far longer, though the strain of work during the second war was intensified by bombing which caused loss of sleep and disrupted transport. An average factory worker might easily spend 15 hours a day at work and travelling to and from work, and in addition take his turn at firewatching. Yet absenteeism was remarkably low, and in 1940 and 1941 the problem was not to get workers to put in sufficient hours, but rather to stop them from over-working and collapsing from sheer exhaustion. Bombing disrupted work, of course, but although factory buildings were often damaged, the machinery itself might survive, and production was interrupted far less seriously than was expected. Female labour was again very prominent in munitions factories: the number of women employed on munitions grew from 7000 in 1939 to 260 000 by October 1944. Numbers also increased in engineering and vehicle building by 770 000, so that the proportion of women employed in these trades increased from 9 per cent to 34 per cent. Women in commerce went up in number from 33 per cent of the total to 62 per cent. No doubt women gained a further degree of social freedom during the war as a result of their widespread participation in war work, but the change was not so marked as during the first war. Some progress was made towards equal pay, but in metal work and engineering the average woman's pay was only half that of the average man in January 1944.

The precedents of the First World War were also followed with respect to dilution and overall control of labour. Agreements on dilution were reached in summer, 1940, while in the same year the Emergency Powers (Defence) Act gave the government such wide powers that under the Act a special regulation (Defence Regulation 58A) could be issued, virtually giving complete control of labour to the Minister of Labour, Ernest Bevin. By Order 1305 strikes and lock-outs became illegal, and wage disputes which could not be solved by the usual negotiations were to go to a National Arbitration Tribunal. This body issued 816 adjudications before the end of the war. By the Restriction on Engagement Order, 1940, labour might be engaged only through an approved trade union or through the labour exchanges. A further order in March 1941, the Essential Work (General Provisions) Order, subjected skilled workers to direction of labour; once in a specified skilled job, the worker could not leave it, though there were to be minimum standards of wages and working conditions by way of compensation in the jobs concerned.

Great efforts were also made to secure good labour relations in industry so that production could be kept at the maximum. Regional Boards of Industry were set up in 1941, a Ministry of Production and a National Production Advisory Council in 1942. Joint Production Committees were established, and by the end of 1944 some 3·5 m workers were represented on these committees. Wages were still left to pre-war methods of negotiation, although in some cases pre-war wages were so low that the government was obliged to interfere. Thus the Central Agricultural Wages Board was established in 1940 to fix national minimum wages for male agricultural workers, while the Catering Wages Act, 1943, set up the Catering Wages Commission. In 1945 the Wages Councils Act converted existing trades boards into wages boards with increased powers. Working conditions in factories were also improved with the better provision of factory doctors (35 whole-time, and 70 part-time before the war; 181 whole-time, 890 part-time by 1944) and of industrial nurses (1500 before the war, increasing to 8000 by 1943). Factory inspectors were given powers to have welfare officers appointed in factories employing more than 250 workers, and to make canteens compulsory in the larger works. Variety shows were given in the dinner hour and were broadcast nationally ('Workers' Playtime'), and there were half-hour BBC programmes of continuous music every day especially for factory workers ('Music While You Work').

There seems no doubt that government interest in the health and well-being of the work force increased greatly during the war. However, the most important reason for good industrial relations was simply the universal acceptance of the need for all-out production. This is shown in the limited number of strikes which occurred. In 1940 fewer working days were lost than in any year since records had been kept. Later on the figures increased, so that 1·8 m days were lost in 1943, and

3·7 m days in 1944. The figure for 1944 was worse than that for any year since 1932. Yet it must be seen in perspective: the trouble was worst in the coal industry where half the number of working days were lost in 1943, and two-thirds in 1944. Disputes arose mostly over piece rates which were low enough before the war, and had not been altered to keep pace with the rise in prices. Generally speaking, although strikes were not infrequent, they were short in duration. In engineering and allied industries nine out of 10 strikes in 1943 and 1944 lasted for less than a week. Further, the number of strikes and the loss of working days were at first far smaller than immeditely after World War I:

Year	No. of Strikes	Working Days Lost
1919	1352	34·97 m
1920	1607	26·57 m
1921	763	85·87 m
1922	576	19·85 m
1940	922	0·94 m
1941	1251	1·08 m
1942	1303	1·52 m
1943	1785	1·80 m
1944	2194	3·71 m

The government wisely avoided prosecuting under Order 1305 whenever possible, so that there were only 71 prosecutions in Scotland and 38 in England and Wales throughout the war. In 1944 there were only three prosecutions in England and Wales, and fines of £5 were normal rather than the maximum permissible of £25.

The role of the trade unions in minimizing labour unrest was very important, of course. As in the first war, the trade unions profited from war-time conditions, not merely because their membership increased under conditions of full employment, but also because their active cooperation was once more essential to the war effort. Their membership in 1938 was 6·05 m, and though it was increasing from year to year it had still not risen to the peak post-war period figure of 8·34 m in 1920. During the war it rose to 8·07 m in 1944, dropping to 7·87 m in 1945, but rising to the largest figure yet of 8·80 m in 1946. As far as influence is concerned, the unions were fortunate in having Bevin as Minister of Labour from October 1940 onwards, after Churchill had become Prime Minister and the Labour Party had joined the government in May 1940. Henceforth the unions took a leading part in the struggle for maximum production, being represented at all levels of the consultative procedures—on the Regional Boards for Industry, on the National Production Advisory Council, and on the joint consultative committees. Their influence was even greater than these facts indicate, because members of the Labour Party occupied key positions in the government—Clement Attlee was Deputy Prime Minister, and Herbert Morrison became Home Secretary. Consequently the trade unions were much better represented in the government through the Labour Party than they had been in 1914–18, and the Labour Movement as a whole was in a strong position when there was a return to party politics in 1945.

The Standard of Living

On a first appraisal it might seem that material conditions so worstened for the average civilian that the standard of living was bound to fall. Long hours were worked in industry, with night shifts often working in ill-ventilated workshops with black-outs up at every window. Rationing of basic foods began in 1940, with other food stuffs and clothing going on 'points' rations in the following year. Petrol became unobtainable except for essential use. As we have seen, bombing rendered many temporarily homeless—for every civilian killed, there were 35 made homeless. There were as many as 60 million changes of address during the war. By 1941 it has been calculated that personal consumption was 14 per cent less than pre-war, and people were spending less on everything except beer, tobacco, the cinema, and public transport.

Yet astonishingly the health of the nation as a whole actually improved after a minor decline in 1940 and 1941. This was due to a variety of causes. School meals were provided for all school children, with cheap milk for younger children and expectant mothers, who were also provided with orange juice, cod liver oil, vitamins and extra eggs. Factory workers benefited from the factory canteens and additional welfare services. The government publicized recipes for economical yet nourishing meals. Local authorities set up 'British Restaurants' to make plain meals available to the general public at cheap prices. Since a maximum limit of five shillings was placed on all meals in public restaurants, and since there was a shortage of goods of all kinds, there was a noticeable levelling down of consumption. It has been estimated that personal consumption settled down at about the pre-war skilled artisan level. This meant a rise in consumption for unskilled workers. Certainly health statistics show an improvement during the war, particularly the Infant Mortality figures which declined further from 56 per 1 000 live births in England in 1936–8 to 45 in 1944–6.

It was not only in health that advances were made. The cost of living increased by about 50 per cent by 1944, while wage rates rose rather less, but actual earnings increased by over 81 per cent as a result of more regular hours, overtime, week-end work, and piecework.

	Wage Rates (September 1938 = 100)	Cost of Living (1938 = 100)	Weekly Earnings (Oct. 1938 = 100)
1939	104	102·5	–
1940	113–14	120	130
1941	122	135	142
1942	131–2	143	160
1943	136–7	146	176
1944	143–4	150	181·5
1945	150–1	–	180·5

The cost of living was also held down by the freezing of house rents in 1939. Women's wage rates rose more than men's, while unskilled rates improved from about 70 per cent of skilled rates to 80 per cent by 1945, so again it was the less well-paid workers whose position improved most substantially. On the whole, however, it was not changes in wage rates which brought higher earnings, but longer hours and harder or more skilled work.

The length of the working week necessarily limited the amount of leisure time available, but public entertainment continued, though affected by wartime restrictions. Professional football was still played, though to reduced crowds at first, while England–Scotland internationals could still have gates of 60 000. The main problem for many clubs was the calling-up of their players, so that scratch sides often had to be fielded. Brighton and Hove Albion once played Norwich City with a team consisting of five Brighton players, two Norwich reserves, and four soldiers who volunteered from the crowd; Norwich won 18–0. Professional cricket also continued. The attendance at Lords in 1943 was less than a third down on attendance in 1939. Greyhound racing also went on. Amateur football and cricket matches were still played, and Army and RAF sides benefited from the help of professionals serving in their ranks. But the major entertainment away from home remained the cinema, where attendances actually increased. Three-quarters of the adult population went regularly to the cinema, and weekly attendances were between 25 and 30 million. The pub remained the working man's club, though beer was in short supply and was weaker. One new social centre, of a kind, was the ARP or Civil Defence Centre, where street fire watchers would gather, and when it was all-clear play darts, cards, or dominoes.

For many, the radio provided a major source of entertainment, the most famous comedy show of all being ITMA, with its star Tommy Handley, and a host of comic characters, all with their own catch phrases, such as Colonel Chinstrap ('I don't mind if I do'), and Mrs Mopp, the cleaner ('Can I do you now, sir?'). There were other comedy shows such as 'Hi Gang' with Bebe Daniels and Ben Lyon. Popular music continued, now in the form of swing, with the American Glen

Miller Orchestra a great favourite, together with record request programmes such as 'Forces Favourites'. The most popular woman singer
was Vera Lynn, universally known for her songs, 'We'll Meet Again
. . .', and 'The White Cliffs of Dover':

> There'll be blue birds over
> The white cliffs of Dover
> Tomorrow, just you wait and see . . .
> There'll be joy and laughter
> And peace ever after
> Tomorrow, when the world is free

The radio also provided more serious fare in the form of talks and
concerts. A new and increasingly popular programme began on 1
January, 1941—the Brains Trust, in which listeners' questions were
answered by a team consisting of Professor Joad, a teacher of philoso-
phy, Julian Huxley, the biologist, and a retired naval officer, Comman-
der A. B. Campbell. As for concerts, classical music became more
popular than before and CEMA (Council for Education in Music and
the Arts) put on public concerts of classical music as well as sponsoring
exhibitions of art, and tours by the Old Vic and opera and ballet
companies. Many young working-class men and women found an
interest in music and the arts which they had hitherto thought beyond
them. For those with lighter tastes, variety shows and the dance halls
were still available, while for the forces themselves, entertainment was
provided by a new organization, ENSA (Entertainments National
Service Association).

Thus, although it was hardly to be expected that there would be any
new and major developments during the war in the field of leisure
activities and entertainment, pre-war patterns of working-class leisure
were continued and in some cases strengthened. It was indeed the
hey-day of popular enjoyment of the cinema and of the radio. The BBC
television service was closed down for the duration, and the only TV
screens in use during the war were to be found in radar sets. It was not
until after the war, and especially in the 1950s, that television came into
its own and replaced both the cinema and the radio as a form of
entertainment.

Social Reform

It seems strange that although the nation was mobilized for war on a
scale never witnessed before, the government still found time to
introduce social reform. Yet the reforms proposed or actually
implemented were so extensive that one historian has recently argued
that the Coalition Government proved to be the greatest reforming

administration since the Liberal governments of 1905–14. The reason for this is that after Dunkirk in May 1940 there was a great change in public opinion which was the result of a heightened sense of common danger and of national unity. Not only was there a great emphasis on equality of sacrifice (as seen in rationing and in service in Civil Defence and the newly formed Home Guard) but there was also much hostility to the pre-war establishment of privilege and vested interests. J. B. Priestley contributed to the discussion in a series of talks broadcast after the news on Sundays under the title *Postscripts*. He stressed the need for change after the war, and for change for the benefit of the community as a whole rather than for the minority, propertied classes:

> Now the war, because it demands a huge collective effort, is compelling us to change not only our ordinary social and economic habits, but also our habits of thought. We're actually changing over from a property view to a sense of community, which simply means that we're all in the same boat.

Discussion was further encouraged by the establishment in June 1941 of the Army Bureau of Current Affairs which issued regular bulletins on both military events and on current affairs, at the same time introducing compulsory weekly discussions among the troops. Churchill was somewhat suspicious of the possibly political consquences of this. In fact, the bulletins of the ABCA were politically neutral, and the discussion groups hardly became centres of political agitation, though they must have helped to stimulate ideas as to what a better future might hold. The entry of Russia into the war in June 1941 brought an increased interest in what might be achieved by planned social reform; while books like *Guilty Men* (published just after Dunkirk) held up to scorn a number of pre-war politicians who, it was alleged, had failed to re-arm Britain and had thereby weakened the British army and air force.

For all these reasons there took place a great swing away from pre-war attitudes, and while Churchill concentrated on gaining military victory, the Labour members of the coalition, together with progressive Conservatives like R. A. Butler, and leading reformers like Keynes and Beveridge, together produced a series of proposals for reform. In 1941 the influence of Keynes was seen in the financial planning contained in the budget, and in December, 1942 the first manpower budget was introduced. Also in 1941 the Board of Education issued proposals for educational reform known as the Green Book. In May, 1942 the Report of the Medical Planning Commission advocated a national health service for all, while in September the Uthwatt Report was issued on post-war town planning. The Labour Party itself produced a new programme of reform in the autumn of 1942 entitled *The Old World and the New Society*. It stressed the need for full employment, wide-ranging social services, and full education for all. But the most famous of all the blueprints for the brave new world to come was the Beveridge Report of December 1942. This was a report on the state of the social insurance services, and in it Beveridge expressed his belief that:

> . . . the purpose of victory is to live in a better world than the old world; that each individual is more likely to concentrate upon his war effort if he feels that his government will be ready with plans for that better world; that, if these plans are to be ready in time, they must be made now.

In examining the social services of the time, Beveridge reached the conclusion that they were excellent in many ways, but that both the medical and the unemployment schemes were too limited, with different rates of benefit, while there was insufficient provision for maternity and funeral benefit. In addition, the workmen's compensation system was inadequate, and the administrative system of the existing schemes was too complex. Beveridge considered that social insurance should be only part of a comprehensive policy of social progress, being an attack on Want, though Want was only one of five giants—the others were Disease, Ignorance, Squalor and Illness. Since the inter-war surveys had shown that three-quarters to five-sixths of Want was due to interruption or loss of earning power, the remainder being due to the family being too large for the family income, two things were needed to abolish Want. The first was better social insurance, and the second was family allowances.

Beveridge then proceeded to elaborate his Plan. In general terms, this was to cover all classes, both of working age and above and below. Everyone was to contribute to insurance against the interruption and destruction of earning power, and for special expenditure at birth, marriage and death. A comprehensive range of benefits could then be provided, to cover unemployment and disability, medical treatment, pensions, maternity benefits, children's allowances, and funeral expenses. Lastly, a Ministry of Social Security should be established to administer the whole scheme.

There is no doubt that the Beveridge Report was extremely popular, offering as it did the prospect of social security from the cradle to the grave, and the setting up of a Welfare State. Sales of the Report reached a total of 635 000 copies. A public opinion poll recorded 86 per cent of those questioned in favour of putting the Report into effect. The Government made known its support of the Report in principle, though it was divided over the cost of the scheme, and over its practicability. Doubts were strongest among the insurance companies, understandably enough, and among older Conservatives, including Churchill. The Labour Party was strongly in favour, Herbert Morrison taking the lead. As he saw it:

The social benefits of the Beveridge Plan are very great. And to remove the plague spots of extreme poverty, undernourishment and its accompanying diseases from the body politic is a measure that will react most favourably and in many different ways upon the economic health and soundness of our society . . .

Not all the Labour ministers supported the Report in every detail, however. Bevin disliked the proposals for children's allowances and workmen's compensation, nor did he think it right that the doctors' private practices should be affected by the new plan.

In the event, the government failed to implement the Beveridge Plan forthwith, preferring to postpone immediate action for the time being. Churchill himself talked of a Four Year Plan of reform to be brought in at the end of the war, without referring directly to the Report. Nevertheless, the Beveridge proposals had enormous influence over attitudes to reform throughout the rest of the war, and a broad consensus of opinion developed between Labour reformers and the younger Conservatives such as Quintin Hogg (later Lord Hailsham), Harold Macmillan, and R. A. Butler. The results were to be seen in 1943 with the setting up of a Ministry of Reconstruction, while in 1944 a number of important government White Papers were issued—the 'White Paper Chase', Beveridge called it. Thus in February 1944 a White Paper was published proposing the instituting of a National Health Service, while in May another White Paper was issued on Employment Policy, in which the government accepted as one of their primary aims and responsibilities: 'the maintenance of a high and stable level of employment after the war.' Moreover, the Paper accepted the need for Keynesian economics to achieve this end. Later in the year (September 1944) a White Paper on Social Insurance adopted the main recommendations of the Beveridge Report. In November Beveridge strengthened his case for an attack on unemployment in a book entitled *Full Employment in a Free Society*.

Meanwhile a bill for the reform of the state educational system became law in August 1944 following the Green Book and a White Paper in July 1943. The Education Act, 1944, was the first major education Act since 1918, and is sometimes referred to as the Butler Act since it was introduced by R. A. Butler, President of the Board of Education. Its thinking was based on the 1926 Hadow Report with its advocacy of secondary education for all, and it was also influenced by the Norwood Report (1943) on the curriculum and examinations; this divided secondary school children into three groups—the academically able, the technically minded, and the remaining majority, those for whom the Hadow Report had recommended the setting up of modern schools. The Act made local authorities responsible for providing education in three stages—primary, secondary, and further; county colleges were to be established for the third stage, providing part-time education up to 18. All education in local authority schools was to become free, so that the fees previously charged in county secondary (grammar) schools were abolished. The school leaving age was to be raised to 15 and later to 16. Church schools were given additional financial help, either as Aided Schools, where the governors contributed 50 per cent towards repairs and alterations but appointed their own staff, or Controlled Schools, where the local authority assumed complete responsibility for buildings and a greater control of staffing. A daily act of corporate worship became obligatory, and so did religious instruction—henceforth the one compulsory subject in the curriculum. There was also a substantial reorganization of local educational authorities, 169 smaller bodies out of the 315 authorities in England and Wales losing their powers. Lastly, as an indication of increased status and responsibility, the old Board of Education was replaced by the Ministry of Education, and the former President became the Minister.

The importance of the Education Act, 1944, is undoubted, and it represented a real effort to provide a system of state education more appropriate to the needs of a democracy. It was clearly of benefit to the working classes that all secondary grammar school places should now be free, and some excellent new secondary modern schools were built in an attempt to achieve what was called at the time 'parity of esteem' for each type of secondary school. The school leaving age was put up to 15 in 1947. The Act said nothing about selection procedures for the different types of secondary schools, simply requiring local authorities to provide 'efficient full-time education suitable to their age, ability and aptitude'. The authorities had therefore to devise their own selection procedures at 11+, usually based on an intelligence test, and tests in English and Arithmetic.

Unfortunately it soon became apparent that 'parity of esteem' could not be achieved as between the grammar school and the secondary modern school because the former was generally housed in better buildings, had a better-qualified staff, and offered 'O' and 'A' Level courses with access to the universities. Hence the grammar school retained its prestige, while the secondary modern school was too often regarded as the school for the 11+ 'failures'; there were so few technical schools in existence that they made little difference to the fundamental choice between grammar school and secondary modern school. Thus, the new tripartite system rapidly came under fire, particularly by the articulate middle-class parents who could no longer buy education in the grammar school, but had to submit their offspring to the hazards of the 11+ examination. Some chose rather to send their children to public schools, or to the new direct grant grammar schools, which were mostly old foundations now receiving grants direct from the government, and charging fees for 50 per cent of their places. Although many secondary modern schools in the course of time developed CSE and 'O' Level courses, and even 'A' Level courses in some instances, they still lacked the prestige of the secondary grammar schools. The 11+ examination was increasingly attacked for its inaccuracy, and so was the basic idea of the Norwood Committee that children could be conveniently sorted out into three neat categories at the age of 11 (though in fairness it must be pointed out that the Committee did not advocate strict segregation of children of different abilities at 11, and was not opposed to multilateral schools containing all three types of children). The Butler Act was therefore severely flawed in its failure to take account of the consequences of secondary reorganization. Yet it was regarded as a valuable step forward at the time, and was the springboard for the further reorganization upon a comprehensive basis of the 1960s and 1970s.

One other reform needs to be mentioned—the Family Allowances Act, passed by Churchill's caretaker government in June 1945. By this Act family allowances of 5s per child were paid for each child in a family after the first. This was a direct response, of course, to Beveridge's claim that a quarter to a sixth of poverty was due to the family income being insufficient for the size of the family. Plans were also announced early in 1945 for the building of 300 000 new houses within two years of the end of the war, together with the spending of £150 m on prefabricated houses, some of which are still in existence today.

The End of the War

The war against Germany ended in May 1945, and the war against Japan in August. Meanwhile, parliament was dissolved, and the General Election took place on 5 July. Both the Labour Party and the Conservative Party campaigned actively on a platform of full employment, a national health service, and social security—a clear indication of the war-time agreement on the need for social reform after the war. In addition, the Labour Party stood for the nationalization of the Bank of England, fuel and power, inland transport, and iron and steel, together with controls of raw materials, food prices, housing, and the putting of necessities for all before luxuries for the few. The pre-war record of the Conservatives, identified as they were with unemployment and appeasement, told heavily against them. The Service vote certainly went against them, though in fact more than half the service men and women did not vote. Labour won a great victory with 393 seats, as against the Conservatives' 213, and the Liberals' 12. Attlee became Prime Minister of the new Labour government, the third of its kind to be formed, but the first to have a clear majority. In his War Memoirs Churchill made a bitter comparison between his gaining the premiership in 1940, and his losing it in 1945:

... I acquired the chief power in the State, which henceforth I wielded in ever-growing measure for five months and three years of world war, at the end of which time, all our enemies having surrendered unconditionally or being about to do so, I was immediately dismissed by the British Electorate from all further conduct of their affairs.

In fact, he remained enormously popular with the people; it was his party that had suffered rejection.

Labour now stood on the threshold of a new world, and it is fitting that its election manifesto should have been called *Let Us Face the Future*. Admittedly the country was in a desperate financial state, there had been massive physical damage during the war, and a third of a million lives had been lost. Nevertheless, the party of the working classes was in power, not as the result of some revolutionary coup d'état, but with the support of the nation as a whole. At the end of an earlier great war in 1815, there was no Labour Party in existence, trade unions were illegal, there was no effective regulation of working conditions or public health, no state educational system, and no social security other than that provided by the Old Poor Law. The average working man then had no vote, nor had any working woman. The working classes formed the basis of a strongly hierarchical society, naturally inferior—or so it was thought—to the classes above them. Between 1815 and 1945 a social revolution had taken place. The representatives of the working classes were now the political masters. It remained to be seen what they would do with their new-found power and responsibilities, and whether a People's War would be followed by a People's Peace.

Select Bibliography

A full bibliography listing all the books, articles, and primary sources upon which this book is based would run into many pages. What follows here is very much of a select bibliography intended merely to guide the earnest enquirer to some of the basic books. Most of the books mentioned have their own extensive bibliographies.

Section A: 1815–1914

General

Best, Geoffrey, *Mid-Victorian Britain 1851–75* (revised edition, 1973)

Checkland, S. G., *The Rise of Industrial Society in England, 1815–1885* (1964)

Clark, G. Kitson, *The Making of Victorian England* (1962)

Clark, G. Kitson, *An Expanding Society: Britain 1830–1900* (1967)

Chambers, J. D., *The Workshop of the World* (1961)

Fraser, Derek, *The Evolution of the British Welfare State* (1973)

Harrison, F. F. C., *The Early Victorians 1832–51* (1971)

Hobsbawm, E. J., *Industry and Empire* (1968)

Landes, D. S., *The Unbound Prometheus* (1969)

Mathias, Peter, *The First Industrial Nation* (1969)

Midwinter, Eric, *Victorian Social Reform* (1968)

Working and Living Conditions

Chadwick, E., *Report on the Sanitary Condition of the Labouring Population of Great Britain* (1842, reprinted with Introduction by M. W. Flinn, 1965)

Dyos, H. J. & Wolff, M., *The Victorian City: Images and Realities* (1973)

Finer, S. E., *The Life and Times of Edwin Chadwick* (1952)

Frazer, W. M., *The History of English Public Health, 1834–1939* (1950)

Hammond, J. L. and Barbara, *The Town Labourer* (2nd edition, 1925)

Hartwell, R. M. (ed.), *The Industrial Revolution* (1970)

Hartwell, R. M. and others, *The Long Debate on Poverty* (1974)

Hobsbawm, E. J., *Labouring Men* (1964)

Lambert, R. J., *Sir John Simon, 1816–1904* (1963)

Taylor, A. J. (ed.), *The Standard of Living in Britain in the Industrial Revolution* (1974)
Thomis, M. I., *The Town Labourer and the Industrial Revolution* (1974)

Government Intervention
Bruce, Maurice, *The Coming of the British Welfare State* (4th edition 1968)
Hay, J. R., *The Origins of the Liberal Welfare Reforms 1906–1914* (1975)
Hutchings, B. L. & Harrison, A., *A History of Factory Legislation* (1926)
MacDonagh, Oliver, *Early Victorian Government 1830–70* (1977)
Taylor, A. J., *Laissez-faire and State Intervention in 19th Century Britain* (1972)
Ward, J. T., *The Factory Movement* (1962)
Ward, J. T., *The Factory System* (2 vols) (1970)

Education and Religion
Curtis, S. J., *History of Education in Great Britain* (7th edition, 1967)
Inglis, K. S., *Churches and the Working Classes in Victorian England* (1963)
Lawson, John and Silver, Harold, *A Social History of Education in England* (1973)
McLeod, Hugh, *Class and Religion in the late Victorian City* (1974)
Sturt, M., *The Education of the People* (1967)
Sutherland, G., *Elementary Education in the Nineteenth Century* (1971)
Wearmouth, R. F., *Methodism and the Struggle of the Working Classes 1850–1900* (1955)

The Poor Law
Fraser, Derek (ed.), *The new Poor Law in the Nineteenth Century* (1976)
Marshall, J. D., *The Old Poor Law 1795–1834* (1968)
Rose, M. E., *The Relief of Poverty, 1834–1914* (1792)
Rose, M. E., *The English Poor Law, 1780–1930* (1971)

Protest, Self-Help and the Labour Movement
Gosden, Peter, *The Friendly Societies in England, 1815–1875* (1961)
Gosden, Peter, *Voluntary Associations in the 19th Century* (1973)
Jones, David, *Chartism and the Chartists* (1975)
Lovell, John, *British Trade Unions* (1977)
Mather, F. C., *Chartism* (with revised postscript, 1972)
Musson, A. E., *British Trade Unions 1800–1875* (1972)
Pelling, H., *Origins of the Labour Party* (1965)
Pelling, H., *Popular Politics and Society in Late Victorian Britain* (1968)
Pelling, H., *A History of British Trade Unionism* (Penguin, 1977)
Pelling, H., *A Short History of the Labour Party* (1965)
Thompson, Dorothy, *The Early Charists* (1971)
Ward, J. T., *Chartism* (1973)
White, R. J., *From Waterloo to Peterloo* (1957)

Class and Family

Anderson, Michael, *Family Structure in Nineteenth Century Lancashire* (1971)
Foster, John, *Class Struggle and the Industrial Revolution* (1974)
Laslett, Peter, *The World we have lost* (1965)
Laslett, Peter, *Household and Family in Past Time* (1972)
Marx, K. and Engels, F., *The Communist Manifesto* (Penguin, intro. By A. J. P. Taylor, 1967)
Smelser, Neil J., *Social Change in the Industrial Revolution* (1969)
Thompson, E. P., *The Making of the English Working Class* (Penguin, 1968)

Section B: 1914–1945

Aldcroft, D. H., *The Inter-War Economy: Britain 1919–1939* (1970)
Alford, B. W. E., *Depression and Recovery in the British Economy 1918–39* (1972)
Ashworth, W., *An Economic History of England, 1870–1939* (1960)
Calder, A., *The People's War* (1969)
Marwick, A., *The Deluge* (Penguin, 1967)
Marwick, A., *Britain in the Century of Total War* (Penguin, 1970)
McKibbin, Ross, *The Evolution of the Labour Party 1910–1924* (1974)
Milward, Alan S., *The Economic Effects of the World Wars on Britain* (1970)
Mowat, C. L., *Britain between the Wars* (1957)
Pollard, S., *The Development of the British Economy 1914–1960* (1962)
Taylor, A. J. P., *England 1914–45* (1965)

Index